# Revolution

# ENCOUNTERS

Series Editors

*Robert J. Nelson,* UNIVERSITY OF ILLINOIS
*Gerald Weales,* UNIVERSITY OF PENNSYLVANIA

A series of collections of plays in which the selection is based on the relationship the plays have to one another in theme or structure. The works chosen are each of intrinsic value, but their "encounter" with one another in the same volume enhances the interest of each.

# Revolution

*A Collection of Plays*

Edited by Gerald Weales
and Robert J. Nelson

DAVID McKAY COMPANY, INC., NEW YORK

# REVOLUTION

*A Collection of Plays*

COPYRIGHT © 1975 BY DAVID MCKAY COMPANY, INC.

International Standard Book Number: 0–679–30272–7 (paper)
0–679–50532–6 (cloth)

LIBRARY OF CONGRESS CATALOG CARD NUMBER: 74–23082
MANUFACTURED IN THE UNITED STATES OF AMERICA
Designed by Angela Foote

# Contents

# Revolution

# Introduction

At the end of Jean Genet's *The Balcony*, a play about revolution, among other things, there is a last offstage burst of machine-gun fire. The audience assumption must be that another, a new, a continuing revolution is underway. If a sound effect could serve as an epigraph, that final a-a-a-a-a-a-a-a might do for this volume. Come to think of it, it might do for a history of revolution as a theatrical subject, or, for that matter, of revolution as a fact in the real world. My assumption here is that revolutions inevitably run one of two courses: they fail, and out of the ashes of that failure, a new revolutionary attempt must be made; they succeed, and out of the sunlight of that success, new conditions are created that make new revolutions necessary. It is a conservative assumption, based on a recognition of human limitations, and it is a radical assumption, based on a faith in human possibility.

Any playwright, like any member of an audience, may be a conservative in the sense that he clings to a particular *status quo* or a radical in his adherence to a specific revolution, and his play will probably in some way reflect his allegiance. Yet, except for narrowly propagandistic plays, *agitprop* designed to convert an audience into an action group, plays tend to use revolutions—real or fictional—in a way that suggests the ambiguous reality I was talking about in the first paragraph. Take Sean O'Casey, for instance. Reading *The Plough and the Stars*, one might assume, correctly, that he had little patience with the nationalist revolution, but, unless one knew something of the man outside the work, it would be difficult to realize that he shared the Covey's political ideas. After all, the

Covey is as much a comic character as the play's most ludicrous nationalist, old Uncle Peter in his canonicals. O'Casey, of course, made a deliberate choice as an artist; he stepped back from himself and his own politics and used revolution as a melodramatic fact seen only in terms of characters who could not share the Rising as a simple, single event. Time would have caught up with him in any case, because historical situations change meaning with the years. For O'Casey's generation of radicals there was a firm line between economic revolution, the dream of the international socialists, and nationalist revolution. Today, that line is very indistinct. A 1970s' variation on the Covey, if he were able to move from words to acts, would probably join some new Jack Clitheroe in smuggling bombs into Northern Ireland. In the same kind of transformation through time, Aristophanes, a conservative in the Athens of fifth century B.C., has become a radical playwright as new causes have been able to put *Lysistrata* and *Peace* to work. On the other hand, Bertolt Brecht, a doctrinaire Communist with a saving sense of irony, seems increasingly conservative, except in those plays in which the irony outdistances the doctrine.

A play, then, is a very uncertain weapon, one likely to turn in the hand that wields it. Even so, a play can be frightening to a certain kind of political mind. Reactionary governments have a way of banishing plays they find revolutionary, and successful revolutions ban other and sometimes similar plays as counterrevolutionary threats to the new state. As I write this, Brazil is a particularly blatant instance of the former and, if the Soviet Union seems too obvious an example of the latter, we can always scramble back in time to 1642 when the Commonwealth closed the British theaters. Such bureaucratic nervousness may have a point. It is true that no group of patriots and/or traitors ever ran out of a theater, inspirited by fine rhetoric, and overthrew a government. Still the theater, even at its most trivial and time-serving, has a way of keeping ideas alive. That fact is much more obvious with plays, like the ones in this volume, in which the ideas are indelibly part of the dramatic substance. These plays are dangerous only as any work of art may be: they may trip up the reader, the viewer, and force him to think.

If one were asked to reduce to one sentence the theme or the plot of any of the four plays collected here, it would be possible to do so without ever using the word *revolution*. Yet, that word is the label that hangs on the cover of this volume. The reason, of course, is that revolution is the one thing—or at least the chief thing—that the four plays have in common. Yet, how different the four revolutions are. O'Casey's is the only historical one. Well, almost. An account of a real mutiny lay behind Herman Melville's *Benito Cereno*, although it came to Robert Lowell as fiction—a surer kind of truth—and Shakespeare's riotous Romans are only as historical as Plutarch ever is. For theatrical purposes, however, the authenticity of a revolution depends not on its historical truth but on its dramatic presentation. The revolutions of these four plays vary according to when we join them. In *The Plough and the Stars*, the audience, like the characters, goes through the disaster of the Rising; it is almost a classic instance of the squashed rebellion. In *Benito Cereno*, the audience, like Captain Delano, arrives once the revolution (the mutiny) has been accomplished, but the revolutionary state (the ship) does not exist in isolation; the successful revolution has barely time to mimic the tyranny it replaced before the outside forces (Delano, certainly; the audience, perhaps) return the state (the ship) to an empty shell of its former condition. The revolution in *The Queen and the Rebels* seems to have been underway for years, to have established its power and—at the same time—to be on the point of dissolution; that machine-gun burst with which I opened this essay can be heard more clearly in Ugo Betti's play than in any of the others in this volume. In *Coriolanus*, the revolutionary impulse has been domesticated, the plebeians have been given tribunes to speak for them, but the noisy opening indicates the tenuous quality of the political agreement and the restlessness that the tribunes can tap when they need it.

The characters in the plays might have a difficult time recognizing their revolutions from the descriptions above. After all, one of the most important elements in all these plays is the conflicting attitudes of the characters toward the struggles in which they are involved. In *The Plough and the Stars*, innocent Jack, defending the dream, and innocent Nora, defending the hearth, could hardly see the Rising from the same vantage point; and their neighbors, able to dissociate rhetoric from reality as Jack is not, can toast the Irish cause in the second act and loot the stores in the third without altering their real relationship to the rebellion. In *Benito Cereno*, Babu and Benito, having exchanged roles as victim and victimizer, in some sense share a view of the mutiny, but Captain Delano, his revolution twenty-five years behind him, sees with difficulty and acts instinctively. He is, almost reluctantly, what Coriolanus is by choice, a turner-back of clocks, and—in both cases—there is the threat of complete disorder in the name of old order. In the Shakespeare play, the range of attitudes toward the citizens, who see themselves alternately as injured parties seeking restitution and as free men asserting their rights, goes from the open contempt of Coriolanus through the placating contempt of Menenius to the implicit contempt of the tribunes who manipulate them. These tribunes are distantly related to Amos of *The Queen and the Rebels*, but Ugo Betti's revolutionary is particularly interesting as a contemporary type, one whose sympathy for the people is more abstract than actual. Yet, the image of Amos as the tough ideologist is not that firmly fixed; when he describes the destruction of the palace, his revolution begins to look like Babu's, but as his negation builds, it is Coriolanus who keeps coming back into my mind. Of course, *The Queen and the Rebels* was not designed as an exercise in understanding Coriolanus. Still, it does no harm to see Amos as Coriolanus or as Babu or as the voice outside the bar in *The Plough and the Stars*, as long as one sees him always and inevitably as Amos with a place—a play—of his own to inhabit.

Although the plays seem to be alive with contending

attitudes—I have barely scratched the surface in the paragraph above—each play must have an overall sense of its revolution. Mustn't it? Well, maybe, but . . . let's take Shakespeare for starters. It would be possible to play *Coriolanus* so that the citizens come across as the fools and rascals that the titular hero thinks they are; what, after all, is the point of that marvelous long scene in the fourth act in which Coriolanus offers his service to Aufidius—plot business that could be done in a few lines—if it is not to use the comedy of the servingmen—their self-importance, their cowardice, their changeability—to reflect on the Roman mob scenes. On the other hand, if we accept the poverty of the citizens as real, their complaints about the corn shortage as justified, and play the brief looting scene (I, v) with the approval that O'Casey seems to bring to his Act Three, their incipient revolution begins to look legitimate. Of course, a final reading of the play depends on how we see Coriolanus, who is after all the central figure. It makes a difference whether he is a stronghold of ancient virtue or a crackpot rightist general home from the wars. Or both at once. So it goes. I find it hard to imagine an audience that could see the rebellion in *The Plough and the Stars* as anything but a painful mistake, but Jack's kind of idealism must have an audience equivalent and, if it does, the line of O'Casey's play may be redrawn by the very naïveté that he is treating in Jack and his fellow rebels. In *Benito Cereno*, however, the line is never very clear. An audience, responding to the conventions of the stage, is likely to cast Babu as the villain and Delano as the fool, until Delano begins shooting (the fool as villain) and the sympathy starts to shift. In the process, does the revolution as butchery begin to find a new acceptance? In the case of *Benito Cereno*, of course, the audience reaction will be strongly influenced by extra-theatrical attitudes toward the Black Power movement at home and Third World anticolonialism abroad. In *The Queen and the Rebels* an easy assumption about Betti's depiction of the revolution is complicated by the conditions under which Argia dies. Her death is, inevitably, a weapon against the revolution, but she goes to that death with a new sense of her own dignity, a discovery that is the play's clearest embodiment of one of Amos's essential revolutionary ideals.

It is possible that these are not really plays about revolution at all, that revolution simply provides the backdrop against which the drama takes place. *The Queen and the Rebels*, then, becomes a play about a woman who never discovers the possibilities in herself until she completely fills a role that has been thrust upon her. A triumph, then, and not a tragedy like *Coriolanus*, in which a man cannot shape his strong sense of self to a think-small society. O'Casey calls his play a "tragedy" too, but he may not be thinking of the pathetic destruction of the Clitheroes, but of a society in dislocation unable to right itself. As Captain Boyle says at the end of another O'Casey play, *Juno and the Paycock*, "I'm telling you . . . Joxer . . . th' whole worl's . . . in a terr . . . ible state o' . . . chassis!" Of course, O'Casey may be undercutting the idea even as he presents it by the vigor with which his comic characters live and by the possibility of real courage (in Fluther, in Bessie) that grows out of necessity rather than romanticism. The title of *Benito Cereno* may be misleading, for Captain Delano is clearly the leading character and Lowell may be most intent—as Melville was before him—in depicting that perennial American stereotype, the obtuse, good man who—under pressure—falls back on his own self-righteousness.

A final comment. These are not revolutionary plays. A revolutionary play, after all, has nothing to do with revolution and everything to do with theatrical technique. None of the plays in this volume attempts to overthrow the conventions of the theater. *Coriolanus* differs from the ordinary Elizabethan history play only insofar as Shakespeare, by virtue of his superiority, outshines his contemporaries. Of the three modern plays, *The Queen and the Rebels* is the most conventional if realistic drama be taken as the standard, but its preoccupation with ideas imposes on that form some of the artificiality of formal discussion. *The Plough and the Stars* mixes melodrama and comedy turns and adds some songs for spice, and *Benito*

*Cereno* attempts to adapt contemporary verse to the stage and to work for visual as well as verbal metaphors; but O'Casey, Betti, and Lowell conserve much more than they alter. Four good plays, then, not four revolutionary ones. I have been circling them, throwing out suggestions, definitions, interpretations, but it should be clear by this time that, for me, they are so fascinatingly slippery that they cannot be pinned down in a short introduction. What is it Babu says? "He had a hundred eyes,/he lived our lives for us."

Gerald Weales

# The Plough and the Stars    (1926)*

## Sean O'Casey    (1880-1964)

Sean O'Casey had already had two plays produced at the Abbey Theatre, Dublin—*The Shadow of a Gunman* (1923) and the much admired *Juno and the Paycock* (1924)—when *The Plough and the Stars* was first performed there, February 8, 1926. There was trouble before and after the new play opened. George O'Brien, one of the directors of the Abbey, hinting that a production might endanger the state subsidy to the theater, objected to much of the play, particularly Act Two, but he was voted down by the other three directors, W. B. Yeats, Lady Gregory, and Lennox Robinson. Earlier, Michael J. Dolan, who played the Covey, had complained to Lady Gregory that the language in the play was "beyond the beyonds," and some of the other actors agreed. Eileen Crowe, who was to play Mrs. Gogan, refused, on the advice of her priest, to say, "any kid, livin' or dead, that Jinnie Gogan's had since, was got between th' bordhers of th' Ten Commandments," and she finally gave up the role to May Craig and played the small part of the frightened woman in Act Three; F. J. McCormick, who played Jack, would not say "snotty." Such objections seem ludicrous today, but that brand of Irish primness is one of the elements that O'Casey uses to define the characters in his play.

The difficulties were overcome and the play, directed by Robinson, with Barry Fitzgerald as Fluther, finally reached the stage, only to be greeted by an audience that was outraged at the suggestion that the beloved Irish flags had ever been seen inside a pub and that an Irish girl could be a prostitute.

* From *Collected Plays* by Sean O'Casey. Reprinted by permission of St. Martin's Press, Inc., and Macmillan & Co., Ltd.

The anger was not exactly spontaneous. On the second night, a number of people—including several widows of Irish heroes, who, according to the anti-O'Casey diarist, Joseph Holloway, "were in the theatre to vindicate the manhood of 1916"— came to make trouble. The police were finally called in to put down the protest, but the high point of the disturbance was apparently the appearance of Yeats on stage, shouting above the uproar that "Dublin has once more rocked the cradle of genius . . . the fame of O'Casey is born here tonight. This is apotheosis." And so it was. A distinguished Abbey cast took the play to London, May 12, 1926, and it was produced in New York on November 26, 1927, under the direction of Arthur Sinclair, who played Fluther in both the New York and the London productions. Not necessarily the most accurate account of the *Plough* riot, but certainly the liveliest and most eloquent, can be found in *Inishfallen Fare Thee Well*, the fourth volume of O'Casey's remarkable autobiography.

In 1937 the play was made into a film (RKO), starring Barbara Stanwyck and Preston Foster and featuring a gaggle of Irish character actors, many of them from the Abbey. There was precious little of O'Casey in it. Although it was directed by John Ford with a script by Dudley Nichols, the two men who had done the celebrated adaptation of Liam O'Flaherty's *The Informer* (1935), the movie tended to romanticize the Nora-Jack story, presumably for the sake of the stars, and to reduce the other characters to standard Irish comic turns. Even more outrageously, it converted O'Casey's play into a sentimental pro-Rising tract. However, if it did nothing else, the film gave Barry Fitzgerald, who again played Fluther, to Hollywood. The movie still shows occasionally on television.

The Easter Rebellion, which takes place during the last two acts of *Plough*, began on Easter Monday, April 24, 1916. The two organizations involved in the fighting were the Irish Volunteers, a nationalist group under the command of P. H. Pearse, and the Irish Citizen Army, under James Connolly. It is the Citizen Army flag, the Plough and the Stars, that gives its name to the play, and, as the Covey explains (p. 27), "it's a

Labour flag, an' was never meant for politics." An outgrowth of the unsuccessful Transport Workers' strike of 1913, the Citizen Army was organized to protect the workers. The more conservative Volunteers never worked very comfortably with the Citizen Army, which was Socialist, but the two groups necessarily merged during the Rising and we find Pearse, the newly proclaimed Commander-in-Chief of the Army of the Irish Republic and President of the Provisional Government, in a dispatch dated April 28, praising the wounded Jim Connolly as "the guiding brain of our resistance." None of the tension between the two organizations is shown in the play; in fact, no distinction is made between the Citizen Army members (Clitheroe, Brennan) and the Volunteers (Langon). O'Casey was a member of the Citizen Army until shortly before the Rising, when he left in a factional dispute; he later wrote *The Story of the Irish Citizen Army* (1919), which was signed P. O'Cathasaigh, the spelling of his name that he was using at that time. The "P" was apparently a misprint. The Irish forces seized the General Post Office and a number of other buildings, including the Imperial Hotel, which did fly the Plough and the Stars, as Brennan says (p. 74), explaining how Jack died. The British landed a large force and brought up the gunboat *Helga* to help with the bombardment. By Friday night the rebellion was broken. Fifteen leaders, including Pearse and Connolly, were executed by the British.

The looting of the shops did take place, and O'Casey, in *Drums Under the Window*, the autobiographical volume covering this period, wrote a spirited and amusing defense of the looters.

# THE PLOUGH AND THE STARS
## A Tragedy in Four Acts
### Sean O'Casey

*To the gay laugh of my mother*
*at the gate of the grave*

## CHARACTERS

JACK CLITHEROE (*a bricklayer*),
*Commandant in the Irish Citizen Army*

NORA CLITHEROE, *his wife*

PETER FLYNN (*a labourer*), *Nora's uncle*

THE YOUNG COVEY (*a fitter*), *Clitheroe's cousin*

BESSIE BURGESS (*a street fruit-vendor*)

MRS. GOGAN (*a charwoman*)

MOLLSER, *her consumptive child*

FLUTHER GOOD (*a carpenter*)

*Residents in the Tenement*

LIEUT. LANGON (*a Civil Servant*), *of the Irish Volunteers*

CAPT. BRENNAN (*a chicken butcher*), *of the Irish Citizen Army*

CORPORAL STODDART, *of the Wiltshires*

SERGEANT TINLEY, *of the Wiltshires*

ROSIE REDMOND, *a daughter of 'the Digs'*

A BAR-TENDER

A WOMAN

THE FIGURE IN THE WINDOW

TIME.—*Acts One and Two, November 1915; Acts Three and Four, Easter Week, 1916. A few days elapse between Acts Three and Four.*

ACT ONE.—*The living-room of the Clitheroe flat in a Dublin tenement.*
ACT TWO.—*A public-house, outside of which a meeting is being held.*
ACT THREE.—*The street outside the Clitheroe tenement.*
ACT FOUR.—*The room of Bessie Burgess.*

## ACT ONE

*The home of the Clitheroes. It consists of the front and back drawing-rooms in a fine old Georgian house, struggling for its life against the assaults of time, and the more savage assaults of the tenants. The room shown is the back drawing-room, wide, spacious, and lofty. At back is the entrance to the front drawing-room. The space, originally occupied by folding doors, is now draped with casement cloth of a dark purple, decorated with a design in reddish-purple and cream. One of the curtains is pulled aside, giving a glimpse of front drawing-room, at the end of which can be seen the wide, lofty windows looking out into the street. The room directly in front of the audience is furnished in a way that suggests an attempt towards a finer expression of domestic life. The large fireplace on right is of wood, painted to look like marble (the original has been taken away by the landlord). On the mantelshelf are two candlesticks of dark carved wood. Between them is a small clock. Over the clock is hanging a calendar which displays a picture of 'The Sleeping Venus'.[1] In the centre of the breast of the chimney hangs a picture of Robert Emmet. On the right of the entrance to the front drawing-room is a copy of 'The Gleaners', on the opposite side a copy of 'The Angelus'. Underneath 'The Gleaners' is a chest of drawers on which stands a green bowl filled with scarlet dahlias and white chrysanthemums. Near to the fireplace is a settee which at night forms a double bed for Clitheroe and Nora. Underneath 'The Angelus' are a number of shelves containing saucepans and a frying-pan. Under these is a table on which are various articles of delf ware. Near the end of the room, opposite to the fireplace, is a gate-legged table, covered with a cloth. On top of the table a huge cavalry sword is lying. To the right is a door which leads to a lobby from which the staircase leads to the hall. The floor is covered with a dark green linoleum. The room is dim except where it is illuminated from the glow of the fire. Through the window of the room at back can be seen the flaring of the flame of a gasolene lamp giving light to workmen repairing the street. Occasionally can be heard the clang of crowbars striking the setts. Fluther Good is repairing the lock of door, Right. A claw-hammer is on a chair beside him, and he has a screw-driver in his hand. He is a man of forty years of age, rarely surrendering to thoughts of anxiety, fond of his 'oil' but determined to conquer the habit before he dies. He is square-jawed and harshly featured; under the left eye is a scar, and his nose is bent from a smashing blow received in a fistic battle long ago. He is bald, save for a few peeping tufts of reddish hair around his ears; and his upper lip is hidden by a scrubby red moustache, embroidered here and*

1. By Giorgione, as Fluther almost says (p. 21). The copies of the Millet paintings must have been put up by Nora, but the picture of Emmet, the leader of the abortive Dublin uprising of 1803, is surely Jack's. To decide which of them hung the calendar is to settle some moot questions about characterization.

*there with a grey hair. He is dressed in a seedy black suit, cotton shirt with a soft collar, and wears a very respectable little black bow. On his head is a faded jerry hat, which, when he is excited, he has a habit of knocking farther back on his head, in a series of taps. In an argument he usually fills with sound and fury generally signifying a row. He is in his shirt-sleeves at present, and wears a soiled white apron, from a pocket in which sticks a carpenter's two-foot rule. He has just finished the job of putting on a new lock, and, filled with satisfaction, he is opening and shutting the door, enjoying the completion of a work well done. Sitting at the fire, airing a white shirt, is Peter Flynn. He is a little, thin bit of a man, with a face shaped like a lozenge; on his cheeks and under his chin is a straggling wiry beard of a dirty-white and lemon hue. His face invariably wears a look of animated anguish, mixed with irritated defiance, as if everybody was at war with him, and he at war with everybody. He is cocking his head in a way that suggests resentment at the presence of Fluther, who pays no attention to him, apparently, but is really furtively watching him. Peter is clad in a singlet, white whipcord knee-breeches, and is in his stocking-feet.*

*A voice is heard speaking outside of door, Left. It is that of Mrs. Gogan.*

MRS. GOGAN (*outside*) Who are you lookin' for, sir? Who? Mrs. Clitheroe? . . . Oh, excuse me. Oh ay, up this way. She's out, I think: I seen her goin'. Oh, you've somethin' for her; oh, excuse me. You're from Arnott's. . . . I see. . . . You've a parcel for her. . . . Righto. . . . I'll take it. . . . I'll give it to her the minute she comes in. . . . It'll be quite safe. . . . Oh, sign that. . . . Excuse me. . . . Where? . . . Here? . . . No, there; righto. Am I to put Maggie or Mrs.? What is it? You dunno? Oh, excuse me.

*Mrs. Gogan opens the door and comes in. She is a doleful-looking little woman of forty, insinuating manner and sallow complexion. She is fidgety and nervous, terribly talkative, has a habit of taking up things that may be near her and fiddling with them while she is speaking. Her heart is aflame with curiosity, and a fly could not come into nor go out of the house without her knowing. She has a draper's parcel in her hand, the knot of the twine tying it is untied. Peter, more resentful of this intrusion than of Fluther's presence, gets up from the chair, and without looking around, his head carried at an angry cock, marches into the room at back.*

MRS. GOGAN (*removing the paper and opening the cardboard box it contains*) I wondher what's this now? A hat! (*She takes out a hat, black, with decorations in red and gold.*) God, she's goin' to th' divil lately for style! That hat, now, cost more than a penny. Such notions of upperosity she's gettin'. (*Putting the hat on her head.*) Oh, swank, what! (*She replaces it in parcel.*)

FLUTHER    She's a pretty little Judy, all the same.

MRS. GOGAN    Ah, she is, an' she isn't. There's prettiness an' prettiness in it. I'm always sayin' that her skirts are a little too short for a married woman. An' to see her, sometimes of an evenin', in her glad-neck gown would make a body's blood run cold. I do be ashamed of me life before her husband. An' th' way she thries to be polite, with her 'Good mornin', Mrs. Gogan', when she's goin' down, an' her 'Good evenin', Mrs. Gogan', when she's comin' up. But there's politeness an' politeness in it.

FLUTHER    They seem to get on well together, all th' same.

MRS. GOGAN    Ah, they do, an' they don't. The pair o' them used to be like two turtle doves always billin' an' cooin'. You couldn't come into th' room but you'd feel, instinctive like, that they'd just been affher kissin' an' cuddlin' each other. . . . It often made me shiver, for, affher all, there's kissin' an' cuddlin' in it. But I'm thinkin' he's beginnin' to take things more quietly; the mystery of havin' a woman's a mystery no longer. . . . She dhresses herself to keep him with her, but it's no use—affher a month or two, th' wondher of a woman wears off.

FLUTHER    I dunno, I dunno. Not wishin' to say anything derogatory, I think it's all a question of location: when a man finds th' wondher of one woman beginnin' to die, it's usually beginnin' to live in another.

MRS. GOGAN    She's always grumblin' about havin' to live in a tenement house. 'I wouldn't like to spend me last hour in one, let alone live me life in a tenement,' says she. 'Vaults,' says she, 'that are hidin' th' dead, instead of homes that are sheltherin' th' livin'.' 'Many a good one,' says I, 'was reared in a tenement house.' Oh, you know, she's a well-up little lassie, too; able to make a shillin' go where another would have to spend a pound. She's wipin' th' eyes[2] of th' Covey an' poor oul' Pether—everybody knows that—screwin' every penny she can out o' them, in ordher to turn th' place

2. Robbing them.

into a babby-house.[3] An' she has th' life frightened out o'
them; washin' their face, combin' their hair, wipin' their
feet, brushin' their clothes, thrimmin' their nails, cleanin'
their teeth—God Almighty, you'd think th' poor men were
undhergoin' penal servitude.

FLUTHER (*with an exclamation of disgust*) A-a-ah, that's goin'
beyond th' beyonds in a tenement house. That's a little bit
too derogatory.

*Peter enters from room, Back, head elevated and resentful fire in his
eyes; he is still in his singlet and trousers, but is now wearing a pair of
unlaced boots—possibly to be decent in the presence of Mrs. Gogan. He
places the white shirt, which he has carried in on his arm, on the back
of a chair near the fire, and, going over to the chest of drawers, he
opens drawer after drawer, looking for something; as he fails to find it
he closes each drawer with a snap; he pulls out pieces of linen neatly
folded, and bundles them back again any way.*

PETER (*in accents of anguish*) Well, God Almighty, give me
patience! (*He returns to room, Back, giving the shirt a vicious turn
as he passes.*)

MRS. GOGAN I wondher what he is foostherin'[4] for now?

FLUTHER He's adornin' himself for th' meeting to-night.
(*Pulling a handbill from his pocket and reading.*) 'Great Demonstration an' torchlight procession around places in th' city
sacred to th' memory of Irish Patriots, to be concluded be a
meetin', at which will be taken an oath of fealty to th' Irish
Republic. Formation in Parnell Square at eight o'clock.'
Well, they can hold it for Fluther. I'm up th' pole; no more
dhrink for Fluther. It's three days now since I touched a
dhrop, an' I feel a new man already.

MRS. GOGAN Isn't oul' Peter a funny-lookin' little man? . . .
Like somethin' you'd pick off a Christmas Tree. . . . When
he's dhressed up in his canonicals, you'd wondher where
he'd been got. God forgive me, when I see him in them, I
always think he must ha' had a Mormon for a father! He
an' th' Covey can't abide each other; th' pair o' them is
always at it, thryin' to best each other. There'll be blood
dhrawn one o' these days.

3. A doll house.
4. Bustling around.

FLUTHER   How is it that Clitheroe himself, now, doesn't have anythin' to do with th' Citizen Army? A couple o' months ago, an' you'd hardly ever see him without his gun, an' th' Red Hand o' Liberty Hall⁵ in his hat.

MRS. GOGAN   Just because he wasn't made a Captain of. He wasn't goin' to be in anything where he couldn't be conspishuous. He was so cocksure o' being made one that he bought a Sam Browne belt, an' was always puttin' it on an' standin' at th' door showing it off till th' man came an' put out th' street lamps on him. God, I think he used to bring it to bed with him! But I'm tellin' you herself was delighted that that cock didn't crow, for she's like a clockin' hen if he leaves her sight for a minute.

*While she is talking, she takes up book after book from the table, looks into each of them in a near-sighted way, and then leaves them back. She now lifts up the sword, and proceeds to examine it.*

MRS. GOGAN   Be th' look of it, this must ha' been a general's sword. . . . All th' gold lace an' th' fine figaries on it. . . . Sure it's twiced too big for him.

FLUTHER   A-ah; it's a baby's rattle he ought to have, an' he as he is with thoughts tossin' in his head of what may happen to him on th' day o' judgement.

*Peter has entered, and seeing Mrs. Gogan with the sword, goes over to her, pulls it resentfully out of her hands, and marches into the room, Back, without speaking.*

MRS. GOGAN (*as Peter whips the sword*)   Oh, excuse me! . . . (*To Fluther.*) Isn't he th' surly oul' rascal!

FLUTHER   Take no notice of him. . . . You'd think he was dumb, but when you get his goat, or he has a few jars up, he's vice versa. (*He coughs.*)

MRS. GOGAN (*she has now sidled over as far as the shirt hanging on the chair*)   Oh, you've got a cold on you, Fluther.

FLUTHER (*carelessly*)   Ah, it's only a little one.

MRS. GOGAN   You'd want to be careful, all th' same. I knew a woman, a big lump of a woman, red-faced an' round-bod-ied, a little awkward on her feet; you'd think, to look at her,

5. Headquarters of the Irish Transport and General Workers' Union, hence of the Citizen Army.

she could put out her two arms an' lift a two-storied house on th' top of her head; got a ticklin' in her throat, an' a little cough, an' th' next mornin' she had a little catchin' in her chest, an' they had just time to wet her lips with a little rum, an' off she went. (*She begins to look at and handle the shirt.*)

FLUTHER (*a little nervously*) It's only a little cold I have; there's nothing derogatory wrong with me.

MRS. GOGAN I dunno; there's many a man this minute lowerin' a pint, thinkin' of a woman, or pickin' out a winner, or doin' work as you're doin', while th' hearse dhrawn be th' horses with the black plumes is dhrivin' up to his own hall door, an' a voice that he doesn't hear is muttherin' in his ear, 'Earth to earth, an' ashes t' ashes, an' dust to dust.'

FLUTHER (*faintly*) A man in th' pink o' health should have a holy horror of allowin' thoughts o' death to be festerin' in his mind, for (*with a frightened cough*) be God, I think I'm afther gettin' a little catch in me chest that time—it's a creepy thing to be thinkin' about.

MRS. GOGAN It is, an' it isn't; it's both bad an' good. . . . It always gives meself a kind o' thresspassin' joy to feel meself movin' along in a mournin' coach, an' me thinkin' that, maybe, th' next funeral 'll be me own, an' glad, in a quiet way, that this is somebody else's.

FLUTHER An' a curious kind of a gaspin' for breath—I hope there's nothin' derogatory wrong with me.

MRS. GOGAN (*examining the shirt*) Frills on it, like a woman's petticoat.

FLUTHER Suddenly gettin' hot, an' then, just as suddenly, gettin' cold.

MRS. GOGAN (*holding out the shirt towards Fluther*) How would you like to be wearin' this Lord Mayor's nightdhress, Fluther?

FLUTHER (*vehemently*) Blast you an' your nightshirt! Is a man fermentin' with fear to stick th' showin' off to him of a thing that looks like a shinin' shroud?

MRS. GOGAN Oh, excuse me!

*Peter has again entered, and he pulls the shirt from the hands of Mrs. Gogan, replacing it on the chair. He returns to room.*

PETER (*as he goes out*)   Well, God Almighty, give me patience!
MRS. GOGAN (*to Peter*)   Oh, excuse me!

*There is heard a cheer from the men working outside on the street, followed by the clang of tools being thrown down, then silence. The glare of the gasolene light diminishes and finally goes out.*

MRS. GOGAN   (*running onto the back room to look out of the window*)   What's the men repairin' th' streets cheerin' for?
FLUTHER (*sitting down weakly on a chair*)   You can't sneeze but that oul' one wants to know th' why an' th' wherefore. . . . I feel as dizzy as bedamned! I hope I didn't give up th' beer too suddenly.

*The Covey comes in by the door, Right. He is about twenty-five, tall, thin, with lines on his face that form a perpetual protest against life as he conceives it to be. Heavy seams fall from each side of nose, down around his lips, as if they were suspenders keeping his mouth from falling. He speaks in a slow, wailing drawl; more rapidly when he is excited. He is dressed in dungarees, and is wearing a vividly red tie. He flings his cap with a gesture of disgust on the table, and begins to take off his overalls.*

MRS. GOGAN (*to the Covey, as she runs back into the room*)   What's after happenin', Covey?
THE COVEY (*with contempt*)   Th' job's stopped. They've been mobilized to march in th' demonstration to-night undher th' Plough an' th' Stars. Didn't you hear them cheerin', th' mugs! They have to renew their political baptismal vows to be faithful in seculo seculorum.[6]
FLUTHER (*forgetting his fear in his indignation*)   There's no reason to bring religion into it. I think we ought to have as great a regard for religion as we can, so as to keep it out of as many things as possible.
THE COVEY (*pausing in the taking off of his dungarees*)   Oh, you're one o' the boys that climb into religion as high as a short Mass on Sunday mornin's? I suppose you'll be singin' songs o' Sion an' songs o' Tara at th' meetin', too.
FLUTHER   We're all Irishmen, anyhow; aren't we?

---

6. Forever. O'Casey likes to sprinkle his characters' speeches with something that suggests ecclesiastical Latin, particularly when they are mocking, or he is.

THE COVEY (*with hand outstretched, and in a professional tone*) Look here, comrade, there's no such thing as an Irishman, or an Englishman, or a German or a Turk; we're all only human bein's. Scientifically speakin', it's all a question of the accidental gatherin' together of mollycewels an' atoms.

*Peter comes in with a collar in his hand. He goes over to mirror, Left, and proceeds to try to put it on.*

FLUTHER Mollycewels an' atoms! D'ye think I'm goin' to listen to you thryin' to juggle Fluther's mind with complicated cunundhrums of mollycewels an' atoms?

THE COVEY (*rather loudly*) There's nothin' complicated in it. There's no fear o' the Church tellin' you that mollycewels is a stickin' together of millions of atoms o' sodium, carbon, potassium o' iodidc, etcetera, that, accordin' to th' way they're mixed, make a flower, a fish, a star that you see shinin' in th' sky, or a man with a big brain like me, or a man with a little brain like you!

FLUTHER (*more loudly still*) There's no necessity to be raisin' your voice; shoutin's no manifestin' forth of a growin' mind.

PETER (*struggling with his collar*) God, give me patience with this thing. . . . She makes these collars as stiff with starch as a shinin' band o' solid steel! She does it purposely to thry an' twart me. If I can't get it on th' singlet, how, in th' Name o' God, am I goin' to get it on th' shirt?

THE COVEY (*loudly*) There's no use o' arguin' with you; it's education you want, comrade.

FLUTHER The Covey an' God made th' world, I suppose, wha'?

THE COVEY When I hear some men talkin' I'm inclined to disbelieve that th' world's eight-hundhred million years old, for it's not long since th' fathers o' some o' them crawled out o' th' sheltherin' slime o' the sea.

MRS. GOGAN (*from room at back*) There, they're afther formin' fours, an' now they're goin' to march away.

FLUTHER (*scornfully*) Mollycewels! (*He begins to untie his apron.*) What about Adam an' Eve?

THE COVEY Well, what about them?

FLUTHER (*fiercely*) What about them, you?

THE COVEY Adam an' Eve! Is that as far as you've got? Are

you still thinkin' there was nobody in th' world before Adam and Eve? (*Loudly.*) Did you ever hear, man, of th' skeleton of th' man o' Java?

PETER (*casting the collar from him*)   Blast it, blast it, blast it!

FLUTHER (*viciously folding his apron*)   Ah, you're not goin' to be let tap your rubbidge o' thoughts into th' mind o' Fluther.

THE COVEY   You're afraid to listen to th' truth!

FLUTHER   Who's afraid?

THE COVEY   You are!

FLUTHER   G'way, you wurum!

THE COVEY   Who's a worum?

FLUTHER   You are, or you wouldn't talk th' way you're talkin'.

THE COVEY   Th' oul', ignorant savage leppin' up in you, when science shows you that th' head of your god is an empty one. Well, I hope you're enjoyin' th' blessin' o' havin' to live be th' sweat of your brow.

FLUTHER   You'll be kickin' an' yellin' for th' priest yet, me boyo. I'm not goin' to stand silent an' simple listenin' to a thick like you makin' a maddenin' mockery o' God Almighty. It 'ud be a nice derogatory thing on me conscience, an' me dyin', to look back in rememberin' shame of talkin' to a word-weavin' little ignorant yahoo of a red flag Socialist!

MRS. GOGAN (*she has returned to the front room, and has wandered around looking at things in general, and is now in front of the fireplace looking at the picture hanging over it*)   For God's sake, Fluther, dhrop it; there's always th' makin's of a row in th' mention of religion . . . (*Looking at picture.*) God bless us, it's a naked woman!

FLUTHER (*coming over to look at it*)   What's undher it? (*Reading.*) 'Georgina: The Sleepin' Vennis'. Oh, that's a terrible picture; oh, that's a shockin' picture! Oh, th' one that got that taken, she must have been a prime lassie!

PETER (*who also has come over to look, laughing, with his body bent at the waist, and his head slightly titled back*)   Hee, hee, hee, hee, hee!

FLUTHER (*indignantly, to Peter*)   What are you hee, hee-in' for? That's a nice thing to be hee, hee-in' at. Where's your morality, man?

MRS. GOGAN   God forgive us, it's not right to be lookin' at it.

FLUTHER   It's nearly a derogatory thing to be in th' room where it is.

MRS. GOGAN (*giggling hysterically*)   I couldn't stop any longer in th' same room with three men, afther lookin' at it! (*She goes out.*)

*The Covey, who has divested himself of his dungarees, throws them with a contemptuous motion on top of Peter's white shirt.*

PETER (*plaintively*)   Where are you throwin' them? Are you thryin' to twart an' torment me again?

THE COVEY   Who's thryin' to twart you?

PETER (*flinging the dungarees violently on the floor*)   You're not goin' to make me lose me temper, me young Covey.

THE COVEY (*flinging the white shirt on the floor*)   If you're Nora's pet, aself, you're not goin' to get your way in everything.

PETER (*plaintively, with his eyes looking up at the ceiling*)   I'll say nothin'. . . . I'll leave you to th' day when th' all-pitiful, all-merciful, all-lovin' God 'll be handin' you to th' angels to be rievin' an' roastin' you, tearin' an' tormentin' you, burnin' an' blastin' you!

THE COVEY   Aren't you th' little malignant oul' bastard, you lemon-whiskered oul' swine!

*Peter runs to the sword, draws it, and makes for the Covey, who dodges him around the table; Peter has no intention of striking, but the Covey wants to take no chance.*

THE COVEY (*dodging*)   Fluther, hold him, there. It's a nice thing to have a lunatic like this lashin' around with a lethal weapon! (*The Covey darts out of the room, Right, slamming the door in the face of Peter.*)

PETER (*battering and pulling at the door*)   Lemme out, lemme out; isn't it a poor thing for a man who wouldn't say a word against his greatest enemy to have to listen to that Covey's twartin' animosities, shovin' poor, patient people into a lashin' out of curses that darken his soul with th' shadow of th' wrath of th' last day!

FLUTHER   Why d'ye take notice of him? If he seen you didn't, he'd say nothin' derogatory.

PETER   I'll make him stop his laughin' an' leerin', jibin' an'

jeerin' an' scarifyin' people with his cornerboy[7] insinuations!
. . . He's always thryin' to rouse me: if it's not a song, it's a
whistle; if it isn't a whistle, it's a cough. But you can taunt
an' taunt—I'm laughin' at you; he, hee, hee, hee, hee, heee!

THE COVEY (*singing through the keyhole*)[8]

Dear harp o' me counthry, in darkness I found thee,
The dark chain of silence had hung o'er thee long—

PETER (*frantically*) Jasus, d'ye hear that? D'ye hear him
soundin' forth his divil-souled song o' provocation?

THE COVEY (*singing as before*)

When proudly, me own island harp, I unbound thee,
An' gave all thy chords to light, freedom an' song!

PETER (*battering at door*) When I get out I'll do for you, I'll do
for you, I'll do for you!

THE COVEY (*through the keyhole*) Cuckoo-oo!

*Nora enters by door, Right. She is a young woman of twenty-two,
alert, swift, full of nervous energy, and a little anxious to get on in the
world. The firm lines of her face are considerably opposed by a soft,
amorous mouth and gentle eyes. When her firmness fails her, she
persuades with her feminine charm. She is dressed in a tailor-made
costume, and wears around her neck a silver fox fur.*

NORA (*running in and pushing Peter away from the door*) Oh, can I
not turn me back but th' two o' yous are at it like a pair o'
fightin' cocks! Uncle Peter . . . Uncle Peter . . . UNCLE
PETER!

PETER (*vociferously*) Oh, Uncle Peter, Uncle Peter be damned!
D'ye think I'm goin' to give a free pass to th' young Covey
to turn me whole life into a Holy Manual o' penances an'
martyrdoms?

THE COVEY (*angrily rushing into the room*) If you won't exercise
some sort o' conthrol over that Uncle Peter o' yours, there'll
be a funeral, an' it won't be me that'll be in th' hearse!

7. Loafer.
8. Here and later in the scene, the Covey uses Thomas Moore's *Irish Melodies* to
taunt Peter. Moore's romantic nationalism makes the songs the right choice for the
Covey, but O'Casey's ironic use of them does not become fully clear until Act Three,
when Bessie refers to one of the most famous of them, "The Minstrel Boy" (p. 66).

NORA (*between Peter and the Covey, to the Covey*)   Are yous always goin' to be tearin' down th' little bit of respectability that a body's thryin' to build up? Am I always goin' to be havin' to nurse yous into th' hardy habit o' thryin' to keep up a little bit of appearance?

THE COVEY   Why weren't you here to see th' way he run at me with th' sword?

PETER   What did you call me a lemon-whiskered oul' swine for?

NORA   If th' two o' yous don't thry to make a generous altheration in your goin's on, an' keep on thryin' t' inaugurate th' customs o' th' rest o' th' house into this place, yous can flit into other lodgin's where your bowsey battlin' 'ill meet, maybe, with an encore.

PETER (*to Nora*)   Would you like to be called a lemon-whiskered oul' swine?

NORA   If you attempt to wag that sword of yours at anybody again, it'll have to be taken off you an' put in a safe place away from babies that don't know th' danger o' them things.

PETER (*at entrance to room, Back*)   Well, I'm not goin' to let anybody call me a lemon-whiskered oul' swine. (*He goes in.*)

FLUTHER (*trying the door*)   Openin' an' shuttin' now with a well-mannered motion, like a door of a select bar in a high-class pub.

NORA (*to the Covey, as she lays table for tea*)   An', once for all, Willie, you'll have to thry to deliver yourself from th' desire of provokin' oul' Pether into a wild forgetfulness of what's proper an' allowable in a respectable home.

THE COVEY   Well, let him mind his own business, then. Yestherday I caught him hee-hee-in' out of him an' he readin' bits out of Jenersky's *Thesis on th' Origin, Development, an' Consolidation of th' Evolutionary Idea of th' Proletariat.*

NORA   Now, let it end at that, for God's sake; Jack'll be in any minute, an' I'm not goin' to have th' quiet of this evenin' tossed about in an everlastin' uproar between you an' Uncle Pether. (*To Fluther.*) Well, did you manage to settle th' lock, yet, Mr. Good?

FLUTHER (*opening and shutting door*)   It's betther than a new one, now, Mrs. Clitheroe; it's almost ready to open and shut of its own accord.

NORA (*giving him a coin*) You're a whole man. How many pints will that get you?

FLUTHER (*seriously*) Ne'er a one at all, Mrs. Clitheroe, for Fluther's on th' wather waggon now. You could stan' where you're stannin' chantin', 'Have a glass o' malt, Fluther; Fluther, have a glass o' malt,' till th' bells would be ringin' th' ould year out an' th' New Year in, an' you'd have as much chance o' movin' Fluther as a tune on a tin whistle would move a deaf man an' he dead.

*As Nora is opening and shutting door, Mrs. Bessie Burgess appears at it. She is a woman of forty, vigorously built. Her face is a dogged one, hardened by toil, and a little coarsened by drink. She looks scornfully and viciously at Nora for a few moments before she speaks.*

BESSIE Puttin' a new lock on her door . . . afraid her poor neighbours ud break through an' steal. . . . (*In a loud tone.*) Maybe, now, they're a damn sight more honest than your ladyship . . . checkin' th' children playin' on th' stairs . . . gettin' on th' nerves of your ladyship. . . . Complainin' about Bessie Burgess singin' her hymns at night, when she has a few up. . . . (*She comes in half-way on the threshold, and screams.*) Bessie Burgess 'll sing whenever she damn well likes!

*Nora tries to shut the door, but Bessie violently shoves it in, and, gripping Nora by the shoulders, shakes her.*

BESSIE You little over-dressed throllop, you, for one pin I'd paste th' white face o' you!

NORA (*frightened*) Fluther, Fluther!

FLUTHER (*running over and breaking the hold of Bessie from Nora*) Now, now, Bessie, Bessie, leave poor Mrs. Clitheroe alone; she'd do no one any harm, an' minds no one's business but her own.

BESSIE Why is she always thryin' to speak proud things, an' lookin' like a mighty one in th' congregation o' th' people!

*Nora sinks frightened on to the couch as Jack Clitheroe enters. He is a tall, well-made fellow of twenty-five. His face has none of the strength of Nora's. It is a face in which is the desire for authority, without the power to attain it.*

CLITHEROE (*excitedly*) What's up? What's afther happenin'?

FLUTHER Nothin', Jack. Nothin'. It's all over now. Come on, Bessie, come on.

CLITHEROE (*to Nora*) What's wrong, Nora? Did she say anything to you?

NORA She was bargin' out of her, an' I only told her to g'up ower o' that to her own place; an' before I knew where I was, she flew at me like a tiger, an' thried to guzzle me!

CLITHEROE (*going to door and speaking to Bessie*) Get up to your own place, Mrs. Burgess, and don't you be interferin' with my wife, or it'll be th' worse for you. . . . Go on, go on!

BESSIE (*as Clitheroe is pushing her out*) Mind who you're pushin', now. . . . I attend me place o' worship, anyhow . . . not like some o' them that go to neither church, chapel nor meetin'-house. . . . If me son was home from th' threnches he'd see me righted.

*Bessie and Fluther depart, and Clitheroe closes the door.*

CLITHEROE (*going over to Nora, and putting his arm round her*) There, don't mind that old bitch, Nora, darling; I'll soon put a stop to her interferin'.

NORA Some day or another, when I'm here be meself, she'll come in an' do somethin' desperate.

CLITHEROE (*kissing her*) Oh, sorra[9] fear of her doin' anythin' desperate. I'll talk to her to-morrow when she's sober. A taste o' me mind that'll shock her into the sensibility of behavin' herself!

*Nora gets up and settles the table. She sees the dungarees on the floor and stands looking at them, then she turns to the Covey, who is reading Jenersky's 'Thesis' at the fire.*

NORA Willie, is that th' place for your dungarees?

THE COVEY (*getting up and lifting them from the floor*) Ah, they won't do th' floor any harm, will they? (*He carries them into room, Back.*)

NORA (*calling*) Uncle Peter, now, Uncle Peter; tea's ready.

*Peter and the Covey come in from room, Back; they all sit down to tea. Peter is in full dress of the Foresters: green coat, gold braided; white*

9. Sorrow. The expression means "little fear."

*breeches, top boots, frilled shirt. He carries the slouch hat, with the white ostrich plume, and the sword in his hands. They eat for a few moments in silence, the Covey furtively looking at Peter with scorn in his eyes. Peter knows it and is fidgety.*

THE COVEY (*provokingly*) Another cut o' bread, Uncle Peter? (*Peter maintains a dignified silence.*)

CLITHEROE It's sure to be a great meetin' to-night. We ought to go, Nora.

NORA (*decisively*) I won't go, Jack; you can go if you wish.

THE COVEY D'ye want th' sugar, Uncle Peter? (*A pause.*)

PETER (*explosively*) Now, are you goin' to start your thryin' an' your twartin' again?

NORA Now, Uncle Peter, you mustn't be so touchy; Willie has only assed you if you wanted th' sugar.

PETER He doesn't care a damn whether I want th' sugar or no. He's only thryin' to twart me!

NORA (*angrily, to the Covey*) Can't you let him alone, Willie? If he wants the sugar, let him stretch his hand out an' get it himself!

THE COVEY (*to Peter*) Now, if you want the sugar, you can stretch out your hand and get it yourself!

CLITHEROE To-night is th' first chance that Brennan has got of showing himself off since they made a Captain of him—why, God only knows. It'll be a treat to see him swankin' it at th' head of the Citizen Army carryin' th' flag of the Plough an' th' Stars. . . . (*Looking roguishly at Nora.*) He was sweet on you, once, Nora?

NORA He may have been. . . . I never liked him. I always thought he was a bit of a thick.

THE COVEY They're bringin' nice disgrace on that banner now.

CLITHEROE (*remonstratively*) How are they bringin' disgrace on it?

THE COVEY (*snappily*) Because it's a Labour flag, an' was never meant for politics. . . . What does th' design of th' field plough, bearin' on it th' stars of th' heavenly plough, mean, if it's not Communism? It's a flag that should only be used when we're buildin' th' barricades to fight for a Workers' Republic!

PETER (*with a puff of derision*)  P-phuh.

THE COVEY (*angrily*)  What are you phuhin' out o' you for? Your mind is th' mind of a mummy. (*Rising.*) I betther go an' get a good place to have a look at Ireland's warriors passin' by. (*He goes into room, Left, and returns with his cap.*)

NORA (*to the Covey*)  Oh, Willie, brush your clothes before you go.

THE COVEY  Oh, they'll do well enough.

NORA  Go an' brush them; th' brush is in th' drawer there.

*The Covey goes to the drawer, muttering, gets the brush, and starts to brush his clothes.*

THE COVEY (*singing at Peter, as he does so*)

Oh, where's th' slave so lowly,
Condemn'd to chains unholy,
Who, could he burst his bonds at first,
Would pine beneath them slowly?

We tread th' land that . . . bore us,
Th' green flag glitters . . . o'er us,
Th' friends we've tried are by our side,
An' th' foe we hate . . . before us!

PETER (*leaping to his feet in a whirl of rage*)  Now, I'm tellin' you, me young Covey, once for all, that I'll not stick any longer these tittherin' taunts of yours, rovin' around to sing your slights an' slandhers, reddenin' th' mind of a man to th' thinkin' an' sayin' of things that sicken his soul with sin! (*Hysterical; lifting up a cup to fling at the Covey.*) Be God, I'll—

CLITHEROE (*catching his arm*)  Now then, none o' that, none o' that!

NORA  Uncle Pether, Uncle Pether, UNCLE PETHER!

THE COVEY (*at the door, about to go out*)  Isn't that th' malignant oul' varmint! Lookin' like th' illegitimate son of an illegitimate child of a corporal in th' Mexican army! (*He goes out.*)

PETER (*plaintively*)  He's afther leavin' me now in such a state of agitation that I won't be able to do meself justice when I'm marchin' to th' meetin'.

NORA (*jumping up*)  Oh, for God's sake, here, buckle your

sword on, and go to your meetin', so that we'll have at least one hour of peace! (*She proceeds to belt on the sword.*)

CLITHEROE (*irritably*) For God's sake hurry him up ou' o' this, Nora.

PETER Are yous all goin' to thry to start to twart me now?

NORA (*putting on his plumed hat*) S-s-sh. Now, your hat's on, your house is thatched; off you pop! (*She gently pushes him from her.*)

PETER (*going, and turning as he reaches the door*) Now, if that young Covey—

NORA Go on, go on. (*He goes.*)

*Clitheroe sits down in the lounge, lights a cigarette, and looks thoughtfully into the fire. Nora takes the things from the table, placing them on the chest of drawers. There is a pause, then she swiftly comes over to him and sits beside him.*

NORA (*softly*) A penny for them, Jack!

CLITHEROE Me? Oh, I was thinkin' of nothing.

NORA You were thinkin' of th' . . . meetin' . . . Jack. When we were courtin' an' I wanted you to go, you'd say, 'Oh, to hell with meetin's,' an' that you felt lonely in cheerin' crowds when I was absent. An' we weren't a month married when you began that you couldn't keep away from them.

CLITHEROE Oh, that's enough about th' meetin'. It looks as if you wanted me to go th' way you're talkin'. You were always at me to give up th' Citizen Army, an' I gave it up; surely that ought to satisfy you.

NORA Ay, you gave it up—because you got th' sulks when they didn't make a Captain of you. It wasn't for my sake, Jack.

CLITHEROE For your sake or no, you're benefitin' by it, aren't you? I didn't forget this was your birthday, did I? (*He puts his arms around her.*) And you liked your new hat; didn't you, didn't you? (*He kisses her rapidly several times.*)

NORA (*panting*) Jack, Jack; please, Jack! I thought you were tired of that sort of thing long ago.

CLITHEROE Well, you're finding out now that I amn't tired of it yet, anyhow. Mrs. Clitheroe doesn't want to be kissed, sure she doesn't? (*He kisses her again.*) Little, little red-lipped Nora!

NORA (*coquettishly removing his arm from around her*)   Oh, yes, your little, little red-lipped Nora's a sweet little girl when th' fit seizes you; but your little, little red-lipped Nora has to clean your boots every mornin', all the same.

CLITHEROE (*with a movement of irritation*)   Oh, well, if we're goin' to be snotty! (*A pause.*)

NORA   It's lookin' like as if it was you that was goin' to be . . . snotty! Bridlin' up with bittherness, th' minute a body attempts t' open her mouth.

CLITHEROE   Is it any wondher, turnin' a tendher sayin' into a meanin' o' malice an' spite!

NORA   It's hard for a body to be always keepin' her mind bent on makin' thoughts that'll be no longer than th' length of your own satisfaction. (*A pause.*)

NORA (*standing up*)   If we're goin' to dhribble th' time away sittin' here like a pair o' cranky mummies, I'd be as well sewin' or doin' something about th' place.

*She looks appealingly at him for a few moments; he doesn't speak. She swiftly sits down beside him, and puts her arm around his neck.*

NORA (*imploringly*)   Ah, Jack, don't be so cross!

CLITHEROE (*doggedly*)   Cross? I'm not cross; I'm not a bit cross. It was yourself started it.

NORA (*coaxingly*)   I didn't mean to say anything out o' the way. You take a body up too quickly, Jack. (*In an ordinary tone as if nothing of an angry nature had been said.*) You didn't offer me me evenin' allowance yet.

*Clitheroe silently takes out a cigarette for her and himself and lights both.*

NORA (*trying to make conversation*)   How quiet th' house is now; they must be all out.

CLITHEROE (*rather shortly*)   I suppose so.

NORA (*rising from the seat*)   I'm longin' to show you me new hat, to see what you think of it. Would you like to see it?

CLITHEROE   Ah, I don't mind.

*Nora suppresses a sharp reply, hesitates for a moment, then gets the hat, puts it on, and stands before Clitheroe.*

NORA   Well, how does Mr. Clitheroe like me new hat?

CLITHEROE    It suits you, Nora, it does right enough. (*He stands up, puts his hand beneath her chin, and tilts her head up. She looks at him roguishly. He bends down and kisses her.*)

NORA    Here, sit down, an' don't let me hear another cross word out of you for th' rest o' the night. (*They sit down.*)

CLITHEROE    (*with his arms around her*)    Little, little, red-lipped Nora!

NORA    (*with a coaxing movement of her body towards him*)    Jack!

CLITHEROE    (*tightening his arms around her*)    Well?

NORA    You haven't sung me a song since our honeymoon. Sing me one now, do . . . please, Jack!

CLITHEROE    What song? 'Since Maggie Went Away'?

NORA    Ah, no, Jack, not that; it's too sad. 'When You Said You Loved Me.'

*Clearing his throat, Clitheroe thinks for a moment and then begins to sing. Nora, putting an arm around him, nestles her head on his breast and listens delightedly.*

CLITHEROE    (*singing verses following to the air of 'When You and I Were Young, Maggie'*)

Th' violets were scenting th' woods, Nora,
    Displaying their charm to th' bee,
When I first said I lov'd only you, Nora,
    An' you said you lov'd only me!

Th' chestnut blooms gleam'd through th' glade, Nora,
    A robin sang loud from a tree,
When I first said I lov'd only you, Nora,
    An' you said you lov'd only me!

Th' golden-rob'd daffodils shone, Nora,
    An' danc'd in th' breeze on th' lea,
When I first said I lov'd only you, Nora,
    An' you said you lov'd only me!

Th' trees, birds, an' bees sang a song, Nora,
    Of happier transports to be.
When I first said I lov'd only you, Nora,
    An' you said you lov'd only me!

*Nora kisses him.*

*A knock is heard at the door, Right; a pause as they listen. Nora clings closely to Clitheroe. Another knock more imperative than the first.*

CLITHEROE   I wonder who can that be, now?

NORA (*a little nervous*)   Take no notice of it, Jack; they'll go away in a minute. (*Another knock, followed by a voice.*)

VOICE   Commandant Clitheroe, Commandant Clitheroe, are you there? A message from General Jim Connolly.

CLITHEROE   Damn it, it's Captain Brennan.

NORA (*anxiously*)   Don't mind him, don't mind, Jack. Don't break our happiness. . . . Pretend we're not in. Let us forget everything to-night but our two selves!

CLITHEROE (*reassuringly*)   Don't be alarmed, darling; I'll just see what he wants, an' send him about his business.

NORA (*tremulously*)   No, no. Please, Jack; don't open it. Please, for your own little Nora's sake!

CLITHEROE (*rising to open the door*)   Now don't be silly, Nora.

*Clitheroe opens the door, and admits a young man in the full uniform of the Irish Citizen Army—green suit; slouch green hat caught up at one side by a small Red Hand badge; Sam Browne belt, with a revolver in the holster. He carries a letter in his hand. When he comes in he smartly salutes Clitheroe. The young man is Captain Brennan.*

CAPT. BRENNAN (*giving the letter to Clitheroe*)   A dispatch from General Connolly.

CLITHEROE (*reading. While he is doing so, Brennan's eyes are fixed on Nora, who droops as she sits on the lounge*)   'Commandant Clitheroe is to take command of the eighth battalion of the I.C.A. which will assemble to proceed to the meeting at nine o'clock. He is to see that all units are provided with full equipment; two days' rations and fifty rounds of ammunition. At two o'clock A.M. the army will leave Liberty Hall for a reconnaissance attack on Dublin Castle.[10]—Com.-Gen. Connolly.'

CLITHEROE   I don't understand this. Why does General Connolly call me Commandant?

CAPT. BRENNAN   Th' Staff appointed you Commandant, and th' General agreed with their selection.

10. The official seat of the British government in Ireland.

CLITHEROE  When did this happen?

CAPT. BRENNAN  A fortnight ago.

CLITHEROE  How is it word was never sent to me?

CAPT. BRENNAN  Word was sent to you. . . . I meself brought it.

CLITHEROE  Who did you give it to, then?

CAPT. BRENNAN  (*after a pause*)  I think I gave it to Mrs. Clitheroe, there.

CLITHEROE  Nora, d'ye hear that? (*Nora makes no answer.*)

CLITHEROE  (*there is a note of hardness in his voice*)  Nora . . . Captain Brennan says he brought a letter to me from General Connolly, and that he gave it to you. . . . Where is it? What did you do with it?

NORA  (*running over to him, and pleadingly putting her arms around him*)  Jack, please, Jack, don't go out to-night an' I'll tell you; I'll explain everything. . . . Send him away, an' stay with your own little red-lipp'd Nora.

CLITHEROE  (*removing her arms from around him*)  None o' this nonsense, now; I want to know what you did with th' letter?

*Nora goes slowly to the lounge and sits down.*

CLITHEROE  (*angrily*)  Why didn't you give me th' letter? What did you do with it? . . . (*He shakes her by the shoulder.*) What did you do with th' letter?

NORA  (*flaming up*)  I burned it, I burned it! That's what I did with it! Is General Connolly an' th' Citizen Army goin' to be your only care? Is your home goin' to be only a place to rest in? Am I goin' to be only somethin' to provide merry-makin' at night for you? Your vanity'll be th' ruin of you an' me yet. . . . That's what's movin' you: because they've made an officer of you, you'll make a glorious cause of what you're doin', while your little red-lipp'd Nora can go on sittin' here, makin' a companion of th' loneliness of th' night!

CLITHEROE  (*fiercely*)  You burned it, did you? (*He grips her arm.*) Well, me good lady—

NORA  Let go—you're hurtin' me!

CLITHEROE  You deserve to be hurt. . . . Any letter that comes to me for th' future, take care that I get it. . . . D'ye hear—take care that I get it!

*He goes to the chest of drawers and takes out a Sam Browne belt,
which he puts on, and then puts a revolver in the holster. He puts on
his hat, and looks towards Nora. While this dialogue is proceeding,
and while Clitheroe prepares himself, Brennan softly whistles 'The
Soldiers' Song'.*[11]

CLITHEROE (*at door, about to go out*)  You needn't wait up for me;
  if I'm in at all, it won't be before six in th' morning.
NORA (*bitterly*)  I don't care if you never come back!
CLITHEROE (*to Capt. Brennan*)  Come along, Ned.

*They go out; there is a pause. Nora pulls her new hat from her head
and with a bitter movement flings it to the other end of the room. There
is a gentle knock at door, Right, which opens, and Mollser comes into
the room. She is about fifteen, but looks to be only about ten, for the
ravages of consumption have shrivelled her up. She is pitifully worn,
walks feebly, and frequently coughs. She goes over to Nora.*

MOLLSER (*to Nora*)  Mother's gone to th' meetin', an' I was
  feelin' terrible lonely, so I come down to see if you'd let me
  sit with you, thinkin' you mightn't be goin' yourself. . . . I
  do be terrible afraid I'll die sometime when I'm be meself.
  . . . I often envy you, Mrs. Clitheroe, seein' th' health you
  have, an' th' lovely place you have here, an' wondherin' if
  I'll ever be sthrong enough to be keepin' a home together for
  a man. Oh, this must be some more o' the Dublin Fusiliers
  flyin' off to the front.[12]

*Just before Mollser ceases to speak, there is heard in the distance the
music of a brass band playing a regiment to the boat on the way to the
front. The tune that is being played is 'It's a Long Way to Tipperary';
as the band comes to the chorus, the regiment is swinging into the street
by Nora's house, and the voices of the soldiers can be heard lustily
singing the chorus of the song:*

11. Written in 1907 by Peadar Kearney (words) and Patrick Heeney (music), it
was simply one of several songs that the Irish nationalists used until the Rising, when
it became such a popular song of defiance that it outdistanced the others. O'Casey's
audience would have recognized it, of course; in fact, it was sung during the riot in the
theater. In July 1926, a few months after *Plough* opened, it became the official national
anthem of the Irish Free State.

12. There were at least half a million Irish in the British Army before World War I
ended. The Dublin Fusiliers were Irishmen fighting for England. Fictionally, Bessie's
son was a Fusilier (see pp. 79–80); actually, O'Casey's brother was.

It's a long way to Tipperary, it's a long way to go;
It's a long way to Tipperary, to th' sweetest girl I know!
Goodbye, Piccadilly, farewell, Leicester Square.
It's a long, long way to Tipperary, but my heart's right
    there!

*Nora and Mollser remain silently listening. As the chorus ends and the music is faint in the distance again, Bessie Burgess appears at door, Right, which Mollser has left open.*

BESSIE (*speaking in towards the room*)   There's th' men marchin' out into th' dhread dimness o' danger, while th' lice is crawlin' about feedin' on th' fatness o' the land! But yous'll not escape from th' arrow that flieth be night, or th' sickness that wasteth be day. . . . An' ladyship an' all, as some o' them may be, they'll be scattered abroad, like th' dust in the darkness!

*Bessie goes away; Nora steals over and quietly shuts the door. She comes back to the lounge and wearily throws herself on it beside Mollser.*

MOLLSER (*after a pause and a cough*)   Is there anybody goin', Mrs. Clitheroe, with a titther o' sense?

**CURTAIN**

# ACT TWO

*A commodious public-house at the corner of the street in which the meeting is being addressed from Platform No. 1. It is the south corner of the public-house that is visible to the audience. The counter, beginning at Back about one-fourth of the width of the space shown, comes across two-thirds of the length of the stage, and, taking a circular sweep, passes out of sight to Left. On the counter are beerpulls, glasses, and a carafe. The other three-fourths of the Back is occupied by a tall, wide, two-paned window. Beside this window at the Right is a small, box-like, panelled snug. Next to the snug is a double swing door, the entrance to that particular end of the house. Farther on is a shelf on which customers may rest their drinks. Underneath the windows is a cushioned seat. Behind the counter at Back can be seen the shelves running the whole length of the counter. On these shelves can be seen the end (or the beginning) of rows of bottles. The Barman is seen wiping the part of the counter which is in view. Rosie is standing at the counter toying with what remains of a half of whisky in a wine-glass. She is a sturdy, well-shaped girl of twenty; pretty, and pert in manner. She is wearing a cream blouse, with an obviously suggestive glad neck; a grey tweed dress, brown stockings and shoes. The blouse and most of the dress are hidden by a black shawl. She has no hat, and in her hair is jauntily set a cheap, glittering, jewelled ornament. It is an hour later.*

BARMAN (*wiping counter*) Nothin' much doin' in your line to-night, Rosie?

ROSIE Curse o' God on th' haporth,[1] hardly, Tom. There isn't much notice taken of a pretty petticoat of a night like this. . . . They're all in a holy mood. Th' solemn-lookin' dials on th' whole o' them an' they marchin' to th' meetin'. You'd think they were th' glorious company of th' saints, an' th' noble army of martyrs thrampin' through th' sthreets of paradise. They're all thinkin' of higher things than a girl's garthers. . . . It's a tremendous meetin'; four platforms they have—there's one o' them just outside opposite th' window.

BARMAN Oh, ay; sure when th' speaker comes (*motioning with his hand*) to th' near end, here, you can see him plain, an' hear nearly everythin' he's spoutin' out of him.

ROSIE It's no joke thryin' to make up fifty-five shillin's a week for your keep an' laundhry, an' then taxin' you a quid for your own room if you bring home a friend for th' night. . . . If I could only put by a couple of quid for a swankier outfit, everythin' in th' garden ud look lovely—

BARMAN Whisht, till we hear what he's sayin'.

*Through the window is silhouetted the figure of a tall man who is speaking to the crowd. The Barman and Rosie look out of the window and listen.*

THE VOICE OF THE MAN[2] It is a glorious thing to see arms in the hands of Irishmen. We must accustom ourselves to the thought of arms, we must accustom ourselves to the sight of

1. Halfpenny worth. The expression means "God help us."
2. O'Casey used a real speech by P. H. Pearse. See pp. 10–11.

arms, we must accustom ourselves to the use of arms. . . . Bloodshed is a cleansing and sanctifying thing, and the nation that regards it as the final horror has lost its manhood. . . . There are many things more horrible than bloodshed, and slavery is one of them! (*The figure moves away towards the Right, and is lost to sight and hearing.*)

ROSIE  It's th' sacred thruth, mind you, what that man's afther sayin'.

BARMAN  If I was only a little younger, I'd be plungin' mad into th' middle of it!

ROSIE (*who is still looking out of the window*)  Oh, here's the two gems runnin' over again for their oil!

*Peter and Fluther enter tumultuously. They are hot, and full and hasty with the things they have seen and heard. Emotion is bubbling up in them, so that when they drink, and when they speak, they drink and speak with the fullness of emotional passion. Peter leads the way to the counter.*

PETER (*splutteringly to Barman*)  Two halves . . . (*To Fluther.*) A meetin' like this always makes me feel as if I could dhrink Loch Erinn dhry!

FLUTHER  You couldn't feel any way else at a time like this when th' spirit of a man is pulsin' to be out fightin' for th' thruth with his feet thremblin' on th' way, maybe to th' gallows, an' his ears tinglin' with th' faint, far-away sound of burstin' rifle–shots that'll maybe whip th' last little shock o' life out of him that's left lingerin' in his body!

PETER  I felt a burnin' lump in me throat when I heard th' band playin' 'The Soldiers' Song', rememberin' last hearin' it marchin' in military formation with th' people starin' on both sides at us, carryin' with us th' pride an' resolution o' Dublin to th' grave of Wolfe Tone.[3]

FLUTHER  Get th' Dublin men goin' an' they'll go on full force for anything that's thryin' to bar them away from what they're wantin', where th' slim thinkin' counthry boyo ud limp away from th' first faintest touch of compromization!

PETER (*hurriedly to the Barman*)  Two more, Tom! . . . (*To Fluther.*) Th' memory of all th' things that was done, an' all

3. The hero of the failed insurrection of 1798. By 1916, the annual pilgrimage to his grave in Bodenstown, usually held in June, was established as an important occasion for Irish nationalists.

th' things that was suffered be th' people, was boomin' in me brain. . . . Every nerve in me body was quiverin' to do somethin' desperate!

FLUTHER   Jammed as I was in th' crowd, I listened to th' speeches patterin' on th' people's head, like rain fallin' on th' corn; every derogatory thought went out o' me mind, an' I said to meself, 'You can die now, Fluther, for you've seen th' shadow-dhreams of th' past leppin' to life in th' bodies of livin' men that show, if we were without a titther o' courage for centuries, we're vice versa now!' Looka here. (*He stretches out his arm under Peter's face and rolls up his sleeve.*) The blood was BOILIN' in me veins!

*The silhouette of the tall figure again moves into the frame of the window speaking to the people.*

PETER (*unaware, in his enthusiasm, of the speaker's appearance, to Fluther*)   I was burnin' to dhraw me sword, an' wave an' wave it over me—

FLUTHER (*overwhelming Peter*)   Will you stop your blatherin' for a minute, man, an' let us hear what he's sayin'!

VOICE OF THE MAN   Comrade soldiers of the Irish Volunteers and of the Citizen Army we rejoice in this terrible war. The old heart of the earth needed to be warmed with the red wine of the battlefields. . . . Such august homage was never offered to God as this: the homage of millions of lives given gladly for love of country. And we must be ready to pour out the same red wine in the same glorious sacrifice, for without shedding of blood there is no redemption! (*The figure moves out of sight and hearing.*)

FLUTHER (*gulping down the drink that remains in his glass, and rushing out*)   Come on, man; this is too good to be missed!

*Peter finishes his drink less rapidly, and as he is going out wiping his mouth with the back of his hand he runs into the Covey coming in. He immediately erects his body like a young cock, and with his chin thrust forward, and a look of venomous dignity on his face, he marches out.*

THE COVEY (*at counter*)   Give us a glass o' malt, for God's sake, till I stimulate meself from the shock o' seein' th' sight that's afther goin' out!

ROSIE (*all business, coming over to the counter, and standing near the*

*Covey*)   Another one for me, Tommy; (*To the Barman.*) th' young gentleman's ordherin' it in th' corner of his eye.

*The Barman brings the drink for the Covey, and leaves it on the counter. Rosie whips it up.*

BARMAN   Ay, houl' on there, houl' on there, Rosie!

ROSIE (*to the Barman*)   What are you houldin' on out o' you for? Didn't you hear th' young gentleman say that he couldn't refuse anything to a nice little bird? (*To the Covey.*) Isn't that right, Jiggs? (*The Covey says nothing.*) Didn't I know, Tommy, it would be all right? It takes Rosie to size a young man up, an' tell th' thoughts that are thremblin' in his mind. Isn't that right, Jiggs?

*The Covey stirs uneasily, moves a little farther away, and pulls his cap over his eyes.*

ROSIE (*moving after him*)   Great meetin' that's gettin' held outside. Well, it's up to us all, anyway, to fight for our freedom.

THE COVEY (*to Barman*)   Two more, please. (*To Rosie.*) Freedom! What's th' use o' freedom, if it's not economic freedom?

ROSIE (*emphasizing with extended arm and moving finger*)   I used them very words just before you come in. 'A lot o' thricksters,' says I, 'that wouldn't know what freedom was if they got it from their mother.' . . . (*To Barman.*) Didn't I, Tommy?

BARMAN   I disremember.

ROSIE   No, you don't disremember. Remember you said, yourself, it was all 'only a flash in th' pan'. Well, 'flash in th' pan, or no flash in th' pan,' says I, 'they're not goin' to get Rosie Redmond,' says I, 'to fight for freedom that wouldn't be worth winnin' in a raffle!'

THE COVEY   There's only one freedom for th' workin' man: conthrol o' th' means o' production, rates of exchange, an' th' means of disthribution. (*Tapping Rosie on the shoulder.*) Look here, comrade, I'll leave here to-morrow night for you a copy of Jenersky's *Thesis on the Origin, Development, an' Consolidation of the Evolutionary Idea of the Proletariat.*

ROSIE (*throwing off her shawl on to the counter, and showing an exemplified glad neck, which reveals a good deal of a white bosom*) If y'ass Rosie, it's heartbreakin' to see a young fella thinkin' of anything, or admirin' anything, but silk transparent stockin's showin' off the shape of a little lassie's legs!

*The Covey, frightened, moves a little away.*

ROSIE (*following on*)  Out in th' park in th' shade of a warm summery evenin', with your little darlin' bridie to be, kissin' an' cuddlin' (*she tries to put her arm around his neck*) kissin' an' cuddlin', ay?

THE COVEY (*frightened*)  Ay, what are you doin'? None o' that, now; none o' that. I've something else to do besides shinannickin' afther Judies!

*He turns away, but Rosie follows, keeping face to face with him.*

ROSIE  Oh, little duckey, oh, shy little duckey! Never held a mot's hand, an' wouldn't know how to tittle a little Judy! (*She clips him under the chin.*) Tittle him undher th' chin, tittle him undher th' chin!

THE COVEY (*breaking away and running out*)  Ay, go on, now; I don't want to have any meddlin' with a lassie like you!

ROSIE (*enraged*)  Jasus, it's in a monasthery some of us ought to be, spendin' our holidays kneelin' on our adorers, tellin' our beads, an' knockin' hell out of our buzzums!

THE COVEY (*outside*)  Cuckoo-oo!

*Peter and Fluther come in again, followed by Mrs. Gogan, carrying a baby in her arms. They go over to the counter.*

PETER (*with plaintive anger*)  It's terrible that young Covey can't let me pass without proddin' at me! Did you hear him murmurin' 'cuckoo' when we were passin'?

FLUTHER (*irritably*)  I wouldn't be everlastin' cockin' me ear to hear every little whisper that was floatin' around about me! It's my rule never to lose me temper till it would be dethrimental to keep it. There's nothin' derogatory in th' use o' th' word 'cuckoo', is there?

PETER (*tearfully*)  It's not th' word; it's th' way he says it: he never says it straight out, but murmurs it with curious quiverin' ripples, like variations on a flute!

FLUTHER  Ah, what odds if he gave it with variations on a

thrombone! (*To Mrs. Gogan.*) What's yours goin' to be, ma'am?

MRS. GOGAN   Ah, a half o' malt, Fluther.

FLUTHER (*to Barman*)   Three halves, Tommy.

*The Barman brings the drinks.*

MRS. GOGAN (*drinking*)   The Foresthers' is a gorgeous dhress! I don't think I've seen nicer, mind you, in a pantomime. . . . Th' loveliest part of th' dhress, I think, is th' osthrichess plume. . . . When yous are goin' along, an' I see them wavin' an' noddin' an' waggin', I seem to be lookin' at each of yous hangin' at th' end of a rope, your eyes bulgin' an' your legs twistin' an' jerkin', gaspin' an' gaspin' for breath while yous are thryin' to die for Ireland!

FLUTHER   If any o' them is hangin' at the end of a rope, it won't be for Ireland!

PETER   Are you goin' to start th' young Covey's game o' proddin' an' twartin' a man? There's not many that's talkin' can say that for twenty-five years he never missed a pilgrimage to Bodenstown!

FLUTHER   You're always blowin' about goin' to Bodenstown. D'ye think no one but yourself ever went to Bodenstown?

PETER (*plaintively*)   I'm not blowin' about it; but there's not a year that I go there but I pluck a leaf off Tone's grave, an' this very day me prayer-book is nearly full of them.

FLUTHER (*scornfully*)   Then Fluther has a vice versa opinion of them that put ivy leaves into their prayer-books, scabbin' it on th' clergy, an' thryin' to out-do th' haloes o' th' saints be lookin' as if he was wearin' around his head a glittherin' aroree boree allis! (*Fiercely.*) Sure, I don't care a damn if you slep' in Bodenstown! You can take your breakfast, dinner, an' tea on th' grave in Bodenstown, if you like, for Fluther!

MRS. GOGAN   Oh, don't start a fight, boys, for God's sake; I was only sayin' what a nice costume it is—nicer than th' kilts, for, God forgive me, I always think th' kilts is hardly decent.

FLUTHER   Ah, sure, when you'd look at him, you'd wondher whether th' man was makin' fun o' th' costume, or th' costume was makin' fun o' th' man!

BARMAN   Now, then, thry to speak asy, will yous? We don't want no shoutin' here.

*The Covey followed by Bessie Burgess comes in. They go over to the opposite end of the counter, and direct their gaze on the other group.*

THE COVEY (*to Barman*)   Two glasses o' malt.

PETER   There he is, now; I knew he wouldn't be long till he folleyed me in.

BESSIE (*speaking to the Covey, but really at the other party*)   I can't for th' life o' me undherstand how they can call themselves Catholics, when they won't lift a finger to help poor little Catholic Belgium.[4]

MRS. GOGAN (*raising her voice*)   What about poor little Catholic Ireland?

BESSIE (*over to Mrs. Gogan*)   You mind your own business, ma'am, an' stupefy your foolishness be gettin' dhrunk.

PETER (*anxiously*)   Take no notice of her; pay no attention to her. She's just tormentin' herself towards havin' a row with somebody.

BESSIE   There's a storm of anger tossin' in me heart, thinkin' of all th' poor Tommies, an' with them me own son, dhrenched in water an' soaked in blood, gropin' their way to a shattherin' death, in a shower o' shells! Young men with th' sunny lust o' life beamin' in them, layin' down their white bodies, shredded into torn an' bloody pieces, on th' althar that God Himself has built for th' sacrifice of heroes!

MRS. GOGAN   Isn't it a nice thing to have to be listenin' to a lassie an' hangin' our heads in a dead silence, knowin' that some persons think more of a ball of malt than they do of th' blessed saints.

FLUTHER   Whisht; she's always dangerous an' derogatory when she's well oiled. Th' safest way to hindher her from havin' any enjoyment out of her spite, is to dip our thoughts into the fact of her bein' a female person that has moved out of th' sight of ordinary sensible people.

BESSIE   To look at some o' th' women that's knockin' about,

4. The Germans invaded Belgium on August 4, 1914, bringing England into the war. Belgian defiance of the invaders became a rallying point for the Allies. Although Belgium has long since fallen when Bessie speaks, she is echoing the early admiration for Belgian resistance in her ironic recognition that it is Protestant England not Catholic Ireland that is on the side of Catholic Belgium.

now, is a thing to make a body sigh. . . . A woman on her own, dhrinkin' with a bevy o' men, is hardly an example to her sex. . . . A woman dhrinkin' with a woman is one thing, an' a woman dhrinkin' with herself is still a woman—flappers may be put in another category altogether—but a middle-aged married woman makin' herself th' centre of a circle of men is as a woman that is loud an' stubborn, whose feet abideth not in her own house.

THE COVEY (*to Bessie*) When I think of all th' problems in front o' th' workers, it makes me sick to be lookin' at oul' codgers goin' about dhressed up like green-accoutred figures gone asthray out of a toyshop!

PETER Gracious God, give me patience to be listenin' to that blasted young Covey proddin' at me from over at th' other end of th' shop!

MRS. GOGAN (*dipping her finger in the whisky, and moistening with it the lips of her baby*) Cissie Gogan's a woman livin' for nigh on twenty-five years in her own room, an' beyond biddin' th' time o' day to her neighbours, never yet as much as nodded her head in th' direction of other people's business, while she knows some as are never content unless they're standin' senthry over other people's doin's!

*Bessie is about to reply, when the tall, dark figure is again silhouetted against the window, and the voice of the speaker is heard speaking passionately.*

VOICE OF SPEAKER The last sixteen months have been the most glorious in the history of Europe. Heroism has come back to the earth. War is a terrible thing, but war is not an evil thing. People in Ireland dread war because they do not know it. Ireland has not known the exhilaration of war for over a hundred years. When war comes to Ireland she must welcome it as she would welcome the Angel of God! (*The figure passes out of sight and hearing.*)

THE COVEY (*towards all present*) Dope, dope. There's only one war worth havin': th' war for th' economic emancipation of th' proletariat.

BESSIE They may crow away out o' them; but it ud be fitther for some o' them to mend their ways, an' cease from havin' scouts out watchin' for th' comin' of th' Saint Vincent de

Paul man,[5] for fear they'd be nailed lowerin' a pint of beer, mockin' th' man with an angel face, shinin' with th' glamour of deceit an' lies!

MRS. GOGAN   An' a certain lassie standin' stiff behind her own door with her ears cocked listenin' to what's being said, stuffed till she's sthrained with envy of a neighbour thryin' for a few little things that may be got be hard sthrivin' to keep up to th' letther an' th' law, an' th' practices of th' Church!

PETER (*to Mrs. Gogan*)   If I was you, Mrs. Gogan, I'd parry her jabbin' remarks be a powerful silence that'll keep her tantalizin' words from penethratin' into your feelin's. It's always betther to leave these people to th' vengeance o' God!

BESSIE   Bessie Burgess doesn't put up to know much, never havin' a swaggerin' mind, thanks be to God, but goin' on packin' up knowledge accordin' to her conscience: precept upon precept, line upon line; here a little, an' there a little. But (*with a passionate swing of her shawl*), thanks be to Christ, she knows when she was got, where she was got, an' how she was got; while there's some she knows, decoratin' their finger with a well-polished weddin' ring, would be hard put to it if they were assed to show their weddin' lines!

MRS. GOGAN (*plunging out into the centre of the floor in a wild tempest of hysterical rage*)   Y' oul' rip of a blasted liar, me weddin' ring's been well earned be twenty years be th' side o' me husband, now takin' his rest in heaven, married to me be Father Dempsey, in th' Chapel o' Saint Jude's, in th' Christmas Week of eighteen hundhred an' ninety-five; an' any kid, livin' or dead, that Jinnie Gogan's had since, was got between th' bordhers of th' Ten Commandments! . . . An' that's more than some o' you can say that are kep' from th' dhread o' desthruction be a few drowsy virtues, that th' first whisper of temptation lulls into a sleep, that'll know one sin from another only on th' day of their last anointin', an' that use th' innocent light o' th' shinin' stars to dip into th' sins of a night's diversion!

5. The Catholic Association of St. Vincent de Paul did charity work in the Dublin slums and, if Bessie is to be believed, the organization must have insisted that the recipients be the "deserving" poor.

BESSIE (*jumping out to face Mrs. Gogan, and bringing the palms of her hands together in sharp claps to emphasize her remarks*)  Liar to you, too, ma'am, y' oul' hardened threspasser on other people's good nature, wizenin' up your soul in th' arts o' dodgeries, till every dhrop of respectability in a female is dhried up in her, lookin' at your ready-made manoeuverin' with th' menkind!

BARMAN  Here, there; here, there; speak asy there. No rowin' here, no rowin' here, now.

FLUTHER (*trying to calm Mrs. Gogan*)  Now Jinnie, Jinnie, it's a derogatory thing to be smirchin' a night like this with a row; it's rompin' with th' feelin's of hope we ought to be, instead o' bein' vice versa!

PETER (*trying to quiet Bessie*)  I'm terrible dawny, Mrs. Burgess, an' a fight leaves me weak for a long time aftherwards. . . . Please, Mrs. Burgess, before there's damage done, try to have a little respect for yourself.

BESSIE (*with a push of her hand that sends Peter tottering to the end of the shop*)  G'way, you little sermonizing, little yella-faced, little consequential, little pudgy, little bum, you!

MRS. GOGAN (*screaming*)  Fluther, leggo! I'm not goin' to keep an unresistin' silence, an' her scattherin' her festherin' words in me face, stirrin' up ever dhrop of decency in a respectable female, with her restless rally o' lies that would make a saint say his prayer backwards!

BESSIE (*shouting*)  Ah, everybody knows well that th' best charity that can be shown to you is to hide th' thruth as much as our thrue worship of God Almighty will allow us!

MRS. GOGAN (*frantically*)  Here, houl' th' kid, one o' yous; houl' th' kid for a minute! There's nothin' for it but to show this lassie a lesson or two. . . . (*To Peter.*) Here, houl' th' kid, you. (*Before Peter is aware of it, she places the infant in his arms.*)

MRS. GOGAN (*to Bessie, standing before her in a fighting attitude*)  Come on, now, me loyal lassie, dyin' with grief for little Catholic Belgium! When Jinnie Gogan's done with you, you'll have a little leisure lyin' down to think an' pray for your king an' counthry!

BARMAN (*coming from behind the counter, getting between the women, and proceeding to push them towards the door*)  Here, now, since yous can't have a little friendly argument quietly, you'll get out o' this place in quick time. Go on, an' settle your differences somewhere else—I don't want to have another endorsement on me licence.

PETER (*anxiously, over to Mrs. Gogan*)  Here, take your kid back, ower this. How nicely I was picked, now, for it to be plumped into me arms!

THE COVEY  She knew who she was givin' it to, maybe.

PETER (*hotly to the Covey*)  Now, I'm givin' you fair warnin', me young Covey, to quit firin' your jibes an' jeers at me. . . . For one o' these days, I'll run out in front o' God Almighty an' take your sacred life!

BARMAN (*pushing Bessie out after Mrs. Gogan*)  Go on, now; out you go.

BESSIE (*as she goes out*)  If you think, me lassie, that Bessie Burgess has an untidy conscience, she'll soon show you to th' differ!

PETER (*leaving the baby down on the floor*)  Ay, be Jasus, wait there, till I give her back her youngster! (*He runs to the door.*) Ay, there, ay! (*He comes back.*) There, she's afther goin' without her kid. What are we goin' to do with it, now?

THE COVEY  What are we goin' to do with it? Bring it outside an' show everybody what you're afther findin'!

PETER (*in a panic to Fluther*)  Pick it up, you, Fluther, an' run afther her with it, will you?

FLUTHER  What d'ye take Fluther for? You must think Fluther's a right gom. D'ye think Fluther's like yourself, destitute of a titther of undherstandin'?

BARMAN (*imperatively to Peter*)  Take it up, man, an' run out afther her with it, before she's gone too far. You're not goin' to leave th' bloody thing here, are you?

PETER (*plaintively, as he lifts up the baby*)  Well, God Almighty, give me patience with all th' scorners, tormentors, an' twarters that are always an' ever thryin' to goad me into prayin' for their blindin' an' blastin' an' burnin' in th' world to come! (*He goes out.*)

FLUTHER  God, it's a relief to get rid o' that crowd. Women is terrible when they start to fight. There's no holdin' them back. (*To the Covey.*) Are you goin' to have anything?

THE COVEY  Ah, I don't mind if I have another half.

FLUTHER (*to Barman*)  Two more, Tommy, me son.

*The Barman gets the drinks.*

FLUTHER   You know, there's no conthrollin' a woman when she loses her head.

*Rosie enters and goes over to the counter on the side nearest to Fluther.*

ROSIE (*to Barman*)   Divil a use i' havin' a thrim little leg on a night like this; things was never worse. . . . Give us a half till to-morrow, Tom, duckey.

BARMAN (*coldly*)   No more tonight, Rosie; you owe me for three already.

ROSIE (*combatively*)   You'll be paid, won't you?

BARMAN   I hope so.

ROSIE   You hope so! Is that th' way with you, now?

FLUTHER (*to Barman*)   Give her one; it'll be all right.

ROSIE (*clapping Fluther on the back*)   Oul' sport!

FLUTHER   Th' meetin' should be soon over, now.

THE COVEY   Th' sooner th' betther. It's all a lot o' blasted nonsense, comrade.

FLUTHER   Oh, I wouldn't say it was all nonsense. Afther all, Fluther can remember th' time, an' him only a dawny chiselur, bein' taught at his mother's knee to be faithful to th' Shan Van Vok! [6]

THE COVEY   That's all dope, comrade; th' sort o' thing that workers are fed on be th' Boorzwawzee.

FLUTHER (*a little sharply*)   What's all dope? Though I'm sayin' it that shouldn't: (*catching his cheek with his hand, and pulling down the flesh from the eye*) d'ye see that mark there, undher me eye? . . . A sabre slice from a dragoon in O'Connell Street! [7] (*Thrusting his head forward towards Rosie.*) Feel that dint in th' middle o' me nut!

ROSIE (*rubbing Fluther's head, and winking at the Covey*)   My God, there's a holla!

FLUTHER (*putting on his hat with quiet pride*)   A skelp from a bobby's baton at a Labour meetin' in th' Phoenix Park!

THE COVEY   He must ha' hitten you in mistake. I don't know what you ever done for th' Labour movement.

6. The Poor Old Woman, i.e., Ireland.
7. This is a reference to a bloody police attack on strikers and bystanders during the Transport Workers' strike, 1913.

FLUTHER (*loudly*)  D'ye not? Maybe, then, I done as much, an' know as much about th' Labour movement as th' chancers[8] that are blowin' about it!

BARMAN  Speak easy, Fluther, thry to speak easy.

THE COVEY  There's no necessity to get excited about it, comrade.

FLUTHER (*more loudly*)  Excited? Who's gettin' excited? There's no one gettin' excited! It would take something more than a thing like you to flutther a feather o' Fluther. Blatherin', an', when all is said, you know as much as th' rest in th' wind up!

THE COVEY  Well, let us put it to th' test, then, an' see what you know about th' Labour movement: what's the mechanism of exchange?

FLUTHER (*roaring, because he feels he is beaten*)  How th' hell do I know what it is? There's nothin' about that in th' rules of our Thrades Union!

BARMAN  For God's sake, thry to speak easy, Fluther.

THE COVEY  What does Karl Marx say about th' Relation of Value to th' Cost o' Production?

FLUTHER (*angrily*)  What th' hell do I care what he says? I'm Irishman enough not to lose me head be follyin' foreigners!

BARMAN  Speak easy, Fluther.

THE COVEY  It's only waste o' time talkin' to you, comrade.

FLUTHER  Don't be comradin' me, mate. I'd be on me last legs if I wanted you for a comrade.

ROSIE (*to the Covey*)  It seems a highly rediculous thing to hear a thing that's only an inch or two away from a kid, swingin' heavy words about he doesn't know th' meanin' of, an' uppishly thryin' to down a man like Misther Fluther here, that's well flavoured in th' knowledge of th' world he's livin' in.

THE COVEY (*savagely to Rosie*)  Nobody's askin' you to be buttin' in with your prate. . . . I have you well taped, me lassie. . . . Just you keep your opinions for your own place. . . . It'll be a long time before th' Covey takes any insthructions or reprimandin' from a prostitute!

ROSIE (*wild with humiliation*)  You louse, you louse, you!

8. Liars.

. . . You're no man. . . . You're no man . . . I'm a woman, anyhow, an' if I'm a prostitute aself, I have me feelin's. . . . Thryin' to put his arm around me a minute ago, an' givin' me th' glad eye, th' little wrigglin' lump o' desolation turns on me now, because he saw there was nothin' doin'. . . . You louse, you! If I was a man, or you were a woman, I'd bate th' puss o' you!

BARMAN   Ay, Rosie, ay! You'll have to shut your mouth altogether, if you can't learn to speak easy!

FLUTHER (*to Rosie*)   Houl' on there, Rosie; houl' on there. There's no necessity to flutther yourself when you're with Fluther. . . . Any lady that's in th' company of Fluther is goin' to get a fair hunt. . . . This is outside your province. . . . I'm not goin' to let you demean yourself be talkin' to a tittherin' chancer. . . . Leave this to Fluther—this is a man's job. (*To the Covey.*) Now if you've anything to say, say it to Fluther, an', let me tell you, you're not goin' to be pass-remarkable to any lady in my company.

THE COVEY   Sure I don't care if you were runnin' all night afther your Mary o' th' Curlin' Hair, but, when you start tellin' luscious lies about what you done for th' Labour movement, it's nearly time to show y'up!

FLUTHER (*fiercely*)   Is it you show Fluther up? G'way, man, I'd beat two o' you before me breakfast!

THE COVEY (*contemptuously*)   Tell us where you bury your dead, will you?

FLUTHER (*with his face stuck into the face of the Covey*)   Sing a little less on th' high note, or, when I'm done with you, you'll put a Christianable consthruction on things, I'm tellin' you!

THE COVEY   You're a big fella, you are.

FLUTHER (*tapping the Covey threateningly on the shoulder*)   Now, you're temptin' Providence when you're temptin' Fluther!

THE COVEY (*losing his temper, and bawling*)   Easy with them hands, there, easy with them hands! You're startin' to take a little risk when you commence to paw the Covey!

*Fluther suddenly springs into the middle of the shop, flings his hat into the corner, whips off his coat, and begins to paw the air.*

FLUTHER (*roaring at the top of his voice*)   Come on, come on, you lowser; put your mits up now, if there's a man's blood in you! Be God, in a few minutes you'll see some snots flyin' around, I'm tellin' you. . . . When Fluther's done with you, you'll have a vice versa opinion of him! Come on, now, come on!

BARMAN (*running from behind the counter and catching hold of the Covey*) Here, out you go, me little bowsey. Because you got a couple o' halves you think you can act as you like. (*He pushes the Covey to the door.*) Fluther's a friend o' mine, an' I'll not have him insulted.

THE COVEY (*struggling with the Barman*) Ay, leggo, leggo there; fair hunt, give a man a fair hunt! One minute with him is all I ask; one minute alone with him, while you're runnin' for th' priest an' th' doctor.

FLUTHER (*to the Barman*) Let him go, let him go, Tom: let him open th' door to sudden death if he wants to!

BARMAN (*to the Covey*) Go on, out you go an' do th' bowsey somewhere else. (*He pushes the Covey out and comes back.*)

ROSIE (*getting Fluther's hat as he is putting on his coat*) Be God, you put th' fear o' God in his heart that time! I thought you'd have to be dug out of him. . . . Th' way you lepped out without any of your fancy side-steppin'! 'Men like Fluther,' say I to meself, 'is gettin' scarce nowadays.'

FLUTHER (*with proud complacency*) I wasn't goin' to let meself be malignified by a chancer. . . . He got a little bit too derogatory for Fluther. . . . Be God, to think of a cur like that comin' to talk to a man like me!

ROSIE (*fixing on his hat*) Did j'ever!

FLUTHER He's lucky he got off safe. I hit a man last week, Rosie, an' he's fallin' yet!

ROSIE Sure, you'd ha' broken him in two if you'd ha' hitten him one clatther!

FLUTHER (*amorously, putting his arm around Rosie*) Come on into th' snug, me little darlin', an' we'll have a few dhrinks before I see you home.

ROSIE Oh, Fluther, I'm afraid you're a terrible man for th' women.

*They go into the snug as Clitheroe, Captain Brennan, and Lieut. Langon of the Irish Volunteers enter hurriedly. Captain Brennan carries the banner of the The Plough and the Stars, and Lieut. Langon a green, white, and orange Tri-colour.[9] They are in a state of emotional excitement. Their faces are flushed and their eyes sparkle; they speak rapidly, as if unaware of the meaning of what they said. They have been mesmerized by the fervency of the speeches.*

CLITHEROE (*almost pantingly*)   Three glasses o' port!

*The Barman brings the drinks.*

CAPT. BRENNAN   We won't have long to wait now.

LIEUT. LANGON   Th' time is rotten ripe for revolution.

CLITHEROE   You have a mother, Langon.

LIEUT. LANGON   Ireland is greater than a mother.

CAPT. BRENNAN   You have a wife, Clitheroe.

CLITHEROE   Ireland is greater than a wife.

LIEUT. LANGON   Th' time for Ireland's battle is now—th' place for Ireland's battle is here.

*The tall, dark figure again is silhouetted against the window. The three men pause and listen.*

VOICE OF THE MAN   Our foes are strong, but strong as they are, they cannot undo the miracles of God, who ripens in the heart of young men the seeds sown by the young men of a former generation. They think they have pacified Ireland; think they have foreseen everything; think they have provided against everything; but the fools, the fools, the fools!—they have left us our Fenian dead, and, while Ireland holds these graves, Ireland, unfree, shall never be at peace!

CAPT. BRENNAN (*catching up The Plough and the Stars*)   Imprisonment for th' Independence of Ireland!

LIEUT. LANGON (*catching up the Tri-colour*)   Wounds for th' Independence of Ireland!

CLITHEROE   Death for th' Independence of Ireland!

THE THREE (*together*)   So help us God!

*They drink. A bugle blows the Assembly. They hurry out. A pause. Fluther and Rosie come out of the snug; Rosie is linking Fluther, who is a little drunk. Both are in a merry mood.*

ROSIE   Come on home, ower o' that, man. Are you afraid

9. The flag of the Republic.

or what? Are you goin' to come home, or are you not?

FLUTHER   Of course I'm goin' home. What ud ail me that I wouldn't go?

ROSIE (*lovingly*)   Come on, then, oul' sport.

OFFICER'S VOICE (*giving command outside*)   Irish Volunteers, by th' right, quick march!

ROSIE (*putting her arm round Fluther and singing*) [10]

> I once had a lover, a tailor, but he could do nothin' for me,
> An' then I fell in with a sailor as strong an' as wild as th' sea.
> We cuddled an' kissed with devotion, till th' night from th' mornin' had fled;
> An' there, to our joy, a bright bouncin' boy
> Was dancin' a jig in th' bed!

> Dancin' a jig in th' bed, an' bawlin' for butther an' bread.
> An' there, to our joy, a bright bouncin' boy
> Was dancin' a jig in th' bed!

*They go out with their arms round each other.*

CLITHEROE'S VOICE (*in command outside*)   Dublin Battalion of the Irish Citizen Army, by th' right, quick march!

CURTAIN

# ACT THREE

*The corner house in a street of tenements: it is the home of the Clitheroes. The house is a long, gaunt, five-story tenement; its brick front is chipped and scarred with age and neglect. The wide and heavy hall door, flanked by two pillars, has a look of having been charred by a fire in the distant past. The door lurches a little to one side, disjointed by the continual and reckless banging when it is being closed by most of the residents. The diamond-paned fanlight is destitute of a single pane, the framework alone*

10. Rosie's naughty song, coming immediately after the revolutionary rhetoric of the toasts, was one of the chief bones of contention when the play was first produced. It was dropped finally. Would its absence noticeably change the effect that O'Casey wanted at the end of this act?

*remaining. The windows, except the two looking into the front parlour (Clitheroe's room), are grimy, and are draped with fluttering and soiled fragments of lace curtains. The front parlour windows are hung with rich, comparatively, casement cloth. Five stone steps lead from the door to the path on the street. Branching on each side are railings to prevent people from falling into the area. At the left corner of the house runs a narrow lane, bisecting the street, and connecting it with another of the same kind. At the corner of the lane is a street lamp.*

*As the house is revealed, Mrs. Gogan is seen helping Mollser to a chair, which stands on the path beside the railings, at the left side of the steps. She then wraps a shawl around Mollser's shoulders. It is some months later.*

MRS. GOGAN (*arranging shawl around Mollser*)  Th' sun'll do you all th' good in th' world. A few more weeks o' this weather, an' there's no knowin' how well you'll be. . . . Are you comfy, now?

MOLLSER (*weakly and wearily*)  Yis, ma; I'm all right.

MRS. GOGAN  How are you feelin'?

MOLLSER  Betther, ma, betther. If th' horrible sinkin' feelin' ud go, I'd be all right.

MRS. GOGAN  Ah, I wouldn't put much pass on that. Your stomach maybe's out of ordher. . . . Is th' poor breathin' any betther, d'ye think?

MOLLSER  Yis, yis, ma; a lot betther.

MRS. GOGAN  Well, that's somethin' anyhow. . . . With th' help o' God, you'll be on th' mend from this out. . . . D'your legs feel any sthronger undher you, d'ye think!

MOLLSER (*irritably*)  I can't tell, ma. I think so. . . . A little.

MRS. GOGAN  Well, a little aself is somethin'. . . . I thought I heard you coughin' a little more than usual last night. . . . D'ye think you were?

MOLLSER  I wasn't, ma, I wasn't.

MRS. GOGAN  I thought I heard you, for I was kep' awake all night with th' shootin'. An' thinkin' o' that madman, Fluther, runnin' about through th' night lookin' for Nora Clitheroe to bring her back when he heard she'd gone to folly her husband, an' in dhread any minute he might come staggerin' in covered with bandages, splashed all over with th' red of his own blood, an' givin' us barely time to bring th' priest to hear th' last whisper of his final confession, as his soul was passin' through th' dark doorway o' death into th' way o' th' wondherin' dead. . . . You don't feel cold, do you?

MOLLSER   No, ma; I'm all right.

MRS. GOGAN   Keep your chest well covered, for that's th' delicate spot in you . . . if there's any danger, I'll whip you in again. . . . (*Looking up the street.*) Oh, here's th' Covey an' oul' Pether hurryin' along. God Almighty, sthrange things is happenin' when them two is pullin' together.

*The Covey and Peter come in, breathless and excited.*

MRS. GOGAN (*to the two men*)   Were yous far up th' town? Did yous see any sign o' Fluther or Nora? How is things lookin'? I hear they're blazin' away out o' th' G.P.O. That th' Tommies is sthretched in heaps around Nelson's Pillar, an' th' Parnell Statue, an' that th' pavin' sets in O'Connell Street is nearly covered be pools o' blood.[1]

PETER   We seen no sign o' Nora or Fluther anywhere.

MRS. GOGAN   We should ha' held her back be main force from goin' to look for her husband. . . . God knows what's happened to her—I'm always seein' her sthretched on her back in some hospital, moanin' with th' pain of a bullet in her vitals, an' nuns thryin' to get her to take a last look at th' crucifix!

THE COVEY   We can do nothin'. You can't stick your nose into O'Connell Street, an' Tyler's is on fire.

PETER   An' we seen th' Lancers—

THE COVEY (*interrupting*)   Throttin' along, heads in th' air; spurs an' sabres jinglin', an' lances quiverin', an' lookin' as if they were assin' themselves, 'Where's these blighters, till we get a prod at them?' when there was a volley from th' Post Office that stretched half o' them, an' sent th' rest gallopin' away wondherin' how far they'd have to go before they'd feel safe.

---

1. This and what follows is a reasonably accurate account of what went on during the Rising. Most of the specific references—Nelson's Pillar, the Parnell statue, O'Connell Street, Tyler's (one of the stores that was looted)—are to the area around the General Post Office, where the heart of the fighting took place. Boland's Mills, a little farther east, was occupied by forces under Eamon de Valera. The Lancers were British troops.

PETER (*rubbing his hands*)    'Damn it,' says I to meself, 'this looks like business!'

THE COVEY    An' then out comes General Pearse an' his staff, an', standin' in th' middle o' th' street, he reads th' Proclamation.

MRS. GOGAN    What proclamation?

PETER    Declarin' an Irish Republic.

MRS. GOGAN    Go to God!

PETER    The gunboat *Helga's* shellin' Liberty Hall, an' I hear the people livin' on th' quays had to crawl on their bellies to Mass with th' bullets that were flyin' around from Boland's Mills.

MRS. GOGAN    God bless us, what's goin' to be th' end of it all!

BESSIE (*looking out of the top window*)    Maybe yous are satisfied now; maybe yous are satisfied now. Go on an' get guns if yous are men—Johnny get your gun, get your gun, get your gun! Yous are all nicely shanghaied now; th' boyo hasn't a sword on his thigh now! Oh, yous are all nicely shanghaied now!

MRS. GOGAN (*warningly to Peter and the Covey*)    S-s-sh, don't answer her. She's th' right oul' Orange[2] bitch! She's been chantin' 'Rule, Britannia' all th' mornin'.

PETER    I hope Fluther hasn't met with any accident, he's such a wild card.

MRS. GOGAN    God grant it; but last night I dreamt I seen gettin' carried into th' house a shtretcher with a figure lyin' on it, stiff an' still, dhressed in th' habit of Saint Francis. An' then, I heard th' murmurs of a crowd no one could see sayin' th' litany for th' dead; an' then it got so dark that nothin' was seen but th' white face of th' corpse, gleamin' like a white wather-lily floatin' on th' top of a dark lake. Then a tiny whisper thrickled into me ear, sayin', 'Isn't the face very like th' face o' Fluther?' an' then, with a thremblin' flutther, th' dead lips opened, an' although I couldn't hear, I knew they were sayin', 'Poor oul' Fluther,

2. The Orange order, founded in 1795, became strong in the late nineteenth century when Home Rule was proposed for Ireland. Largely Ulster based, it is a Protestant organization. Mrs. Gogan is using the epithet "Orange" in a more general way, meaning simply that Bessie is a Protestant and loyal to England.

afther havin' handed in his gun at last, his shakin' soul moored in th' place where th' wicked are at rest an' th' weary cease from throublin'.'

PETER (*who has put on a pair of spectacles, and has been looking down the street*)   Here they are, be God, here they are; just afther turnin' th' corner—Nora an' Fluther!

THE COVEY   She must be wounded or something—he seems to be carryin' her.

*Fluther and Nora enter. Fluther has his arm around her and is half leading, half carrying her in. Her eyes are dim and hollow, her face pale and strained-looking; her hair is tossed, and her clothes are dusty.*

MRS. GOGAN (*running over to them*)   God bless us, is it wounded y'are, Mrs. Clitheroe, or what?

FLUTHER   Ah, she's all right, Mrs. Gogan; only worn out from thravellin' an' want o' sleep. A night's rest, now, an' she'll be as fit as a fiddle. Bring her in, an' make her lie down.

MRS. GOGAN (*to Nora*)   Did you hear e'er a whisper o' Mr. Clitheroe?

NORA (*wearily*)   I could find him nowhere, Mrs. Gogan. None o' them would tell me where he was. They told me I shamed my husband an' th' women of Ireland be carryin' on as I was. . . . They said th' women must learn to be brave an' cease to be cowardly. . . . Me who risked more for love than they would risk for hate. . . . (*Raising her voice in hysterical protest.*) My Jack will be killed, my Jack will be killed! . . . He is to be butchered as a sacrifice to th' dead!

BESSIE (*from upper window*)   Yous are all nicely shanghaied now! Sorra mend th' lasses that have been kissin' an' cuddlin' their boys into th' sheddin' of blood! . . . Fillin' their minds with fairy tales that had no beginnin', but, please God, 'll have a bloody quick endin'! . . . Turnin' bitther into sweet, an' sweet into bitther. . . . Stabbin' in th' back th' men that are dyin' in th' threnches for them! It's a bad thing for any one that thries to jilt th' Ten Commandments, for judgements are prepared for scorners an' sthripes for th' back o' fools! (*Going away from window as she sings*)

Rule, Britannia, Britannia rules th' waves,
Britons never, never, never shall be slaves!

FLUTHER (*with a roar up at the window*) Y'ignorant oul' throllop, you!

MRS. GOGAN (*to Nora*) He'll come home safe enough to you, you'll find, Mrs. Clitheroe; afther all, there's a power o' women that's handed over sons an' husbands to take a runnin' risk in th' fight they're wagin'.

NORA I can't help thinkin' every shot fired 'll be fired at Jack, an' every shot fired at Jack 'll be fired at me. What do I care for th' others? I can think only of me own self. . . . An' there's no woman gives a son or a husband to be killed—if they say it, they're lyin', lyin', against God, Nature, an' against themselves! . . . One blasted hussy at a barricade told me to go home an' not to be thryin' to dishearten th' men. . . . That I wasn't worthy to bear a son to a man that was out fightin' for freedom. . . . I clawed at her, an' smashed her in th' face till we were separated. . . . I was pushed down th' street, an' I cursed them—cursed the rebel ruffians an' Volunteers that had dhragged me ravin' mad into th' sthreets to seek me husband!

PETER You'll have to have patience, Nora. We all have to put up with twarters an' tormentors in this world.

THE COVEY If they were fightin' for anything worth while, I wouldn't mind.

FLUTHER (*to Nora*) Nothin' derogatory 'll happen to Mr. Clitheroe. You'll find, now, in th' finish up it'll be vice versa.

NORA Oh, I know that wherever he is, he's thinkin' of wantin' to be with me. I know he's longin' to be passin' his hand through me hair, to be caressin' me neck, to fondle me hand an' to feel me kisses clingin' to his mouth. . . . An' he stands wherever he is because he's brave? (*Vehemently.*) No, but because he's a coward, a coward, a coward!

MRS. GOGAN Oh, they're not cowards anyway.

NORA (*with denunciatory anger*) I tell you they're afraid to say they're afraid! . . . Oh, I saw it, I saw it, Mrs. Gogan. . . . At th' barricade in North King Street I saw fear glowin' in all their eyes. . . . An' in th' middle o' th' sthreet was somethin' huddled up in a horrible tangled heap. . . . His face was jammed again th' stones, an' his arm was twisted round his back. . . . An' every twist of his body was a cry against th' terrible thing that had happened to him. . . .

An' I saw they were afraid to look at it. . . . An' some o' them laughed at me, but th' laugh was a frightened one. . . . An' some o' them shouted at me, but th' shout had in it th' shiver o' fear. . . . I tell you they were afraid, afraid, afraid!

MRS. GOGAN (*leading her towards the house*)  Come on in, dear. If you'd been a little longer together, th' wrench asundher wouldn't have been so sharp.

NORA  Th' agony I'm in since he left me has thrust away every rough thing he done, an' every unkind word he spoke; only th' blossoms that grew out of our lives are before me now; shakin' their colours before me face, an' breathin' their sweet scent on every thought springin' up in me mind, till, sometimes, Mrs. Gogan, sometimes I think I'm goin' mad!

MRS. GOGAN  You'll be a lot betther when you have a little lie down.

NORA (*turning towards Fluther as she is going in*)  I don't know what I'd have done, only for Fluther. I'd have been lyin' in th' streets, only for him. . . . (*As she goes in.*) They have dhriven away th' little happiness life had to spare for me. He has gone from me for ever, for ever. . . . Oh, Jack, Jack, Jack!

*She is led in by Mrs. Gogan, as Bessie comes out with a shawl around her shoulders. She passes by them with her head in the air. When they have gone in, she gives a mug of milk to Mollser silently.*

FLUTHER  Which of yous has th' tossers?

THE COVEY  I have.

BESSIE (*as she is passing them to go down the street*)  You an' your Leadhers an' their sham-battle soldiers has landed a body in a nice way, havin' to go an' ferret out a bit o' bread God knows where. . . . Why aren't yous in th' G.P.O. if yous are men? It's paler an' paler yous are gettin'. . . . A lot o' vipers, that's what th' Irish people is! (*She goes out.*)

FLUTHER  Never mind her. . . . (*To the Covey.*) Make a start an' keep us from th' sin o' idleness. (*To Mollser.*) Well, how are you to-day, Mollser, oul' son? What are you dhrinkin', milk?

MOLLSER  Grand, Fluther, grand, thanks. Yis, milk.

FLUTHER  You couldn't get a better thing down you. . . . This turn-up has done one good thing, anyhow; you can't get dhrink anywhere, an' if it lasts a week, I'll be so used to it that I won't think of a pint.

THE COVEY  (*who has taken from his pocket two worn coins and a thin strip of wood about four inches long*) What's th' bettin'?

PETER  Heads, a juice.

FLUTHER  Harps, a tanner.[3]

*The Covey places the coins on the strip of wood, and flips them up into the air. As they jingle on the ground the distant boom of a big gun is heard. They stand for a moment listening.*

FLUTHER  What th' hell's that?

THE COVEY  It's like th' boom of a big gun!

FLUTHER  Surely to God they're not goin' to use artillery on us?

THE COVEY (*scornfully*)  Not goin'! (*Vehemently.*) Wouldn't they use anything on us, man?

FLUTHER  Aw, holy Christ, that's not playin' th' game!

PETER  (*plaintively*) What would happen if a shell landed here now?

THE COVEY (*ironically*)  You'd be off to heaven in a fiery chariot.

PETER  In spite of all th' warnin's that's ringin' around us, are you goin' to start your pickin' at me again?

FLUTHER  Go on, toss them again, toss them again. . . . Harps, a tanner.

PETER  Heads, a juice.

*The Covey tosses the coins.*

FLUTHER (*as the coins fall*)  Let them roll, let them roll. Heads, be God!

*Bessie runs in excitedly. She has a new hat on her head, a fox fur round her neck over her shawl, three umbrellas under her right arm, and a box of biscuits under her left. She speaks rapidly and breathlessly.*

BESSIE  They're breakin' into th' shops, they're breakin' into th' shops! Smashin' th' windows, battherin' in th' doors, an' whippin' away everything! An' th' Volunteers is firin' on

3. Irish coins have a harp on one side.

them. I seen two men an' a lassie pushin' a piano down th' sthreet, an' th' sweat rollin' off them thryin' to get it up on th' pavement; an' an oul' wan that must ha' been seventy lookin' as if she'd dhrop every minute with th' dint o' heart beatin', thryin' to pull a big double bed out of a broken shop window! I was goin' to wait till I dhressed meself from th' skin out.

MOLLSER (*to Bessie, as she is going in*)  Help me in, Bessie; I'm feelin' curious. (*Bessie leaves the looted things in the house, and, rapidly returning, helps Mollser in.*)

THE COVEY  Th' selfishness of that one—she waited till she got all she could carry before she'd come to tell anyone!

FLUTHER (*running over to the door of the house and shouting in to Bessie*)  Ay, Bessie, did you hear of e'er a pub gettin' a shake up?

BESSIE (*inside*)  I didn't hear o' none.

FLUTHER (*in a burst of enthusiasm*)  Well, you're goin' to hear of one soon!

THE COVEY  Come on, man, an' don't be wastin' time.

PETER (*to them as they are about to run off*)  Ay, ay, are you goin' to leave me here?

FLUTHER  Are you goin' to leave yourself here?

PETER (*anxiously*)  Didn't yous hear her sayin' they were firin' on them?

THE COVEY AND FLUTHER (*together*)  Well?

PETER  Supposin' I happened to be potted?

FLUTHER  We'd give you a Christian burial, anyhow.

THE COVEY (*ironically*)  Dhressed up in your regimentals.

PETER (*to the Covey, passionately*)  May th' all-lovin' God give you a hot knock one o' these days, me young Covey, tuthorin' Fluther up now to be tiltin' at me, an' crossin' me with his mockeries an' jibin'!

*A fashionably dressed, middle-aged, stout woman comes hurriedly in, and makes for the group. She is almost fainting with fear.*

THE WOMAN  For Gawd's sake, will one of you kind men show any safe way for me to get to Wrathmines? [4] . . . I was

---

4. Rathmines, a pleasant Dublin suburb. O'Casey's spelling joke would have been lost in the theater. The whole scene with the Woman was dropped from the play when it was produced in London, and it was not printed in the Acting Edition (Samuel French, 1932), a version that is reprinted in a number of standard anthologies. Since the Woman is an extraneous satiric bit, she is still cut from most productions.

foolish enough to visit a friend, thinking the howl thing was a joke, and now I cawn't get a car or a tram to take me home—isn't it awful?

FLUTHER  I'm afraid, ma'am, one way is as safe as another.

WOMAN  And what am I gowing to do? Oh, isn't this awful? . . . I'm so different from others. . . . The mowment I hear a shot, my legs give way under me—I cawn't stir, I'm paralysed—isn't it awful?

FLUTHER (*moving away*)  It's a derogatory way to be, right enough, ma'am.

WOMAN (*catching Fluther's coat*)  Creeping along the street there, with my head down and my eyes half shut, a bullet whizzed past within an inch of my nowse. . . . I had to lean against the wall for a long time, gasping for breath—I nearly passed away—it was awful! . . . I wonder, would you kind men come some of the way and see me safe?

FLUTHER  I have to go away, ma'am, to thry an' save a few things from th' burnin' buildin's.

THE COVEY  Come on, then, or there won't be anything left to save. (*The Covey and Fluther hurry away.*)

WOMAN (*to Peter*)  Wasn't it an awful thing for me to leave my friend's house? Wasn't it an idiotic thing to do? . . . I haven't the slightest idea where I am. . . . You have a kind face, sir. Could you possibly come and pilot me in the direction of Wrathmines?

PETER (*indignantly*)  D'ye think I'm goin' to risk me life throttin' in front of you? An' maybe get a bullet that would gimme a game leg or something that would leave me a jibe an' a jeer to Fluther an' th' young Covey for th' rest o' me days! (*With an indignant toss of his head he walks into the house.*)

THE WOMAN (*going out*)  I know I'll fall down in a dead faint if I hear another shot go off anyway near me—isn't it awful!

*Mrs. Gogan comes out of the house pushing a pram before her. As she enters the street, Bessie rushes out, follows Mrs. Gogan, and catches hold of the pram, stopping Mrs. Gogan's progress.*

BESSIE  Here, where are you goin' with that? How quick you were, me lady, to clap your eyes on th' pram. . . . Maybe you don't know that Mrs. Sullivan, before she went to spend Easther with her people in Dunboyne, gave me sthrict injunctions to give an accasional look to see if it was still standin' where it was left in th' corner of th' lobby.

MRS. GOGAN  That remark of yours, Mrs. Bessie Burgess, requires a little considheration, seein' that th' pram was left on our lobby, an' not on yours; a foot or two a little to th' left of th' jamb of me own room door; nor is it needful to mention th' name of th' person that gave a squint to see if it was there th' first thing in th' mornin', an' th' last thing in th' stillness o' th' night; never failin' to realize that her eyes couldn't be goin' wrong, be sthretchin' out her arm an' runnin' her hand over th' pram, to make sure that th' sight was no deception! Moreover, somethin's tellin' me that th' runnin' hurry of an inthrest you're takin' in it now is a sudden ambition to use th' pram for a purpose that a loyal woman of law an' ordher would stagger away from! (*She gives the pram a sudden push that pulls Bessie forward.*)

BESSIE (*still holding the pram*)  There's not as much as one body in th' house that doesn't know that it wasn't Bessie Burgess that was always shakin' her voice complainin' about people leavin bassinettes in th' way of them that, week in an' week out, had to pay their rent, an' always had to find a regular accommodation for her own furniture in her own room. . . . An' as for law an' ordher, puttin' aside th' harp an' shamrock, Bessie Burgess 'll have as much respect as she wants for th' lion an' unicorn!

PETER (*appearing at the door*)  I think I'll go with th' pair of yous an' see th' fun. A fella might as well chance it, anyhow.

MRS. GOGAN (*taking no notice of Peter, and pushing the pram on another step*)  Take your rovin' lumps o' hands from pattin' th' bassinette, if you please, ma'am; an', steppin' from th' threshold of good manners, let me tell you, Mrs. Burgess, that it's a fat wondher to Jennie Gogan that a lady-like singer o' hymns like yourself would lower her thoughts from sky-thinkin' to stretch out her arm in a sly-seekin' way to pinch anything dhriven asthray in th' confusion of th' battle our boys is makin' for th' freedom of their counthry!

PETER (*laughing and rubbing his hands together*)  Hee, hee, hee, hee, hee! I'll go with th' pair o' yous an' give yous a hand.

MRS. GOGAN (*with a rapid turn of her head as she shoves the pram forward*)  Get up in th' prambulator an' we'll wheel you down.

BESSIE (*to Mrs. Gogan*)  Poverty an' hardship has sent Bessie Burgess to abide with sthrange company, but she always knew them she had to live with from backside to breakfast time; an' she can tell them, always havin' had a Christian kinch[5] on her conscience, that a passion for thievin' an' pinchin' would find her soul a foreign place to live in, an' that her present intention is quite th' lofty-hearted one of pickin' up anything shaken up an' scatthered about in th' loose confusion of a general plundher!

*By this time they have disappeared from view. Peter is following, when the boom of a big gun in the distance brings him to a quick halt.*

PETER  God Almighty, that's th' big gun again! God forbid any harm would happen to them, but sorra mind I'd mind if they met with a dhrop in their mad endeyvours to plundher an' desthroy.

*He looks down the street for a moment, then runs to the hall door of the house, which is open, and shuts it with a vicious pull; he then goes to the chair in which Mollser had sat, sits down, takes out his pipe, lights it and begins to smoke with his head carried at a haughty angle. The Covey comes staggering in with a ten-stone sack of flour on his back. On the top of the sack is a ham. He goes over to the door, pushes it with his head, and finds he can't open it; he turns slightly in the direction of Peter.*

THE COVEY (*to Peter*)  Who shut th' door? . . . (*He kicks at it.*)  Here, come on an' open it, will you? This isn't a mot's hand-bag I've got on me back.

PETER  Now, me young Covey, d'ye think I'm goin' to be your lackey?

THE COVEY (*angrily*)  Will you open th' door, y'oul'—

PETER (*shouting*)  Don't be assin' me to open any door, don't be assin' me to open any door for you. . . . Makin' a shame an' a sin o' th' cause that good men are fightin' for. . . . Oh, God forgive th' people that, instead o' burnishin' th' work

5. Kink, perhaps in the sense of a twisted rope; i.e., she is not easy on her conscience.

th' boys is doin' to-day with quiet honesty an' patience, is
revilin' their sacrifices with a riot of lootin' an' roguery!

THE COVEY  Isn't your own eyes leppin' out o' your head with
envy that you haven't th' guts to ketch a few o' th' things
that God is givin' to His chosen people? . . . Y'oul'
hypocrite, if everyone was blind you'd steal a cross off an
ass's back!

PETER (*very calmly*)  You're not going to make me lose me
temper; you can go on with your proddin' as long as you
like; goad an' goad an' goad away; hee, hee, heee! I'll not
lose me temper. (*Somebody opens door and the Covey goes in.*)

THE COVEY (*inside, mockingly*)  Cuckoo-oo!

PETER (*running to the door and shouting in a blaze of passion as he
follows the Covey in*)  You lean, long, lanky lath of a lowsey
bastard. . . . (*Following him in.*) Lowscy bastard, lowsey
bastard!

*Bessie and Mrs. Gogan enter, the pride of a great joy illuminating
their faces. Bessie is pushing the pram, which is filled with clothes and
boots; on the top of the boots and clothes is a fancy table, which Mrs.
Gogan is holding on with her left hand, while with her right hand she
holds a chair on the top of her head. They are heard talking to each
other before they enter.*

MRS. GOGAN (*outside*)  I don't remember ever havin' seen such
lovely pairs as them, (*they appear*) with th' pointed toes an'
th' cuban heels.

BESSIE  They'll go grand with th' dhresses we're afther liftin',
when we've stitched a sthray bit o' silk to lift th' bodices up
a little higher, so as to shake th' shame out o' them, an'
make them fit for women that hasn't lost themselves in th'
nakedness o' th' times.

*They fussily carry in the chair, the table, and some of the other goods.
They return to bring in the rest.*

PETER (*at the door, sourly to Mrs. Gogan*)  Ay, you. Mollser looks
as if she was goin' to faint, an' your youngster is roarin' in
convulsions in her lap.

MRS. GOGAN (*snappily*)  She's never any other way but faintin'!

*She goes to go in with some things in her arms, when a shot from a rifle rings out. She and Bessie make a bolt for the door, which Peter, in a panic, tries to shut before they have got inside.*

MRS. GOGAN    Ay, ay, ay, you cowardly oul' fool, what are you thryin' to shut th' door on us for?

*They retreat tumultuously inside. A pause; then Captain Brennan comes in supporting Lieutenant Langon, whose arm is around Brennan's neck. Langon's face, which is ghastly white, is momentarily convulsed with spasms of agony. He is in a state of collapse, and Brennan is almost carrying him. After a few moments Clitheroe, pale, and in a state of calm nervousness, follows, looking back in the direction from which he came, a rifle, held at the ready, in his hands.*

CAPT. BRENNAN *(savagely to Clitheroe)*    Why did you fire over their heads? Why didn't you fire to kill?

CLITHEROE    No, no, Bill; bad as they are they're Irish men an' women.

CAPT. BRENNAN *(savagely)*    Irish be damned! Attackin' an' mobbin' th' men that are riskin' their lives for them. If these slum lice gather at our heels again, plug one o' them, or I'll soon shock them with a shot or two meself!

LIEUT. LANGON *(moaningly)*    My God, is there ne'er an ambulance knockin' around anywhere? . . . Th' stomach is ripped out o' me; I feel it—o-o-oh, Christ!

CAPT. BRENNAN    Keep th' heart up, Jim; we'll soon get help, now.

*Nora rushes wildly out of the house and flings her arms round the neck of Clitheroe with a fierce and joyous insistence. Her hair is down, her face is haggard, but her eyes are agleam with the light of happy relief.*

NORA    Jack, Jack, Jack; God be thanked . . . be thanked. . . . He has been kind and merciful to His poor handmaiden. . . . My Jack, my own Jack, that I thought was lost is found, that I thought was dead is alive again! . . . Oh, God be praised for ever, evermore! . . . My poor Jack. . . . Kiss me, kiss me, Jack, kiss your own Nora!

CLITHEROE *(kissing her, and speaking brokenly)*    My Nora; my little, beautiful Nora, I wish to God I'd never left you.

NORA    It doesn't matter—not now, not now, Jack. It will make us dearer than ever to each other. . . . Kiss me, kiss me again.

CLITHEROE  Now, for God's sake, Nora, don't make a scene.

NORA  I won't, I won't; I promise, I promise, Jack; honest to God. I'll be silent an' brave to bear th' joy of feelin' you safe in my arms again. . . . It's hard to force away th' tears of happiness at th' end of an awful agony.

BESSIE (*from the upper window*)  Th' Minsthrel Boys aren't feelin' very comfortable now. Th' big guns has knocked all th' harps out of their hands.[6] General Clitheroe'd rather be unlacin' his wife's bodice than standin' at a barricade. . . . An' th' professor of chicken-butcherin' there, finds he's up against somethin' a little tougher even than his own chickens, an' that's sayin' a lot!

CAPT. BRENNAN (*up to Bessie*)  Shut up, y'oul' hag!

BESSIE (*down to Brennan*)  Choke th' chicken, choke th' chicken, choke th' chicken!

LIEUT. LANGON  For God's sake, Bill, bring me some place where me wound 'll be looked afther. . . . Am I to die before anything is done to save me?

CAPT. BRENNAN (*to Clitheroe*)  Come on, Jack. We've got to get help for Jim, here—have you no thought for his pain an' danger?

BESSIE  Choke th' chicken, choke th' chicken, choke th' chicken!

CLITHEROE (*to Nora*)  Loosen me, darling, let me go.

NORA (*clinging to him*)  No, no, no, I'll not let you go! Come on, come up to our home, Jack, my sweetheart, my lover, my husband, an' we'll forget th' last few terrible days! . . . I look tired now, but a few hours of happy rest in your arms will bring back th' bloom of freshness again, an' you will be glad, you will be glad, glad . . . glad!

LIEUT. LANGON  Oh, if I'd kep' down only a little longer, I mightn't ha' been hit! Everyone else escapin', an' me gettin' me belly ripped asundher! . . . I couldn't scream, couldn't even scream. . . . D'ye think I'm really badly wounded, Bill? Me clothes seem to be all soakin' wet. . . . It's blood . . . My God, it must be me own blood!

CAPT. BRENNAN (*to Clitheroe*)  Go on, Jack, bid her good-bye

---

6. See note, p. 23. Thomas Moore's Minstrel Boy was killed when he went to war with "his wild harp slung behind him." It is his death, not "his proud soul" that Bessie has in mind.

with another kiss, an' be done with it! D'ye want Langon to die in me arms while you're dallyin' with your Nora?

CLITHEROE (*to Nora*)   I must go, I must go, Nora. I'm sorry we met at all. . . . It couldn't be helped—all other ways were blocked be th' British. . . . Let me go, can't you, Nora? D'ye want me to be unthrue to me comrades?

NORA   No, I won't let you go. . . . I want you to be thrue to me, Jack. . . . I'm your dearest comrade; I'm your thruest comrade. . . . They only want th' comfort of havin' you in th' same danger as themselves. . . . Oh, Jack, I can't let you go!

CLITHEROE   You must, Nora, you must.

NORA   All last night at th' barricades I sought you, Jack. . . . I didn't think of th' danger—I could only think of you. . . . I asked for you everywhere. . . . Some o' them laughed. . . . I was pushed away, but I shoved back. . . . Some o' them even sthruck me . . . an' I screamed an' screamed your name!

CLITHEROE (*in fear her action would give him future shame*)   What possessed you to make a show of yourself, like that? . . . What way d'ye think I'll feel when I'm told my wife was bawlin' for me at th' barricades? What are you more than any other woman?

NORA   No more, maybe; but you are more to me than any other man, Jack. . . . I didn't mean any harm, honestly, Jack. . . . I couldn't help it. . . . I shouldn't have told you. . . . My love for you made me mad with terror.

CLITHEROE (*angrily*)   They'll say now that I sent you out th' way I'd have an excuse to bring you home. . . . Are you goin' to turn all th' risks I'm takin' into a laugh?

LIEUT. LANGON   Let me lie down, let me lie down, Bill; th' pain would be easier, maybe, lyin' down. . . . Oh, God, have mercy on me!

CAPT. BRENNAN (*to Langon*)   A few steps more, Jim, a few steps more; thry to stick it for a few steps more.

LIEUT. LANGON   Oh, I can't, I can't, I can't!

CAPT. BRENNAN (*to Clitheroe*)   Are you comin', man, or are you goin' to make an arrangement for another honeymoon? . . . If you want to act th' renegade, say so, an' we'll be off!

BESSIE (*from above*)   Runnin' from th' Tommies—choke th'

chicken. Runnin' from th' Tommies—choke th' chicken!

CLITHEROE (*savagely to Brennan*) Damn you, man, who wants to act th' renegade? (*To Nora.*) Here, let go your hold; let go, I say!

NORA (*clinging to Clitheroe, and indicating Brennan*) Look, Jack, look at th' anger in his face; look at th' fear glintin' in his eyes. . . . He himself's afraid, afraid, afraid! . . . He wants you to go th' way he'll have th' chance of death sthrikin' you an' missin' him! . . . Turn round an' look at him, Jack, look at him, look at him! . . . His very soul is cold . . . shiverin' with th' thought of what may happen to him. . . . It is his fear that is thryin' to frighten you from recognizin' th' same fear that is in your own heart!

CLITHEROE (*struggling to release himself from Nora*) Damn you, woman, will you let me go!

CAPT. BRENNAN (*fiercely, to Clitheroe*) Why are you beggin' her to let you go? Are you afraid of her, or what? Break her hold on you, man, or go up, an' sit on her lap!

*Clitheroe trying roughly to break her hold.*

NORA (*imploringly*) Oh, Jack. . . . Jack. . . . Jack!

LIEUT. LANGON (*agonizingly*) Brennan, a priest; I'm dyin', I think, I'm dyin'!

CLITHEROE (*to Nora*) If you won't do it quietly, I'll have to make you! (*To Brennan.*) Here, hold this gun, you, for a minute. (*He hands the gun to Brennan.*)

NORA (*pitifully*) Please, Jack. . . . You're hurting me, Jack. . . . Honestly. . . . Oh, you're hurting . . . me! . . . I won't, I won't, I won't! . . . Oh, Jack, I gave you everything you asked of me. . . . Don't fling me from you, now! (*He roughly loosens her grip, and pushes her away from him. Nora sinks to the ground and lies there.*)

NORA (*weakly*) Ah, Jack. . . . Jack. . . . Jack!

CLITHEROE (*taking the gun back from Brennan*) Come on, come on.

*They go out. Bessie looks at Nora lying on the street, for a few moments, then, leaving the window, she comes out, runs over to Nora, lifts her up in her arms, and carries her swiftly into the house. A short pause, then down the street is heard a wild, drunken yell; it comes nearer, and Fluther enters, frenzied, wild-eyed, mad, roaring drunk. In his arms is an earthen half-gallon jar of whisky; streaming from one of the pockets of his coat is the arm of a new tunic shirt; on his head is a woman's vivid blue hat with gold lacing, all of which he has looted.*

FLUTHER (*singing in a frenzy*)

Fluther's a jolly good fella! . . . Fluther's a jolly good
    fella!
Up th' rebels! . . . That nobody can deny!

(*He beats on the door.*) Get us a mug or a jug, or somethin', some o' yous, one o' yous, will yous, before I lay one o' yous out! . . . (*Looking down the street.*) Bang an' fire away for all Fluther cares. . . . (*Banging at door.*) Come down an' open th' door, some of yous, one of yous, will yous, before I lay some o' yous out! . . . Th' whole city can topple home to hell, for Fluther!

*Inside the house is heard a scream from Nora, followed by a moan.*

FLUTHER (*singing furiously*)

That nobody can deny, that nobody can deny,
For Fluther's a jolly good fella, Fluther's a jolly good
    fella,
Fluther's a jolly good fella . . . Up th' rebels! That
    nobody can deny!

(*His frantic movements cause him to spill some of the whisky out of the jar.*) Blast you, Fluther, don't be spillin' th' precious liquor! (*He kicks at the door.*) Ay, give us a mug or a jug, or somethin', one o' yous, some o' yous, will yous, before I lay one o' yous out!

*The door suddenly opens, and Bessie, coming out, grips him by the collar.*

BESSIE (*indignantly*) You bowsey, come in ower o' that. . . . I'll thrim your thricks o' dhrunken dancin' for you, an' none of us knowin' how soon we'll bump into a world we were never in before!

FLUTHER (*as she is pulling him in*) Ay, th' jar, th' jar, th' jar!

*A short pause, then again is heard a scream of pain from Nora. The door opens and Mrs. Gogan and Bessie are seen standing at it.*

BESSIE  Fluther would go, only he's too dhrunk. . . . Oh, God, isn't it a pity he's so dhrunk! We'll have to thry to get a docthor somewhere.

MRS. GOGAN  I'd be afraid to go. . . . Besides, Mollser's terrible bad. I don't think you'll get a docthor to come. It's hardly any use goin'.

BESSIE  (*determinedly*)  I'll risk it. . . . Give her a little of Fluther's whisky. . . . It's th' fright that's brought it on her so soon. . . . Go on back to her, you.

*Mrs. Gogan goes in, and Bessie softly closes the door. She is moving forward, when the sound of some rifle shots, and the tok, tok, tok of a distant machine-gun brings her to a sudden halt. She hesitates for a moment, then she tightens her shawl round her, as if it were a shield, then she firmly and swiftly goes out.*

BESSIE  (*as she goes out*)  Oh, God, be Thou my help in time o' throuble. An' shelter me safely in th' shadow of Thy wings!

CURTAIN

## ACT FOUR

*The living-room of Bessie Burgess. It is one of two small attic rooms (the other, used as a bedroom, is to the Left), the ceiling slopes up towards the back, giving to the apartment a look of compressed confinement. In the centre of the ceiling is a small skylight. There is an unmistakable air of poverty bordering on destitution. The paper on the walls is torn and soiled, particularly near the fire where the cooking is done, and near the washstand where the washing is done. The fireplace is to the Left. A small armchair near fire. One small window at Back. A pane of this window is starred by the entrance of a bullet. Under the window to the Right is an oak coffin standing on two kitchen chairs. Near the coffin is a home-manufactured stool, on which are two lighted candles. Beside the window is a worn-out dresser on which is a small quantity of delf. Tattered remains of cheap lace curtains drape the window. Standing near the window on Left is a brass standard-lamp with a fancy shade; hanging on the wall near the same window is a vividly crimson silk dress, both of which have been looted. A door on Left leading to the bedroom. Another opposite giving a way to the rest of the house. To the*

*Left of this door a common washstand. A tin kettle, very black, and an old saucepan inside the fender. There is no light in the room but that given from the two candles and the fire. The dusk has well fallen, and the glare of the burning buildings in the town can be seen through the window, in the distant sky. The Covey and Fluther have been playing cards, sitting on the floor by the light of the candles on the stool near the coffin. When the curtain rises the Covey is shuffling the cards, Peter is sitting in a stiff, dignified way beside him, and Fluther is kneeling beside the window, cautiously looking out. It is a few days later.*

FLUTHER (*furtively peeping out of the window*)  Give them a good shuffling. . . . Th' sky's gettin' reddher an' reddher. . . . You'd think it was afire. . . . Half o' th' city must be burnin'.

THE COVEY  If I was you, Fluther, I'd keep away from that window. . . . It's dangerous, an', besides, if they see you, you'll only bring a nose on th' house.

PETER  Yes; an' he knows we had to leave our own place th' way they were riddlin' it with machine-gun fire. . . . He'll keep on pimpin' an' pimpin' there, till we have to fly out o' this place too.

FLUTHER (*ironically*)  If they make any attack here, we'll send you out in your green an' glory uniform, shakin' your sword over your head, an' they'll fly before you as th' Danes flew before Brian Boru!

THE COVEY (*placing the cards on the floor, after shuffling them*)  Come on, an' cut.

*Fluther comes over, sits on floor, and cuts the cards.*

THE COVEY (*having dealt the cards*)  Spuds up again.

*Nora moans feebly in room on Left.*

FLUTHER  There, she's at it again. She's been quiet for a long time, all th' same.

THE COVEY  She was quiet before, sure, an' she broke out again worse than ever. . . . What was led that time?

PETER  Thray o' Hearts, Thray o' Hearts, Thray o' Hearts.

FLUTHER  It's damned hard lines to think of her dead-born kiddie lyin' there in th' arms o' poor little Mollser. Mollser snuffed it sudden too, afther all.

THE COVEY  Sure she never got any care. How could she get it, an' th' mother out day an' night lookin' for work, an' her consumptive husband leavin' her with a baby to be born before he died!

VOICES IN A LILTING CHANT TO THE LEFT IN A DISTANT STREET  Red Cr . . . oss, Red Cr . . . oss! . . . Ambu . . . lance, Ambu . . . lance!

THE COVEY (*to Fluther*)  Your deal, Fluther.

FLUTHER (*shuffling and dealing the cards*)  It'll take a lot out o' Nora—if she'll ever be th' same.

THE COVEY  Th' docthor thinks she'll never be th' same; thinks she'll be a little touched here. (*He touches his forehead.*) She's ramblin' a lot; thinkin' she's out in th' counthry with Jack; or gettin' his dinner ready for him before he comes home; or yellin' for her kiddie. All that, though, might be th' chloroform she got. . . . I don't know what we'd have done only for oul' Bessie; up with her for th' past three nights, hand runnin'.

FLUTHER  I always knew there was never anything really derogatory wrong with poor oul' Bessie. (*To Peter, who is taking a trick.*) Ay, houl' on, there, don't be so damn quick—that's my thrick.

PETER  What's your thrick? It's my thrick, man.

FLUTHER (*loudly*)  How is it your thrick?

PETER (*answering as loudly*)  Didn't I lead th' deuce!

FLUTHER  You must be gettin' blind, man; don't you see th' ace?

BESSIE (*appearing at the door of room, Left; in a tense whisper*)  D'ye want to waken her again on me, when she's just gone asleep? If she wakes will yous come an' mind her? If I hear a whisper out o' one o' yous again, I'll . . . gut yous!

THE COVEY (*in a whisper*)  S-s-s-h. She can hear anything above a whisper.

PETER (*looking up at the ceiling*)  Th' gentle an' merciful God 'll give th' pair o' yous a scawldin' an' a scarifyin' one o' these days!

*Fluther takes a bottle of whisky from his pocket, and takes a drink.*

THE COVEY (*to Fluther*)  Why don't you spread that out, man, an' thry to keep a sup for to-morrow?

FLUTHER  Spread it out? Keep a sup for to-morrow? How th'

hell does a fella know there'll be any to-morrow? If I'm goin' to be whipped away, let me be whipped away when it's empty, an' not when it's half full! (*To Bessie, who has seated herself in an armchair at the fire.*) How is she, now, Bessie?

BESSIE   I left her sleeping quietly. When I'm listenin' to her babblin', I think she'll never be much betther than she is. Her eyes have a hauntin' way of lookin' in instead of lookin' out, as if her mind had been lost alive in madly minglin' memories of th' past. . . . (*Sleepily.*) Crushin' her thoughts . . . together . . . in a fierce . . . an' fanciful . . . (*she nods her head and starts wakefully*) idea that dead things are livin', an' livin' things are dead. . . . (*With a start.*) Was that a scream I heard her give? (*Reassured.*) Blessed God, I think I hear her screamin' every minute! An' it's only there with me that I'm able to keep awake.

THE COVEY   She'll sleep, maybe, for a long time, now. Ten there.

FLUTHER   Ten here. If she gets a long sleep, she might be all right. Peter's th' lone five.

THE COVEY   Whisht! I think I hear somebody movin' below. Whoever it is, he's comin' up.

*A pause. Then the door opens and Captain Brennan comes into the room. He has changed his uniform for a suit of civvies. His eyes droop with the heaviness of exhaustion; his face is pallid and drawn. His clothes are dusty and stained here and there with mud. He leans heavily on the back of a chair as he stands.*

CAPT. BRENNAN   Mrs. Clitheroe; where's Mrs. Clitheroe? I was told I'd find her here.

BESSIE   What d'ye want with Mrs. Clitheroe?

CAPT. BRENNAN   I've a message, a last message for her from her husband.

BESSIE   Killed! He's not killed, is he!

CAPT. BRENNAN (*sinking stiffly and painfully on to a chair*)   In th' Imperial Hotel; we fought till th' place was in flames. He was shot through th' arm, an' then through th' lung. . . . I could do nothin' for him—only watch his breath comin' an' goin' in quick, jerky gasps, an' a tiny sthream o' blood thricklin' out of his mouth, down over his lower lip. . . . I said a prayer for th' dyin', an' twined his Rosary beads around his fingers. . . . Then I had to leave him to save meself. . . . (*He shows some holes in his coat.*) Look at th' way a machine-gun tore at me coat, as I belted out o' the buildin' an' darted across th' sthreet for shelter.[1] . . . An' then, I seen The Plough an' th' Stars fallin' like a shot as th' roof crashed in, an' where I'd left poor Jack was nothin' but a leppin' spout o' flame!

BESSIE (*with partly repressed vehemence*)  Ay, you left him! You twined his Rosary beads round his fingers, an' then you run like a hare to get out o' danger!

CAPT. BRENNAN  I took me chance as well as him. . . . He took it like a man. His last whisper was to 'Tell Nora to be brave; that I'm ready to meet my God, an' that I'm proud to die for Ireland.' An' when our General heard it he said that 'Commandant Clitheroe's end was a gleam of glory.' Mrs. Clitheroe's grief will be a joy when she realizes that she has had a hero for a husband.

BESSIE  If you only seen her, you'd know to th' differ.

*Nora appears at door, Left. She is clad only in her nightdress; her hair, uncared for some days, is hanging in disorder over her shoulders. Her pale face looks paler still because of a vivid red spot on the tip of each cheek. Her eyes are glimmering with the light of incipient insanity; her hands are nervously fiddling with her nightgown. She halts at the door for a moment, looks vacantly around the room, and then comes slowly in. The rest do not notice her till she speaks.*

NORA (*in a quiet and monotonous tone*)  No . . . Not there, Jack. . . . I can feel comfortable only in our own familiar place beneath th' bramble tree. . . . We must be walking for a long time; I feel very, very tired. . . . Have we to go farther, or have we passed it by? (*Passing her hand across her eyes.*) Curious mist on my eyes. . . . Why don't you hold my hand, Jack. . . . (*Excitedly.*) No, no, Jack, it's not. Can't you see it's a goldfinch. Look at th' black-satiny wings with th' gold bars, an' th' splash of crimson on its head. . . . (*Wearily.*) Something ails me, something ails me. . . . Don't kiss me like that; you take my breath away, Jack. . . . Why do you frown at me? . . . You're going away, and (*frightened*)

1. Brennan is supposed to have changed his clothes since he left the Imperial. See p. 73 and p. 76. An oversight on O'Casey's part?

I can't follow you. Something's keeping me from moving.
. . . (*Crying out.*) Jack, Jack, Jack!

BESSIE (*who has gone over and caught Nora's arm*) Now, Mrs.
Clitheroe, you're a terrible woman to get up out of bed. . . .
You'll get cold if you stay here in them clothes.

NORA Cold? I'm feelin' very cold; it's chilly out here in th'
counthry. . . . (*Looking around frightened.*) What place is this?
Where am I?

BESSIE (*coaxingly*) You're all right, Nora; you're with friends,
an' in a safe place. Don't you know your uncle an' your
cousin, an' poor oul' Fluther?

PETER (*about to go over to Nora*) Nora, darlin', now—

FLUTHER (*pulling him back*) Now, leave her to Bessie, man. A
crowd 'll only make her worse.

NORA (*thoughtfully*) There is something I want to remember,
an' I can't. (*With agony.*) I can't, I can't, I can't! My head,
my head! (*Suddenly breaking from Bessie, and running over to the
men, and gripping Fluther by the shoulders.*) Where is it? Where's
my baby? Tell me where you've put it, where've you hidden
it? My baby, my baby; I want my baby! My head, my poor
head. . . . Oh, I can't tell what is wrong with me.
(*Screaming.*) Give him to me, give me my husband!

BESSIE Blessin' o' God on us, isn't this pitiful!

NORA (*struggling with Bessie*) I won't go away for you; I won't.
Not till you give me back my husband. (*Screaming.*) Murderers, that's what yous are; murderers, murderers!

BESSIE S-s-sh. We'll bring Mr. Clitheroe back to you, if you'll
only lie down an' stop quiet. . . . (*Trying to lead her in.*) Come
on, now, Nora, an' I'll sing something to you.

NORA I feel as if my life was thryin' to force its way out of my
body. . . . I can hardly breathe . . . I'm frightened, I'm
frightened, I'm frightened! For God's sake, don't leave me,
Bessie. Hold my hand, put your arms around me!

FLUTHER (*to Brennan*) Now you can see th' way she is, man.

PETER An' what way would she be if she heard Jack had
gone west?

THE COVEY (*to Peter*) Shut up, you, man!

BESSIE (*to Nora*) We'll have to be brave, an' let patience clip
away th' heaviness of th' slow-movin' hours, rememberin'
that sorrow may endure for th' night, but joy cometh in th'

mornin'. . . . Come on in, an' I'll sing to you, an' you'll rest quietly.

NORA (*stopping suddenly on her way to the room*)  Jack an' me are goin' out somewhere this evenin'. Where I can't tell. Isn't it curious I can't remember. . . . Maura, Maura, Jack, if th' baby's a girl; any name you like, if th' baby's a boy! . . . He's there. (*Screaming.*) He's there, an' they won't give him back to me!

BESSIE  S-ss-s-h, darlin', s-ssh. I won't sing to you, if you're not quiet.

NORA (*nervously holding Bessie*)  Hold my hand, hold my hand, an' sing to me, sing to me!

BESSIE  Come in an' lie down, an' I'll sing to you.

NORA (*vehemently*)  Sing to me, sing to me; sing, sing!

BESSIE (*singing as she leads Nora into room*)

Lead, kindly light, amid th' encircling gloom,
    Lead Thou me on;
Th' night is dark an' I am far from home,
    Lead Thou me on.
Keep Thou my feet; I do not ask to see
Th' distant scene—one step enough for me.
So long that Thou hast blessed me, sure Thou still
    Wilt lead me on;

*They go in.*

BESSIE (*singing in room*)

O'er moor an' fen, o'er crag an' torrent, till
    Th' night is gone.
An' in th' morn those angel faces smile
That I have lov'd long since, an' lost awhile!

THE COVEY (*to Brennan*)  Now that you've seen how bad she is, an' that we daren't tell her what has happened till she's betther, you'd best be slippin' back to where you come from.

CAPT. BRENNAN  There's no chance o' slippin' back now, for th' military are everywhere: a fly couldn't get through. I'd never have got here, only I managed to change me uniform for what I'm wearin'. . . . I'll have to take me chance, an' thry to lie low here for a while.

THE COVEY (*frightened*) There's no place here to lie low. Th' Tommies 'll be hoppin' in here, any minute!

PETER (*aghast*) An' then we'd all be shanghaied!

THE COVEY Be God, there's enough afther happenin' to us!

FLUTHER (*warningly, as he listens*) Whisht, whisht, th' whole o' yous. I think I heard th' clang of a rifle butt on th' floor of th' hall below. (*All alertness.*) Here, come on with th' cards again. I'll deal. (*He shuffles and deals the cards to all.*)

FLUTHER Clubs up. (*To Brennan.*) Thry to keep your hands from shakin', man. You lead, Peter. (*As Peter throws out a card.*) Four o' Hearts led.

*The door opens and Corporal Stoddart of the Wiltshires enters in full war kit; steel helmet, rifle and bayonet, and trench tool. He looks round the room. A pause and a palpable silence.*

FLUTHER (*breaking the silence*) Two tens an' a five.

CORPORAL STODDART 'Ello. (*Indicating the coffin.*) This the stiff?

THE COVEY Yis.

CORPORAL STODDART Who's gowing with it? Ownly one allowed to gow with it, you know.

THE COVEY I dunno.

CORPORAL STODDART You dunnow?

THE COVEY I dunno.

BESSIE (*coming into the room*) She's afther slippin' off to sleep again, thanks be to God. I'm hardly able to keep me own eyes open. (*To the soldier.*) Oh, are yous goin' to take away poor little Mollser?

CORPORAL STODDART Ay; 'oo's agowing with 'er?

BESSIE Oh, th' poor mother, o' course. God help her, it's a terrible blow to her!

FLUTHER A terrible blow? Sure, she's in her element now, woman, mixin' earth to earth, an' ashes t'ashes an' dust to dust, an' revellin' in plumes an' hearses, last days an' judgements!

BESSIE (*falling into chair by the fire*) God bless us! I'm jaded!

CORPORAL STODDART Was she plugged?

THE COVEY Ah, no; died o' consumption.

CORPORAL STODDART Ow, is that all? Thought she moight 'ave been plugged.

THE COVEY Is that all? Isn't it enough? D'ye know, comrade,

that more die o' consumption than are killed in th' wars? An' it's all because of th' system we're livin' undher?

CORPORAL STODDART   Ow, I know. I'm a Sowcialist moiself, but I 'as to do my dooty.

THE COVEY (*ironically*)   Dooty! Th' only dooty of a Socialist is th' emancipation of th' workers.

CORPORAL STODDART   Ow, a man's a man, an 'e 'as to foight for 'is country, 'asn't 'e?

FLUTHER (*aggressively*)   You're not fightin' for your counthry here, are you?

PETER (*anxiously, to Fluther*)   Ay, ay, Fluther, none o' that, none o' that!

THE COVEY   Fight for your counthry! Did y'ever read, comrade, Jenersky's *Thesis on the Origin, Development, an' Consolidation of th' Evolutionary Idea of the Proletariat?*

CORPORAL STODDART   Ow, cheese it, Paddy, cheese it!

BESSIE (*sleepily*)   How is things in th' town, Tommy?

CORPORAL STODDART   Ow, I fink it's nearly hover. We've got 'em surrounded, and we're clowsing in on the bloighters. Ow, it was only a little bit of a dawg-foight.

*The sharp ping of the sniper's rifle is heard, followed by a squeal of pain.*

VOICES TO THE LEFT IN A CHANT   Red Cr . . . oss, Red Cr . . . oss! Ambu . . . lance, Ambu . . . lance!

CORPORAL STODDART (*excitedly*)   Christ, that's another of our men 'it by that blawsted sniper! 'E's knocking abaht 'ere, somewheres. Gawd, when we get th' bloighter, we'll give 'im the cold steel, we will. We'll jab the belly aht of 'im, we will!

*Mrs. Gogan comes in tearfully, and a little proud of the importance of being directly connected with death.*

MRS. GOGAN (*to Fluther*)   I'll never forget what you done for me, Fluther, goin' around at th' risk of your life settlin' everything with th' undhertaker an' th' cemetery people. When all me own were afraid to put their noses out, you plunged like a good one through hummin' bullets, an' they knockin' fire out o' th' road, tinklin' through th' frightened windows, an' splashin' themselves to pieces on th' walls! An' you'll find, that Mollser, in th' happy place she's gone to, won't forget to whisper, now an' again, th' name o' Fluther.

CORPORAL STODDART   Git it aht, mother, git it aht.

BESSIE (*from the chair*)   It's excusin' me you'll be, Mrs. Gogan, for not stannin' up, seein' I'm shaky on me feet for want of a little sleep, an' not desirin' to show any disrespect to poor little Mollser.

FLUTHER   Sure, we all know, Bessie, that it's vice versa with you.

MRS. GOGAN (*to Bessie*)   Indeed, it's meself that has well chronicled, Mrs. Burgess, all your gentle hurryin's to me little Mollser, when she was alive, bringin' her somethin' to dhrink, or somethin' t'eat, an' never passin' her without liftin' up her heart with a delicate word o' kindness.

CORPORAL STODDART (*impatiently, but kindly*)   Git it aht, git it aht, mother.

*The Covey, Fluther, Brennan, and Peter carry out the coffin, followed by Mrs. Gogan.*

CORPORAL STODDART (*to Bessie, who is almost asleep*)   'Ow many men is in this 'ere 'ouse? (*No answer. Loudly.*) 'Ow many men is in this 'ere 'ouse?

BESSIE (*waking with a start*)   God, I was nearly asleep! . . . How many men? Didn't you see them?

CORPORAL STODDART   Are they all that are in the 'ouse?

BESSIE   Oh, there's none higher up, but there may be more lower down. Why?

CORPORAL STODDART   All men in the district 'as to be rounded up. Somebody's giving 'elp to the snipers, an we 'as to take precautions. If I 'ad my woy, I'd make 'em all join hup, and do their bit! But I suppowse they and you are all Shinners.[2]

BESSIE (*who has been sinking into sleep, waking up to a sleepy vehemence*)   Bessie Burgess is no Shinner, an' never had no thruck with anything spotted be th' fingers o' th' Fenians; but always made it her business to harness herself for Church whenever she knew that God Save the King was goin' to be sung at t'end of th' service; whose only son went

2. Members of the Sinn Féin ("We Ourselves"), a party that advocated complete economic and political separation from England. Although it was the Irish Republican Brotherhood rather than the Sinn Féin that organized the Rising, to an outsider like Corporal Stoddart all anti-English Irish must have seemed alike. Bessie is accepting his generalization even as she disdains the label.

to th' front in th' first contingent of the Dublin Fusiliers, an' that's on his way home carryin' a shatthered arm that he got fightin' for his King an' counthry!

*Her head sinks slowly forward again. Peter comes into the room; his body is stiffened and his face is wearing a comically indignant look. He walks to and fro at the back of the room, evidently repressing a violent desire to speak angrily. He is followed in by Fluther, the Covey, and Brennan, who slinks into an obscure corner of the room, nervous of notice.*

FLUTHER (*after an embarrassing pause*) Th' air in th' sthreet outside's shakin' with the firin' o' rifles an' machine-guns. It must be a hot shop in th' middle o' th' scrap.

CORPORAL STODDART We're pumping lead in on 'em from every side, now; they'll soon be shoving up th' white flag.

PETER (*with a shout*) I'm tellin' you either o' yous two lowsers 'ud make a betther hearse-man than Peter; proddin' an' pokin' at me an' I helpin' to carry out a corpse!

FLUTHER It wasn't a very derogatory thing for th' Covey to say that you'd make a fancy hearse-man, was it?

PETER (*furiously*) A pair o' red-jesthered bowseys pondherin' from mornin' till night on how they'll get a chance to break a gap through th' quiet nature of a man that's always endeavourin' to chase out of him any sthray thought of venom against his fella-man!

THE COVEY Oh, shut it, shut it, shut it!

PETER As long as I'm a livin' man, responsible for me thoughts, words, an' deeds to th' Man above, I'll feel meself instituted to fight again' th' sliddherin' ways of a pair o' picaroons, whisperin', concurrin', concoctin', an' conspirin' together to rendher me unconscious of th' life I'm thryin' to live!

CORPORAL STODDART (*dumbfounded*) What's wrong, Daddy; wot 'ave they done to you?

PETER (*savagely to the Corporal*) You mind your own business! What's it got to do with you, what's wrong with me?

BESSIE (*in a sleepy murmur*) Will yous thry to conthrol your- selves into quietness? Yous'll waken her . . . up . . . on . . . me . . . again. (*She sleeps.*)

FLUTHER    Come on, boys, to th' cards again, an' never mind him.

CORPORAL STODDART    No use of you gowing to start cawds; you'll be gowing out of 'ere, soon as Sergeant comes.

FLUTHER    Goin' out o' here? An' why're we goin' out o' here?

CORPORAL STODDART    All men in district to be rounded up, and 'eld in till the scrap is hover.

FLUTHER    An' where're we goin' to be held in?

CORPORAL STODDART    They're puttin 'em in a church.

THE COVEY    A church?

FLUTHER    What sort of a church? Is it a Protestan' Church?

CORPORAL STODDART    I dunnow; I suppowse so.

FLUTHER (*dismayed*)    Be God, it'll be a nice thing to be stuck all night in a Protestan' Church!

CORPORAL STODDART    Bring the cawds; you moight get a chance of a goime.

FLUTHER    Ah, no, that wouldn't do. . . . I wondher? (*After a moment's thought.*) Ah, I don't think we'd be doin' anything derogatory be playin' cards in a Protestan' Church.

CORPORAL STODDART    If I was you I'd bring a little snack with me; you moight be glad of it before the mawning. (*Sings.*)

I do loike a snoice mince poy,
I do loike a snoice mince poy!

*The snap of the sniper's rifle rings out again, followed simultaneously by a scream of pain. Corporal Stoddart goes pale, and brings his rifle to the ready, listening.*

VOICES CHANTING TO THE RIGHT    Red Cro . . . ss, Red Cro . . . ss! Ambu . . . lance, Ambu . . . lance!

*Sergeant Tinley comes rapidly in, pale, agitated, and fiercely angry.*

CORPORAL STODDART (*to Sergeant*)    One of hour men 'it, Sergeant?

SERGEANT TINLEY    Private Taylor; got 'it roight through the chest, 'e did; an 'ole in front of 'im as 'ow you could put your fist through, and 'arf 'is back blown awoy! Dum-dum bullets they're using. Gang of Hassassins potting at us from behind roofs. That's not playing the goime: why down't they come into the owpen and foight fair!

FLUTHER (*unable to stand the slight*)   Fight fair! A few hundhred scrawls o' chaps with a couple o' guns an' Rosary beads, again' a hundhred thousand thrained men with horse, fut, an' artillery . . . an' he wants us to fight fair! (*To Sergeant.*) D'ye want us to come out in our skins an' throw stones?

SERGEANT TINLEY (*to Corporal*)   Are these four all that are 'ere?

CORPORAL STODDART   Four; that's all, Sergeant.

SERGEANT TINLEY (*vindictively*)   Come on, then; get the blighters aht. (*To the men.*) 'Ere, 'op it aht! Aht into the streets with you, and if a snioper sends another of our men west, you gow with 'im! (*He catches Fluther by the shoulder.*) Gow on, git aht!

FLUTHER   Eh, who are you chuckin', eh?

SERGEANT TINLEY (*roughly*)   Gow on, git aht, you blighter.

FLUTHER   Who arc you callin' a blighter to, eh? I'm a Dublin man,[3] born an' bred in th' city, see?

SERGEANT TINLEY   I down't care if you were Broin Buroo; git aht, git aht.

FLUTHER (*halting as he is going out*)   Jasus, you an' your guns! Leave them down, an' I'd beat th' two o' yous without sweatin'!

*Peter, Brennan, the Covey, and Fluther, followed by the soldiers, go out. Bessie is sleeping heavily on the chair by the fire. After a pause, Nora appears at door, Left, in her nightdress. Remaining at door for a few moments she looks vaguely around the room. She then comes in quietly, goes over to the fire, pokes it, and puts the kettle on. She thinks for a few moments, pressing her hand to her forehead. She looks questioningly at the fire, and then at the press at back. She goes to the press, opens it, takes out a soiled cloth and spreads it on the table. She then places things for tea on the table.*

NORA   I imagine th' room looks very odd somehow. . . . I was nearly forgetting Jack's tea . . . Ah, I think I'll have everything done before he gets in. . . . (*She lilts gently, as she arranges the table.*)

Th' violets were scenting th' woods, Nora,
   Displaying their charms to th' bee,

3. Fluther is presumably confusing "blighter" with "Blighty" and insisting that he is no Englishman.

When I first said I lov'd only you, Nora,
   An' you said you lov'd only me.

Th' chestnut blooms gleam'd through th' glade, Nora,
   A robin sang loud from a tree,
When I first said I lov'd only you, Nora,
   An' you said you lov'd only me.

*She pauses suddenly, and glances round the room.*

NORA (*doubtfully*) I can't help feelin' this room very strange. . . . What is it? . . . What is it? . . . I must think. . . . I must thry to remember. . . .

VOICES CHANTING IN A DISTANT STREET Ambu . . . lance, Ambu . . . lance! Red Cro . . . ss, Red Cro . . . ss!

NORA (*startled and listening for a moment, then resuming the arrangement of the table*)

Trees, birds, an' bees sang a song, Nora,
   Of happier transports to be,
When I first said I lov'd only you, Nora,
   An' you said you lov'd only me.

*A burst of rifle fire is heard in a street near by, followed by the rapid rok, tok, tok of a machine-gun.*

NORA (*staring in front of her and screaming*) Jack, Jack, Jack! My baby, my baby, my baby!

BESSIE (*waking with a start*) You divil, are you afther gettin' out o' bed again! (*She rises and runs towards Nora, who rushes to the window, which she frantically opens.*)

NORA (*at window, screaming*) Jack, Jack, for God's sake, come to me!

SOLDIERS (*outside, shouting*) Git away, git away from that window, there!

BESSIE (*seizing hold of Nora*) Come away, come away, woman, from that window!

NORA (*struggling with Bessie*) Where is it; where have you hidden it? Oh, Jack, Jack, where are you?

BESSIE (*imploringly*) Mrs. Clitheroe, for God's sake, come away!

NORA (*fiercely*) I won't; he's below. Let . . . me . . . go!

You're thryin' to keep me from me husband. I'll follow him. Jack, Jack, come to your Nora!

BESSIE    Hus-s-sh, Nora, Nora! He'll be here in a minute. I'll bring him to you, if you'll only be quiet—honest to God, I will.

*With a great effort Bessie pushes Nora away from the window, the force used causing her to stagger against it herself. Two rifle shots ring out in quick succession. Bessie jerks her body convulsively; stands stiffly for a moment, a look of agonized astonishment on her face, then she staggers forward, leaning heavily on the table with her hands.*

BESSIE    (*with an arrested scream of fear and pain*)    Merciful God, I'm shot, I'm shot, I'm shot! . . . Th' life's pourin' out o' me! (*To Nora.*) I've got this through . . . through you . . . through you, you bitch, you! . . . O God, have mercy on me! . . . (*To Nora.*) You wouldn't stop quiet, no, you wouldn't, you wouldn't, blast you! Look at what I'm afther gettin', look at what I'm afther gettin' . . . I'm bleedin' to death, an' no one's here to stop th' flowin' blood! (*Calling.*) Mrs. Gogan, Mrs. Gogan! Fluther, Fluther, for God's sake, somebody, a doctor, a doctor!

*She staggers frightened towards the door, to seek for aid, but, weakening half-way across the room, she sinks to her knees, and bending forward, supports herself with her hands resting on the floor. Nora is standing rigidly with her back to the wall opposite, her trembling hands held out a little from the sides of her body, her lips quivering, her breast heaving, staring wildly at the figure of Bessie.*

NORA    (*in a breathless whisper*)    Jack, I'm frightened. . . . I'm frightened, Jack. . . . Oh, Jack, where are you?

BESSIE    (*moaning*)    This is what's afther comin' on me for nursin' you day an' night. . . . I was a fool, a fool, a fool! Get me a dhrink o' wather, you jade, will you? There's a fire burnin' in me blood! (*Pleadingly.*) Nora, Nora, dear, for God's sake, run out an' get Mrs. Gogan, or Fluther, or somebody to bring a doctor, quick, quick, quick! (*As Nora does not stir.*) Blast you, stir yourself, before I'm gone!

NORA    Oh, Jack, Jack, where are you?

BESSIE    (*in a whispered moan*)    Jesus Christ, me sight's goin'! It's all dark, dark! Nora, hold me hand! (*Bessie's body lists over and she sinks into a prostrate position on the floor.*) I'm dyin', I'm dyin' . . . I feel it. . . . Oh God, oh God! (*She feebly sings.*)

I do believe, I will believe
   That Jesus died for me;
That on th' cross He shed His blood,
   From sin to set me free. . . .
I do believe . . . I will believe
   . . . Jesus died . . . me;
. . . th' cross He shed . . . blood,
   From sin . . . free.

*She ceases singing, and lies stretched out, still and very rigid. A pause. Then Mrs. Gogan runs hastily in.*

MRS. GOGAN. (*quivering with fright*) Blessed be God, what's afther happenin'? (*To Nora.*) What's wrong, child, what's wrong? (*She sees Bessie, runs to her and bends over the body.*) Bessie, Bessie! (*She shakes the body.*) Mrs. Burgess, Mrs. Burgess! (*She feels Bessie's forehead.*) My God, she's as cold as death. They're after murdherin' th' poor inoffensive woman!

*Sergeant Tinley and Corporal Stoddart enter agitatedly, their rifles at the ready.*

SERGEANT TINLEY (*excitedly*) This is the 'ouse. That's the window!

NORA (*pressing back against the wall*) Hide it, hide it; cover it up, cover it up!

SERGEANT TINLEY (*going over to the body*) 'Ere, what's this? Who's this? (*Looking at Bessie.*) Oh Gawd, we've plugged one of the women of the 'ouse.

CORPORAL STODDART Whoy the 'ell did she gow to the window? Is she dead?

SERGEANT TINLEY Oh, dead as bedamned. Well, we couldn't afford to toike any chawnces.

NORA (*screaming*) Hide it, hide it; don't let me see it! Take me away, take me away, Mrs. Gogan!

*Mrs. Gogan runs into room, Left, and runs out again with a sheet which she spreads over the body of Bessie.*

MRS. GOGAN (*as she spreads the sheet*)  Oh, God help her, th' poor woman, she's stiffenin' out as hard as she can! Her face has written on it th' shock o' sudden agony, an' her hands is whitenin' into th' smooth shininess of wax.

NORA (*whimperingly*)  Take me away, take me away; don't leave me here to be lookin' an' lookin' at it!

MRS. GOGAN (*going over to Nora and putting her arm around her*)  Come on with me, dear, an' you can doss in poor Mollser's bed, till we gather some neighbours to come an' give th' last friendly touches to Bessie in th' lonely layin' of her out. (*Mrs. Gogan and Nora go slowly out.*)

CORPORAL STODDART (*who has been looking around, to Sergeant Tinley*)  Tea here, Sergeant. Wot abaht a cup of scald?

SERGEANT TINLEY  Pour it aht, Stoddart, pour it aht. I could scoff hanything just now.

*Corporal Stoddart pours out two cups of tea, and the two soldiers begin to drink. In the distance is heard a bitter burst of rifle and machine-gun fire, interspersed with the boom, boom of artillery. The glare in the sky seen through the window flares into a fuller and deeper red.*

SERGEANT TINLEY  There gows the general attack on the Powst Office.

VOICES IN A DISTANT STREET  Ambu . . . lance, Ambu . . . lance! Red Cro . . . ss, Red Cro . . . ss!

*The voices of soldiers at a barricade outside the house are heard singing:*

> They were summoned from the 'illside,
> They were called in from the glen,
> And the country found 'em ready
> At the stirring call for men.
> Let not tears add to their 'ardship,
> As the soldiers pass along,
> And although our 'eart is breaking,
> Make it sing this cheery song.

SERGEANT TINLEY AND CORPORAL STODDART (*joining in the chorus, as they sip the tea*)

Keep the 'owme fires burning,
While your 'earts are yearning;
Though your lads are far away
They dream of 'owme;
There's a silver loining
Through the dark cloud shoining,
Turn the dark cloud inside out,
Till the boys come 'owme!

# Benito Cereno     (1964)*

## *Robert Lowell*   (*b.1917*)

*Benito Cereno* is one of three short plays that make up Robert Lowell's *The Old Glory*, a trilogy that is unified by the themes of violence and revolution in an American setting and—as the title suggests—by the ways in which the playwright uses flags, symbolically and dramatically. The other two plays are *Endecott and the Red Cross* and *My Kinsman, Major Molineux*. The trilogy—then spelled *The Old Gloary*—was first produced in a staged reading at the American Place Theatre, New York, for one performance, March 1, 1964. The three plays have not been performed as a single work since then, a fact that is not surprising because, although together they form an aesthetic whole, each of them can also stand alone. *Benito Cereno*—with *Major Molineux*—reached full production, again at the American Place, on November 1, 1964; the double bill, directed by Jonathan Miller, used the trilogy title. Although the pair of plays were honored together—five Obie (Off-Broadway) awards—it was *Benito Cereno* that received the greatest critical praise, and on January 14, 1965, it opened at the Theatre de Lys for a brief off-Broadway run on its own. It was televised later that year; Columbia issued an original-cast recording (DOS 719).

The play is based on Herman Melville's *Benito Cereno*, one of the stories in *The Piazza Tales* (1856), which the reader may want to consult as much for pleasure as for scholarly comparison. Among the changes that Lowell makes in the Melville original is the date of the action. Melville's 1799

---

becomes Lowell's "About the year 1800," presumably so that the imprecision of the latter may encompass the many events that are mentioned in the play, directly or by implication: the election of Thomas Jefferson (1800); the war against the Barbary pirates of Tripoli (1801–1805); Napoleon's rise to power after the French Revolution (1799, when he became first consul, or 1802, when he became consul for life); Haiti's proclamation of independence (1804).

Anyone interested in the way plays develop may want to consult an earlier version of *Benito Cereno*, published in *Show* (August 1964). For a discussion of the play and of its relation to the trilogy, see Gerald Weales's *The Jumping-Off Place* (1969).

# BENITO CERENO

*Robert Lowell*

## CHARACTERS
*(In order of appearance)*

CAPTAIN AMASA DELANO  FRANCESCO
JOHN PERKINS  AMERICAN SAILORS
DON BENITO CERENO  SPANISH SAILORS
BABU  NEGRO SLAVES
ATUFAL

*About the year 1800, an American sealing vessel, the* President Adams, *at anchor in an island harbor off the coast of Trinidad. The stage is part of the ship's deck. Everything is unnaturally clean, bare and ship-shape. To one side, a polished, coal-black cannon. The American captain, Amasa Delano from Duxbury, Massachusetts, sits in a cane chair. He is a strong, comfortable looking man in his early thirties who wears a spotless blue coat and white trousers. Incongruously, he has on a straw hat and smokes a corncob pipe. Beside him stands John Perkins, his bosun, a very stiff, green young man, a relative of Delano's. Three Sailors, one carrying an American flag, enter. Everyone stands at attention and salutes with machinelike exactitude. Then the Three Sailors march off-stage. Delano and Perkins are alone.*

DELANO  There goes the most beautiful woman in South America.

PERKINS  We never see any women, Sir;
  just this smothering, overcast Equator,
  a seal or two,
  the flat dull sea,
  and a sky like a gray wasp's nest.

DELANO  I wasn't talking about women,
  I was calling your attention to the American flag.

PERKINS  Yes, Sir! I wish we were home in Duxbury.

DELANO    We are home. America is wherever her flag flies.
My own deck is the only place in the world
where I feel at home.

PERKINS    That's too much for me, Captain Delano.
I mean I wish I were at home with my wife;
these world cruises are only for bachelors.

DELANO    Your wife will keep. You should smoke, Perkins.
Smoking turns men into philosophers
and swabs away their worries.
I can see my wife and children or not see them
in each puff of blue smoke.

PERKINS    You are always tempting me, Sir!
I try to keep fit,
I want to return to my wife as fit as I left her.

DELANO    You're much too nervous, Perkins.
Travel will shake you up. You should let
a little foreign dirt rub off on you.
I've taught myself to speak Spanish like a Spaniard.
At each South American port, they mistake me for a
Castilian Don.

PERKINS    Aren't you lowering yourself a little, Captain?
Excuse me, Sir, I have been wanting to ask you a question,
Don't you think our President, Mr. Jefferson, is
    lowering himself
by being so close to the French?
I'd feel a lot safer in this unprotected place
if we'd elected Mr. Adams instead of Mr. Jefferson.

DELANO    The better man ran second!
Come to think of it, he rather let us down
by losing the election just after we had named this ship,
the *President Adams*. Adams is a nervous dry fellow.
When you've travelled as much as I have,
you'll learn that that sort doesn't export, Perkins.
Adams didn't get a vote outside New England!

PERKINS    He carried every New England state;
that was better than winning the election.
I'm afraid I'm a dry fellow, too, Sir.

DELANO    Not when I've educated you!
When I am through with you, Perkins,

you'll be as worldly as the Prince Regent of England,[1]
only you'll be a first class American officer.
I'm all for Jefferson, he has the popular touch.
Of course he's read too many books,
but I've always said an idea or two won't sink
   our Republic.
I'll tell you this, Perkins,
Mr. Jefferson is a gentleman and an American.

PERKINS   They say he has two illegitimate Negro children.

DELANO   The more the better! That's the quickest way
to raise the blacks to our level.
I'm surprised you swallow such Federalist bilge, Perkins!
I told you Mr. Jefferson is a gentleman and an American;
when a man's in office, Sir, we all pull behind him!

PERKINS   Thank God our Revolution ended where the French
   one began.

DELANO   Oh the French! They're like the rest of the Latins,
they're hardly white people,
they start with a paper republic
and end with a toy soldier, like Bonaparte.

PERKINS   Yes, Sir. I see a strange sail making for the harbor.
They don't know how to sail her.

DELANO   Hand me my telescope.

PERKINS   Aye, aye, Sir!

DELANO (*with telescope*)
I see an ocean undulating in long scoops of swells;
it's set like the beheaded French Queen's[2] high wig;
the sleek surface is like waved lead,
cooled and pressed in the smelter's mould.
I see flights of hurried gray fowl,
patches of fluffy fog.
They skim low and fitfully above the decks,
like swallows sabering flies before a storm.
This gray boat foreshadows something wrong.

---

1. This is stretching that inexact 1800 a little more than necessary. The Prince of Wales, later George IV, was Regent only during the last nine years of his father's reign (1811–20). Historical accuracy aside, the Prince's reputation for dissolution and a certain vulgar elegance suit Delano's comparison.
2. Marie Antoinette.

PERKINS   It does, Sir!
   They don't know how to sail her!
DELANO   I see a sulphurous haze above her cabin,
   the new sun hangs like a silver dollar to her stern;
   low creeping clouds blow on from them to us.
PERKINS   What else, Sir?
DELANO   The yards are woolly
   the ship is furred with fog.
   On the cracked and rotten head-boards,
   the tarnished, gilded letters say, the *San Domingo.*[3]
   A rat's-nest messing up the deck,
   black faces in white sheets are fussing with the ropes.
   I think it's a cargo of Dominican monks.
PERKINS   Dominican monks, Sir! God help us,
   I thought they were outlawed in the new world.
DELANO   No, it's nothing. I see they're only slaves.
   The boat's transporting slaves.
PERKINS   Do you believe in slavery, Captain Delano?
DELANO   In a civilized country, Perkins,
   everyone disbelieves in slavery,
   everyone disbelieves in slavery and wants slaves.
   We have the perfect uneasy answer;
   in the North, we don't have them and want them;
   Mr. Jefferson has them and fears them.
PERKINS   Is that how you answer, Sir,
   when a little foreign dirt has rubbed off on you?
DELANO   Don't ask me such intense questions.
   You should take up smoking, Perkins.
   There was a beautiful, dumb English actress—
   I saw her myself once in London.
   They wanted her to look profound,
   so she read Plato and the Bible and Benjamin Franklin,
   and thought about them every minute.
   She still looked like a moron.
   Then they told her to think about nothing.
   She thought about nothing, and looked like Socrates.
   That's smoking, Perkins, you think about nothing and
     look deep.

3. Santo Domingo was another name for Haiti.

PERKINS    I don't believe in slavery, Sir.

DELANO    You don't believe in slavery or Spaniards
or smoking or long cruises or monks or Mr. Jefferson!
You are a Puritan, all faith and fire.

PERKINS    Yes, Sir.

DELANO    God save America from Americans!

*Takes up the telescope.*

I see octagonal network bagging out
from her heavy top like decayed beehives.
The battered forecastle looks like a raped Versailles.
On the stern-piece, I see the fading arms of Spain.
There's a masked satyr, or something
with its foot on a big white goddess.
She has quite a figure.

PERKINS    They oughtn't to be allowed on the ocean!

DELANO    Who oughtn't? Goddesses?

PERKINS    I mean Spaniards, who cannot handle a ship,
and mess up its hull with immoral statues.

DELANO    You're out of step. You're much too dry.
Bring me my three-cornered hat.
Order some men to clear a whaleboat.
I am going to bring water and fresh fish to the
*San Domingo.*
These people have had some misfortune, Perkins!

PERKINS    Aye, aye, Sir.

DELANO    Spaniards? The name gets you down,
you think their sultry faces and language
make them Zulus.
You take the name *Delano—*
I've always thought it had some saving
Italian or Spanish virtue in it.

PERKINS    Yes, Sir.

DELANO    A Spaniard isn't a Negro under the skin,
particularly a Spaniard from Spain—
these South American ones mix too much with the Indians.
Once you get inside a Spaniard,
he talks about as well as your wife in Duxbury.

PERKINS (*shouting*)
A boat for the captain! A whaleboat for Captain Delano!

*A bosun's whistle is heard, the lights dim. When they come up, we are
on the deck of the* San Domingo, *the same set, identical except for
litter and disorder. Three American Sailors climb on board. They are
followed by Perkins and Delano, now wearing a three-cornered hat.
Once on board, the American Sailors salute Delano and stand stiffly at
attention like toys. Negroes from the* San Domingo *drift silently and
furtively forward.*

DELANO    I see a wen of barnacles hanging to the waterline of
  this ship.
It sticks out like the belly of a pregnant woman.
Have a look at our dory Bosun.
PERKINS    Aye, aye, Sir!

*By now, about twenty blacks and two Spanish Sailors have drifted in.
They look like some gaudy, shabby, unnautical charade, and pay no
attention to the Americans, until an unseen figure in the rigging calls
out a single sharp warning in an unknown tongue. Then they all rush
forward, shouting, waving their arms and making inarticulate cries
like birds. Three shrill warnings come from the rigging. Dead silence.
The men from the* San Domingo *press back in a dense semi-circle.
One by one, individuals come forward, make showy bows to Delano,
and speak.*

FIRST NEGRO    Scurvy, Master Yankee!
SECOND NEGRO    Yellow fever, Master Yankee!
THIRD NEGRO    Two men knocked overboard rounding Cape
  Horn,
Master Yankee!
FOURTH NEGRO    Nothing to eat, Master Yankee!
NEGRO WOMAN    Nothing to drink, Master Yankee!
SECOND NEGRO WOMAN    Our mouths are dead wood, Master
  Yankee!
DELANO    You see, Perkins,
these people have had some misfortune.

*General hubbub, muttering, shouts, gestures, ritual and dumbshow of
distress. The rigging, hitherto dark, lightens, as the sun comes out of a
cloud, and shows Three Old Negroes, identical down to their shabby
patches. They perch on cat's-heads; their heads are grizzled like dying
willow tops; each is picking bits of unstranded rope for oakum. It is
they who have been giving the warnings that control the people below.*

*Everyone, Delano along with the rest, looks up. Delano turns aside
and speaks to Perkins.*

It is like a Turkish bazaar.

PERKINS   They are like gypsies showing themselves for money
at a county fair, Sir.

DELANO   This is enchanting after the blank gray roll of the
ocean!

Go tell the Spanish captain I am waiting for him.

*Perkins goes off. Sharp warnings from the Oakum-Pickers. A big
black spread of canvas is pulled creakingly and ceremoniously aside.
Six Figures stand huddled on a platform about four feet from the deck.
They look like weak old invalids in bathrobes and nightcaps until they
strip to the waist and turn out to be huge, shining young Negroes.
Saying nothing, they set to work cleaning piles of rusted hatchets. From
time to time, they turn and clash their hatchets together with a
rhythmic shout. Perkins returns.*

PERKINS   Their captain's name is Don Benito Cereno,
he sends you his compliments, Sir.
He looks more like a Mexican planter than a seaman.
He's put his fortune on his back:
he doesn't look as if he had washed since they left port.

DELANO   Did you tell him I was waiting for him?
A captain should be welcomed by his fellow-captain.
I can't understand this discourtesy.

PERKINS   He's coming, but there's something wrong with him.

*Benito Cereno, led by his Negro servant, Babu, enters. Benito, looking
sick and dazed, is wearing a sombrero and is dressed with a singular
but shabby richness. Head bent to one side, he leans in a stately coma
against the rail, and stares unseeingly at Delano. Babu, all in scarlet,
and small and quick, keeps whispering, pointing and pulling at
Benito's sleeve. Delano walks over to them.*

DELANO   Your hand, Sir. I am Amasa Delano,
captain of the *President Adams,*
a sealing ship from the United States.
This is your lucky day,
the sun is out of hiding for the first time in two weeks,
and here I am aboard your ship

like the Good Samaritan with fresh food and water.
BENITO    The Good Samaritan? Yes, yes,
we mustn't use the Scriptures lightly.
Welcome, Captain. It is the end of the day.
DELANO    The end? It's only morning.
I loaded and lowered a whaleboat
as soon as I saw how awkwardly your ship was making for
    the harbor.
BENITO    Your whaleboat's welcome, Captain.
I am afraid I am still stunned by the storm.
DELANO    Buck up. Each day is a new beginning.
Assign some sailors to help me dole out my provisions.
BENITO    I have no sailors.
BABU (*in a quick sing-song*)
Scurvy, yellow fever,
ten men knocked off on the Horn,
doldrums, nothing to eat, nothing to drink!
By feeding us, you are feeding the King of Spain.
DELANO    Sir, your slave has a pretty way of talking.
What do you need?

*Delano waits for Benito to speak. When nothing more is said, he shifts
awkwardly from foot to foot, then turns to his Sailors.*

Stand to, men!

*The American Sailors, who have been lounging and gaping, stand in a
row, as if a button had been pressed.*

Lay our fish and water by the cabin!

*The Sailors arrange the watercans and baskets of fish by the cabin. A
sharp whistle comes from the Oakum-Pickers. Almost instantly, the
provisions disappear.*

Captain Cereno, you are surely going to taste my water!
BENITO    A captain is a servant, almost a slave, Sir.
DELANO    No, a captain's a captain.
I am sending for more provisions.
Stand to!

*The American Sailors stand to.*

Row back to the ship. When you get there,

take on five hogsheads of fresh water,
and fifty pounds of soft bread.

*First Sailor salutes and goes down the ladder.*

Bring all our remaining pumpkins!

*Second and Third Sailors salute and go down the ladder.*

My bosun and I will stay on board,
until our boat returns.
I imagine you can use us.

BENITO   Are you going to stay here alone?
Won't your ship be lost without you?
Won't you be lost without your ship?

BABU   Listen to Master!
He is the incarnation of courtesy, Yankee Captain.
Your ship doesn't need you as much as we do.

DELANO   Oh, I've trained my crew.
I can sail my ship in my sleep.

*Leaning over the railing and calling.*

Men, bring me a box of lump sugar,
and six bottles of my best cider.

*Turning to Benito.*

Cider isn't my favorite drink, Don Benito,
but it's a New England specialty;
I'm ordering six bottles for your table.

*Babu whispers and gestures to Don Benito, who is exhausted and silent.*

BABU   *Une bouteille du vin (To Negroes.)*
My master wishes to give you a bottle
of the oldest wine in Seville.

*He whistles. A Negro woman rushes into the cabin and returns with a dusty beribboned bottle, which she holds like a baby. Babu ties a rope around the bottle.*

I am sending this bottle of wine to your cabin.
When you drink it, you will remember us.

Do you see these ribbons? The crown of Spain is tied
    to one.
Forgive me for tying a rope around the King of
    Spain's neck.

*Lowers the wine on the rope to the whaleboat.*

DELANO (*shouting to his Sailors*)
    Pick up your oars!
SAILORS  Aye, aye, Sir!
DELANO  We're New England Federalists;
    we can drink the King of Spain's health.

*Benito stumbles offstage on Babu's arm.*

PERKINS  Captain Cereno hasn't travelled as much as you
    have;
    I don't think he knew what you meant by the New England
    Federalists.
DELANO (*leaning comfortably on the rail; half to himself and half to
    Perkins*)
    The wind is dead. We drift away.
    We will be left alone all day,
    here in this absentee empire.
    Thank God, I know my Spanish!
PERKINS  You'll have to watch them, Sir.
    Brown men in charge of black men—
    it doesn't add up to much!
    This Babu, I don't trust him!
    Why doesn't he talk with a Southern accent,
    Like Mr. Jefferson? They're out of hand, Sir!
DELANO  Nothing relaxes order more than misery.
    They need severe superior officers.
    They haven't one.
    Now, if this Benito were a man of energy . . .
    a Yankee . . .
PERKINS  How can a Spaniard sail?
DELANO  Some can. There was Vasco da Gama and Colum-
    bus . . .
    No, I guess they were Italians. Some can,
    but this captain is tubercular.
PERKINS  Spaniards and Negroes have no business on a ship.

DELANO   Why is this captain so indifferent to me?
  If only I could stomach his foreign reserve!
  This absolute dictator of his ship
  only gives orders through his slaves!
  He is like some Jesuit-haunted Hapsburg king
  about to leave the world and hope the world will end.
PERKINS   He said he was lost in the storm.
DELANO   Perhaps it's only policy,
  a captain's icy dignity
  obliterating all democracy—
PERKINS   He's like someone walking in his sleep.
DELANO   Ah, slumbering dominion!
  He is so self-conscious in his imbecility . . .
  No, he's sick. He sees his men no more than me.
  This ship is like a crowded immigration boat;
  it needs severe superior officers,
  the friendly arm of a strong mate.
  Perhaps, I ought to take it over by force.
  No, they're sick, they've been through the plague.
  I'll go and speak and comfort my fellow captain.
  I think you can help me, Captain. I'm feeling useless.
  My own thoughts oppress me, there's so much to do.
  I wonder if you would tell me the whole sad story of
    your voyage.
  Talk to me as captain to captain.
  We have sailed the same waters.
  Please tell me your story.
BENITO[4]   A story? A story! That's out of place.
  When I was a child, I used to beg for stories back in Lima.
  Now my tongue's tied and my heart is bleeding.

*Stops talking, as if his breath were gone. He stares for a few moments, then looks up at the rigging, as if he were counting the ropes one by one. Delano turns abruptly to Perkins.*

DELANO   Go through the ship, Perkins,
  and see if you can find me a Spaniard who can talk.
BENITO   You must be patient, Captain Delano;
  if we only see with our eyes,

---

4. Lowell forgets that he sent Benito offstage (p. 100) and has not provided for his return.

sometimes we cannot see at all.

DELANO    I stand corrected, Captain;
   tell me about your voyage.

BENITO    It's now a hundred and ninety days . . .
   This ship, well manned, well officered, with several
      cabin passengers,
   carrying a cargo of Paraguay tea and Spanish cutlery.
   That parcel of Negro slaves, less than four score now,
   was once three hundred souls.
   Ten sailors and three officers fell from the mainyard off
      the Horn;
   part of our rigging fell overboard with them,
   as they were beating down the icy sail.
   We threw away all our cargo,
   Broke our waterpipes,
   Lashed them on deck
   this was the chief cause of our suffering.

DELANO    I must interrupt you, Captain.
   How did you happen to have three officers on
      the mainyard?
   I never heard of such a disposal,
   it goes against all seamanship.

BABU    Our officers never spared themselves;
   if there was any danger, they rushed in
   to save us without thinking.

DELANO    I can't understand such an oversight.

BABU    There was no oversight. My master had a hundred
      eyes.
   He had an eye for everything.
   Sometimes the world falls on a man.
   The sea wouldn't let Master act like a master,
   yet he saved himself and many lives.
   He is still a rich man, and he saved the ship.

BENITO    Oh my God, I wish the world had fallen on me,
   and the terrible cold sea had drowned me;
   that would have been better than living through what I've
   lived through!

BABU    He is a good man, but his mind is off;
   he's thinking about the fever when the wind stopped—
   poor, poor Master!

Be patient, Yankee Captain, these fits are short,
Master will be the master once again.

BENITO   The scurvy was raging through us.
We were on the Pacific. We were invalids
and couldn't man our mangled spars.
A hurricane blew us northeast through the fog.
Then the wind died.
We lay in irons fourteen days in unknown waters,
our black tongues stuck through our mouths,
but we couldn't mend our broken waterpipes.

BABU   Always those waterpipes,
he dreams about them like a pile of snakes!

BENITO   Yellow fever followed the scurvy,
the long heat thickened in the calm,
my Spaniards turned black and died like slaves,
The blacks died too. I am my only officer left.

BABU   Poor, poor Master! He had a hundred eyes,
he lived our lives for us.
He is still a rich man.

BENITO   In the smart winds beating us northward,
our torn sails dropped like sinkers in the sea;
each day we dropped more bodies.
Almost without a crew, canvas, water, or a wind,
we were bounced about by the opposing waves
through cross-currents and the weedy calms,
and dropped our dead.
Often we doubled and redoubled on our track
like children lost in jungle. The thick fog
hid the Continent and our only port from us.

BABU   We were poor kidnapped jungle creatures.
We only lived on what he could give us.
He had a hundred eyes, he was the master.

BENITO   These Negroes saved me, Captain.
Through the long calamity,
they were as gentle as their owner, Don Aranda, promised.
Don Aranda took away their chains before he died.

BABU   Don Aranda saved our lives, but we couldn't save his.
Even in Africa I was a slave.
He took away my chains.

BENITO   I gave them the freedom of my ship.

I did not think they were crates or cargo or cannibals.
But it was Babu—under God, I swear I owe my life
   to Babu!
He calmed his ignorant, wild brothers,
never left me, saved the *San Domingo.*
BABU   Poor, poor Master. He is still a rich man.
Don't speak of Babu. Babu is the dirt under your feet.
He did his best.
DELANO   You are a good fellow, Babu.
You are the salt of the earth. I envy you, Don Benito;
he is no slave, Sir, but your friend.
BENITO   Yes, he is salt in my wounds.
I can never repay him, I mean.
Excuse me, Captain, my strength is gone.
I have done too much talking. I want to rest.

*Babu leads Benito to a shabby straw chair at the side. Benito sits.*
*Babu fans him with his sombrero.*

PERKINS   He's a fine gentleman, but no seaman.
A cabin boy would have known better
than to send his three officers on the mainyard.
DELANO *(paying no attention)*
A terrible story. I would have been unhinged myself.

*Looking over toward Babu and Benito.*

There's a true servant. They do things better
in the South and in South America—
trust in return for trust!
The beauty of that relationship is unknown
in New England. We're too much alone
in Massachusetts, Perkins.
How do our captains and our merchants live,
each a republic to himself.
Even Sam Adams had no friends and only loved the mob.
PERKINS   Sir, you are forgetting that
New England seamanship brought them their slaves.
DELANO   Oh, just our Southern slaves;
we had nothing to do with these fellows.
PERKINS   The ocean would be a different place
if every Spaniard served an apprenticeship on an

American ship
before he got his captain's papers.
DELANO   This captain's a gentleman, not a sailor.
His little yellow hands
got their command before they held a rope—
in by the cabin-window, not the hawse-hole!
Do you want to know why
they drifted hog-tied in those easy calms—
inexperience, sickness, impotence and aristocracy!
PERKINS   Here comes Robinson Crusoe and his good man
Friday.
DELANO   We don't beat a man when he's down.

*Benito advances uncertainly on Babu's arm.*

I am glad to see you on your feet again,
That's the only place for a Captain, sir!
I have the cure for you, I have decided
to bring you medicine and a sufficient supply of water.
A first class deck officer, a man from Salem,
shall be stationed on your quarter deck,
a temporary present from my owners.
We shall refit your ship and clear this mess.
BENITO   You will have to clear away the dead.
BABU   This excitement is bad for him, Yankee Master.
He's lived with death. He lives on death still;
this sudden joy will kill him. You've heard
how thirsty men die from overdrinking!
His heart is with his friend, our owner, Don Aranda.
BENITO   I am the only owner. (*He looks confused and shaken.*)

*Babu scurries off and brings up the straw chair. Benito sits.*

DELANO   Your friend is dead? He died of fever?
BENITO   He died very slowly and in torture.
He was the finest man in Lima.
We were brought up together,
I am lost here.
DELANO   Pardon me, Sir. You are young at sea.
My experience tells me what your trouble is:
this is the first body you have buried in the ocean.
I had a friend like yours, a warm honest fellow,

who would look you in the eye—
we had to throw him to the sharks.
Since then I've brought embalming gear on board.
Each man of mine shall have a Christian grave on land.
You wouldn't shake so, if Don Aranda were on board,
I mean, if you'd preserved the body.

BENITO   If he were on board this ship?
If I had preserved his body?

BABU   Be patient, Master!
We still have the figurehead.

DELANO   You have the figurehead?

BABU   You see that thing wrapped up in black cloth?
It's a figurehead Don Aranda bought us in Spain.
It was hurt in the storm. It's very precious.
Master takes comfort in it,
he is going to give it to Don Aranda's widow.
It's time for the pardon ceremony, Master.

*Sound of clashing hatchets.*

DELANO   I am all for these hatchet-cleaners.
They are saving cargo. They make
an awful lot of pomp and racket though
about a few old, rusty knives.

BENITO   They think steel is worth its weight in gold.

*A slow solemn march is sounded on the gongs and other instruments. A
gigantic coal-black Negro comes up the steps. He wears a spiked iron
collar to which a chain is attached that goes twice around his arms and
ends padlocked to a broad band of iron. The Negro comes clanking
forward and stands dumbly and like a dignitary in front of Benito.
Two small black boys bring Benito a frail rattan cane and a silver
ball, which they support on a velvet cushion. Benito springs up, holds
the ball, and raises the cane rigidly above the head of the Negro in
chains. For a moment, he shows no trace of sickness. The assembled
blacks sing, "Evviva, Benito!" three times.*

BABU (*at one side with the Americans, but keeping an eye on Benito*)
You are watching the humiliation of King Atufal,
once a ruler in Africa. He ruled as much land there
   as your President.
Poor Babu was a slave even in Africa,

a black man's slave, and now a white man's.

BENITO (*in a loud, firm voice*)
Former King Atufal, I call on you to kneel!
Say, "My sins are black as night,
I ask the King of Spain's pardon
through his servant, Don Benito."

*Pause. Atufal doesn't move.*

NEGROES   Your sins are black as night, King Atufal!
Your sins are black as night, King Atufal!
DELANO   What has King Atufal done?
BABU   I will tell you later, Yankee Captain.
BENITO   Ask pardon, King Atufal.
If you will kneel,
I will strike away your chains.

*Atufal slowly raises his chained arms and lets them drop.*

Ask pardon!
WOMAN SLAVE   Ask pardon, King Atufal.
BENITO   Go!

*Sound of instruments. The Black Boys take Benito's ball and cane.
The straw chair is brought up. Benito sits. Francesco then leads him
offstage.*

BABU   Francesco!
I will be with you in a moment, Master.
You mustn't be afraid,
Francesco will serve you like a second Babu.
BENITO   Everyone serves me alike here,
but no one can serve me as you have.
BABU   I will be with you in a moment.
The Yankee master is at sea on our ship.
He wants me to explain our customs.

*Benito is carried offstage.*

You would think Master's afraid of dying,
if Babu leaves him!
DELANO   I can imagine your tenderness during his sickness.
You were part of him,
you were almost a wife.

BABU    You say such beautiful things,
 the United States must be a paradise for people like Babu.
DELANO    I don't know.
 We have our faults. We have many states,
 some of them could stand improvement.
BABU    The United States must be heaven.
DELANO    I suppose we have fewer faults than other countries.
 What did King Atufal do?
BABU    He used the Spanish flag for toilet paper.
DELANO    That's treason.
 Did Atufal know what he was doing?
 Perhaps the flag was left somewhere it shouldn't have been.
 Things aren't very strict here.
BABU    I never thought of that.
 I will go and tell Master.
DELANO    Oh, no, you mustn't do that!
 I never interfere with another man's ship.
 Don Benito is your lord and dictator.
 How long has this business with King Atufal been
  going on?
BABU    Ever since the yellow fever,
 and twice a day.
DELANO    He did a terrible thing, but he looks like a royal
  fellow.
 You shouldn't call him a king, though,
 it puts ideas into his head.
BABU    Atufal had gold wedges in his ears in Africa;
 now he wears a padlock and Master bears the key.
DELANO    I see you have a feeling for symbols of power.
 You had better be going now,
 Don Benito will be nervous about you.

*Babu goes off.*

 That was a terrible thing to do with a flag;
 everything is untidy and unravelled here—
 this sort of thing would never happen on the
  *President Adams.*
PERKINS    Your ship is as shipshape as our country, Sir.
DELANO    I wish people wouldn't take me as representative of
  our country:

America's one thing, I am another;
we shouldn't have to bear one another's burdens.
PERKINS    You are a true American for all your talk, Sir;
I can't believe you were mistaken for a Castilian Don.
DELANO    No one would take me for Don Benito.
PERKINS    I wonder if he isn't an impostor, some travelling
actor from a circus?
DELANO    No, Cereno is a great name in Peru, like Winthrop
or Adams with us.
I recognize the family features in our captain.

*An Old Spanish Sailor, grizzled and dirty, is seen crawling on all
fours with an armful of knots toward the Americans. He points to
where Benito and Babu have disappeared and whistles. He holds up
the knots as though he were in chains, then throws them out loosely on
the deck in front of him. A Group of Negroes forms a circle around
him, holding hands and singing childishly. Then, laughing, they carry
the Spaniard offstage on their shoulders.*

These blacks are too familiar!
We are never alone!

*Sound of gongs. Full minute's pause, as if time were passing. Delano
leans on the railing. The sun grows brighter.*

This ship is strange.
These people are too spontaneous—all noise and show,
no character!
Real life is a simple monotonous thing.
I wonder about that story about the calms;
it doesn't stick.
Don Benito hesitated himself in telling it.
No one could run a ship so stupidly,
and place three officers on one yard.

*Benito and Babu return.*

A captain has unpleasant duties;
I am sorry for you, Don Benito.
BENITO    You find my ship unenviable, Sir?
DELANO    I was talking about punishing Atufal;
he acted like an animal!
BENITO    Oh, yes, I was forgetting . . .

He was a King,
How long have you lain in at this island, Sir?
DELANO  Oh, a week today.
BENITO  What was your last port, Sir?
DELANO  Canton.
BENITO  You traded seal-skins and American muskets
for Chinese tea and silks, perhaps?
DELANO  We took in some silks.
BENITO  A little gold and silver too?
DELANO  Just a little silver. We are only merchants.
We take in a dollar here and there. We have no Peru,
or a Pizarro who can sweat gold out of the natives.
BENITO  You'll find things have changed
a little in Peru since Pizarro, Captain.

*Starts to move away. Babu whispers to him, and he comes back
abruptly, as if he had forgotten something important.*

How many men have you on board, Sir?
DELANO  Some twenty-five, Sir. Each man is at his post.
BENITO  They're all on board, Sir, now?
DELANO  They're all on board. Each man is working.
BENITO  They'll be on board tonight, Sir?
DELANO  Tonight? Why do you ask, Don Benito?
BENITO  Will they all be on board tonight, Captain?
DELANO  They'll be on board for all I know.

*Perkins makes a sign to Delano.*

Well, no, to tell the truth, today's our Independence Day.
A gang is going ashore to see the village.
A little diversion improves their efficiency,
a little regulated corruption.
BENITO  You North Americans take no chances. Generally,
I suppose,
even your merchant ships go more or less armed?
DELANO  A rack of muskets, sealing spears and cutlasses.
Oh, and a six-pounder or two; we are a sealing ship,
but with us each merchant is a privateer—
only in case of oppression, of course.
You've heard about how we shoot pirates.
BABU  Boom, boom, come Master.

*Benito walks away on Babu's arm and sits down, almost offstage in his straw chair. They whisper. Meanwhile, a Spanish sailor climbs the rigging furtively, spread-eagles his arms and shows a lace shirt under his shabby jacket. He points to Benito and Babu and winks. At a cry from One of the Oakum-Pickers, Three Negroes help the Spaniard down with servile, ceremonious attentions.*

PERKINS   Did you see that sailor's lace shirt, Sir?
He must have robbed one of the cabin passengers.
I hear that people strip the dead
in these religious countries.

DELANO   No, you don't understand the Spaniards.
In these old Latin countries,
each man's a beggar or a noble, often both;
they have no middle class. With them it's customary
to sew a mess of gold and pearls on rags—
that's how an aristocracy that's going to the dogs
keeps up its nerve.
It's odd though,
that Spanish sailor seemed to want to tell me something.
He ought to dress himself properly and speak his mind.
That's what we do. That's why we're strong:
everybody trusts us. Nothing gets done
when every man's a noble. I wonder why
the captain asked me all those questions?

PERKINS   He was passing the time of day, Sir;
It's a Latin idleness.

DELANO   It's strange. Did you notice how Benito stopped
rambling?
He was conventional . . . consecutive for the first time
since we met him.
Something's wrong. Perhaps, they've men below the decks,
a sleeping volcano of Spanish infantry. The Malays do it,
play sick and cut your throat.
A drifting boat, a dozen doped beggars on deck,
two hundred sweating murderers packed below
like sardines—
that's rot! Anyone can see these people are really sick,
sicker than usual. Our countries are at peace.
I wonder why he asked me all those questions?

PERKINS  Just idle curiosity. I hear
the gentlemen of Lima sit at coffee-tables from sun to sun
and gossip. They don't even have women to look at;
they're all locked up with their aunts.

DELANO  Their sun is going down. These old empires go.
They are much too familiar with their blacks.
I envy them though, they have no character,
they feel no need to stand alone.
We stand alone too much,
that's why no one can touch us for sailing a ship;
When a country loses heart, it's easier to live.
Ah, Babu! I suppose Don Benito's indisposed again!
Tell him I want to talk to his people;
there's nothing like a well man to help the sick.

BABU  Master is taking his siesta, Yankee Master.
His siesta is sacred, I am afraid to disturb it.
Instead, let me show you our little entertainment.

DELANO  Let's have your entertainment;
if you know a man's pleasure
you know his measure.

BABU  We are a childish people. Our pleasures are childish.
No one helped us, we know nothing
about your important amusements,
such as killing seals and pirates.

DELANO  I'm game. Let's have your entertainment.

*Babu signals. The gong sounds ten times and the canvas is pulled from the circular structure. Enclosed in a triangular compartment, an Old Spanish Sailor is dipping naked white dolls in a tar-pot.*

BABU  This little amusement keeps him alive, Yankee Master.
He is especially fond of cleaning the dolls
after he has dirtied them.

*The Old Spanish Sailor laughs hysterically, and then smears his whole face with tar.*

OLD SPANISH SAILOR  My soul is white!

BABU  The yellow fever destroyed his mind.

DELANO  Let's move on. This man's brain,
as well as his face, is defiled with pitch!

BABU  He says his soul is white.

*The structure is pushed around and another triangular compartment appears. A Negro Boy is playing chess against a splendid Spanish doll with a crown on its head. He stops and holds two empty wine bottles to his ears.*

This boy is deaf.
The yellow fever destroyed his mind.
DELANO   Why is he holding those bottles to his ears?
BABU   He is trying to be a rabbit,
or listening to the ocean, his mother—
who knows?
DELANO   If he's deaf, how can he hear the ocean?
Anyway, he can't hear me.
I pass, let's move on.

*The structure is pushed around to a third compartment. A Spanish Sailor is holding a big armful of rope.*

What are you knotting there, my man?
SPANISH SAILOR   The knot.
DELANO   So I see, but what's it for?
SPANISH SAILOR   For someone to untie. Catch!

*Throws the knot to Delano.*

BABU (*snatching the knot from Delano*)
It's dirty, it will dirty your uniform.
DELANO   Let's move on. Your entertainment
is rather lacking in invention, Babu.
BABU   We have to do what we can
We are just beginners at acting.
This next one will be better.

*The structure is pushed around and shows a beautiful Negro Woman. She is dressed and posed as the Virgin Mary. A Christmas crèche is arranged around her. A Very White Spaniard dressed as Saint Joseph stands behind her. She holds a Christ-child, the same crowned doll, only black, the Negro Boy was playing chess against.*

She is the Virgin Mary. That man is not the father.
DELANO   I see. I suppose her son is the King of Spain.
BABU   The Spaniards taught us everything,
there's nothing we can learn from you, Yankee Master.

When they took away our country, they gave us a
    better world.
Things do not happen in that world as they do here.
DELANO    That's a very beautiful,
    though unusual Virgin Mary.
BABU    Yes, the Bible says, "I am black not white."
When Don Aranda was dying,
    we wanted to give him the Queen of Heaven
    because he took away our chains.
PERKINS    The Spaniards must have taught them everything;
    they're all mixed up, they don't even know their religion.
DELANO    No, no! The Catholic Church doesn't just teach,
    it knows how to take from its converts.
BABU    Do you want to shake hands with the Queen of Heaven,
    Yankee Master?
DELANO    No, I'm not used to royalty.
Tell her I believe in freedom of religion,
    if people don't take liberties.
Let's move on.
BABU (*kneeling to the Virgin Mary*)
I present something Your Majesty has never seen,
a white man who doesn't believe in taking liberties,
Your Majesty.

*The structure is pushed around and shows Atufal in chains but with a
crown on his head.*

BABU    This is the life we believe in.
THE NEGROES ALL TOGETHER    Ask pardon, King Atufal!
Kiss the Spanish flag!
DELANO    Please don't ask me to shake hands with King
    Atufal!

*The canvas is put back on the structure.*

BABU    You look tired and serious, Yankee Master.
We have to have what fun we can.
We never would have lived through the deadly calms
without a little amusement. (*Bows and goes off.*)

*The Negroes gradually drift away. Delano sighs with relief.*

DELANO    Well, that wasn't much!

I suppose Shakespeare started that way.

PERKINS   Who cares?
I see a speck on the blue sea, Sir,
our whaleboat is coming.

DELANO   A speck? My eyes are speckled.
I seem to have been dreaming. What's solid?

*Touches the ornate railing; a piece falls onto the deck.*

This ship is nothing, Perkins!
I dreamed someone was trying to kill me!
How could he? Jack-of-the-beach,
they used to call me on the Duxbury shore.
Carrying a duck-satchel in my hand, I used to paddle
along the waterfront from a hulk to school.
I didn't learn much there. I was always shooting duck
or gathering huckleberries along the marsh with
     Cousin Nat!
I like nothing better than breaking myself on the surf.
I used to track the seagulls down the five-mile stretch
     of beach for eggs.
How can I be killed now at the ends of the earth
by this insane Spaniard?
Who could want to murder Amasa Delano?
My conscience is clean. God is good.
What am I doing on board this nigger-pirate ship?

PERKINS   You're not talking like a skipper, Sir.
Our boat's a larger spot now.

DELANO   I am childish.
I am doddering and drooling into my second childhood.
God help me, nothing's solid!

PERKINS   Don Benito, Sir. Touch him,
he's as solid as his ship.

DELANO   Don Benito? He's a walking ghost!

*Benito comes up to Delano. Babu is a few steps behind him.*

BENITO   I am the ghost of myself, Captain.
Excuse me, I heard you talking about dreams
     and childhood.
I was a child, too, once, I have dreams about it.

DELANO (*starting*)

I'm sorry.

This jumping's just a nervous habit.

I thought you were part of my dreams.

BENITO    I was taking my siesta,

I dreamed I was a boy back in Lima.

I was with my brothers and sisters,

and we were dressed for the festival of Corpus Christi

like people at our Bourbon court.

We were simple children, but something went wrong;

little black men came on us with beetle backs.

They had caterpillar heads and munched away on our

fine clothes.

They made us lick their horned and varnished insect legs.

Our faces turned brown from their spit,

we looked like bugs, but nothing could save our lives!

DELANO    Ha, ha, Captain. We are like two dreams meeting

head-on.

My whaleboat's coming,

we'll both feel better over a bottle of cider.

*Babu blows a bosun's whistle. The gongs are sounded with descending
notes. The Negroes assemble in ranks.*

BABU    It's twelve noon, Master Yankee.

Master wants his midday shave.

ALL THE NEGROES    Master wants his shave! Master wants his

shave!

BENITO    Ah, yes, the razor! I have been talking too much.

You can see how badly I need a razor.

I must leave you, Captain.

BABU    No, Don Amasa wants to talk.

Come to the cabin, Don Amasa.

Don Amasa will talk, Master will listen.

Babu will lather and strop.

DELANO    I want to talk to you about navigation.

I am new to these waters.

BENITO    Doubtless, doubtless, Captain Delano.

PERKINS    I think I'll take my siesta, Sir. (*He walks off.*)

*Benito, Babu, and Delano walk toward the back of the stage. A scrim
curtain lifts, showing a light deck cabin that forms a sort of attic. The*

*floor is matted, partitions that still leave splintered traces have been knocked out. To one side, a small table screwed to the floor; on it, a dirty missal; above it, a small crucifix, rusty crossed muskets on one side, rusty crossed cutlasses on the other. Benito sits down in a broken thronelike and gilded chair. Babu begins to lather. A magnificent array of razors, bottles and other shaving equipment lies on a table beside him. Behind him: a hammock with a pole in it and a dirty pillow.*

DELANO   So this is where you took your siesta.

BENITO   Yes, Captain, I rest here when my fate will let me.

DELANO   This seems like a sort of dormitory, sitting-room, sail-loft, chapel, armory, and private bedroom all together.

BENITO   Yes, Captain: events have not been favorable
to much order in my personal arrangements.

*Babu moves back and opens a locker. A lot of flags, torn shirts and socks tumble out. He takes one of the flags, shakes it with a flourish, and ties it around Benito's neck.*

BABU   Master needs more protection.
I do everything I can to save his clothes.

DELANO   The Castle and the Lion of Spain.
Why, Don Benito, this is the flag of Spain you're using!
It's well it's only I and not the King of Spain who sees this!
All's one, though, I guess, in this carnival world.
I see you like gay colors as much as Babu.

BABU *(giggling)*
The bright colors draw the yellow fever
from Master's mind. *(Raises the razor.)*

*Benito begins to shake.*

Now, Master, now, Master!

BENITO   You are talking while you hold the razor.

BABU   You mustn't shake so, Master.
Look, Don Amasa, Master always shakes when I shave him,
though he is braver than a lion and stronger than a castle.
Master knows Babu has never yet drawn blood.
I may, though, sometime, if he shakes so much.
Now, Master!
Come, Don Amasa, talk to Master about the gales
and calms,

he'll answer and forget to shake.

DELANO    Those calms, the more I think of them the more I
wonder.

You say you were two months sailing here;
I made that stretch in less than a week.
We never met with any calms.
If I'd not heard your story from your lips,
and seen your ruined ship,
I would have said something was missing,
I would have said this was a mystery ship.

BENITO    For some men the whole world is a mystery;
they cannot believe their senses.

*Benito shakes, the razor gets out of hand and cuts his cheek.*

Santa Maria!

BABU    Poor, poor Master, see, you shook so;
this is Babu's first blood.
Please answer Don Amasa, while I wipe
this ugly blood from the razor and strop it again.

BENITO    The sea was like the final calm of the world
On, on it went. It sat on us and drank our strength,
cross-currents eased us out to sea,
the yellow fever changed our blood to poison.

BABU    You stood by us. Some of us stood by you!

BENITO    Yes, my Spanish crew was weak and surly, but
the blacks,
the blacks were angels. Babu has kept me in this world.
I wonder what he is keeping me for?
You belong to me. I belong to you forever.

BABU    Ah, Master, spare yourself.
Forever is a very long time;
nothing's forever.

*With great expertness, delicacy and gentleness, Babu massages
Benito's cheeks, shakes out the flag, pours lotion from five bottles on
Benito's hair, cleans the shaving materials, and stands off admiring
his work.*

Master looks just like a statue.
He's like a figurehead, Don Amasa!

*Delano looks, then starts to walk out leaving Benito and Babu. The curtain drops upon them. Delano rejoins Perkins, lounging at the rail.*

PERKINS   Our boat is coming.

DELANO (*gaily*)
I know!
I don't know how I'll explain this pomp
and squalor to my own comfortable family of a crew.
Even shaving here is like a High Mass.
There's something in a Negro, something
that makes him fit to have around your person.
His comb and brush are castanets.
What tact Babu had!
What noiseless, gliding briskness!

PERKINS   Our boat's about along side, Sir.

DELANO   What's more, the Negro has a sense of humor.
I don't mean their boorish giggling and teeth-showing,
I mean his easy cheerfulness in every glance and gesture.
You should have seen Babu toss that Spanish flag like
      a juggler,
and change it to a shaving napkin!

PERKINS   The boat's here, Sir.

DELANO   We need inferiors, Perkins,
more manners, more docility, no one has an inferior mind
      in America.

PERKINS   Here is your crew, Sir.

*Babu runs out from the cabin. His cheek is bleeding.*

DELANO   Why, Babu, what has happened?

BABU   Master will never get better from his sickness.
His bad nerves and evil fever made him use me so.
I gave him one small scratch by accident,
the only time I've nicked him, Don Amasa.
He cut me with his razor. Do you think I will die?
I'd rather die than bleed to death!

DELANO   It's just a pinprick, Babu. You'll live.

BABU   I must attend my master. (*Runs back into cabin.*)

DELANO   Just a pinprick, but I wouldn't have thought
Don Benito had the stuff to swing a razor.
Up north we use our fists instead of knives.

I hope Benito's not dodging around some old grindstone
in the hold, and sharpening a knife for me.
Here, Perkins, help our men up the ladder.

*Two immaculate American Sailors appear carrying great casks of
water. Two more follow carrying net baskets of wilted pumpkins. The
Negroes begin to crowd forward, shouting, "We want Yankee food, we
want Yankee drink!" Delano grandiosely holds up a pumpkin; an Old
Negro rushes forward, snatches at the pumpkin, and knocks Delano
off-balance into Perkins's arms. Delano gets up and knocks the Negro
down with his fist. All is tense and quiet. The Six Hatchet-Cleaners
lift their hatchets above their heads.*

DELANO (*furious*)
Americans, stand by me! Stand by your captain!

*Like lightning, the Americans unsling their muskets, fix bayonets, and
kneel with their guns pointing at the Negroes.*

Don Benito, Sir, call your men to order!
BABU    We're starving, Yankee Master. We mean no harm;
we've never been so scared.
DELANO    You try my patience, Babu.
I am talking to Captain Cereno;
call your men to order, Sir.
BENITO    Make them laugh, Babu. The Americans aren't
going to shoot.

*Babu airily waves a hand. The Negroes smile. Delano turns to Benito.*

You mustn't blame them too much; they're sick
and hungry.
We have kept them cooped up for ages.
DELANO (*as the Negroes relax*)
Form them in lines, Perkins!
Each man shall have his share.
That's how we run things in the States—
to each man equally, no matter what his claims.
NEGROES (*standing back, bleating like sheep*)
Feed me, Master Yankee! Feed me, Master Yankee!
DELANO    You are much too close.
Here, Perkins, take the provisions aft.
You'll save lives by giving each as little as you can,

Be sure to keep a tally.

*Francesco, a majestic, yellow-colored mulatto, comes up to Delano.*

FRANCESCO  My master requests your presence at dinner, Don
  Amasa.
DELANO   Tell him I have indigestion.
  Tell him to keep better order on his ship.
  It's always the man of good will that gets hurt;
  my fist still aches from hitting that old darky.
FRANCESCO  My master has his own methods of discipline
  that are suitable for our unfortunate circumstances.
  Will you come to dinner, Don Amasa?
DELANO   I'll come. When in Rome, do as the Romans.
  Excuse my quick temper, Sir.
  It's better to blow up than to smoulder.

*The scrim curtain is raised. In the cabin, a long table loaded with
silver has been laid out. The locker has been closed and the Spanish
flag hangs on the wall. Don Benito is seated, Babu stands behind him.
As soon as Delano sits down, Francesco begins serving with great
dignity and agility.*

FRANCESCO  A finger bowl, Don Amasa.

*After each statement, he moves about the table.*

A napkin, Don Amasa.
A glass of American water, Don Amasa.
A slice of American pumpkin, Don Amasa.
A goblet of American cider, Don Amasa.

*Delano drinks a great deal of cider, Benito hardly touches his.*

DELANO   This is very courtly for a sick ship, Don Benito.
  The Spanish Empire will never go down, if she keeps her
    chin up.
BENITO   I'm afraid I shan't live long enough to enjoy your
  prophecy.
DELANO   I propose a toast to the Spanish Empire
  on which the sun never sets;
  may you find her still standing, when you land, Sir!
BENITO   Our Empire has lasted three hundred years,
  I suppose she will last another month.

I wish I could say the same for myself. My sun is setting,
I hear the voices of the dead in this calm.

DELANO    You hear the wind lifting;
it's bringing our two vessels together.
We are going to take you into port, Don Benito.

BENITO    You are either too late or too early with your good
works.
Our yellow fever may break out again.
You aren't going to put your men in danger, Don Amasa?

DELANO    My boys are all healthy, Sir.

BENITO    Health isn't God, I wouldn't trust it.

FRANCESCO    May I fill your glass, Don Amasa?

BABU    New wine in new bottles,
that's the American spirit, Yankee Master.
They say all men are created equal in North America.

DELANO    We prefer merit to birth, boy.

*Babu motions imperiously for Francesco to leave. As he goes, bowing to
the Captains, Four Negroes play the* "Marseillaise."

Why are they playing the *"Marseillaise"*?

BABU    His uncle is supposed to have been in the French
Convention,[5]
and voted for the death of the French King.

DELANO    This polite and royal fellow is no anarchist!

BABU    Francesco is very *ancien régime,*
he is even frightened of the Americans.
He doesn't like the way you treated King George.
Babu is more liberal.

DELANO    A royal fellow,
this usher of yours, Don Benito!
He is as yellow as a goldenrod.
He is a king, a king of kind hearts.
What a pleasant voice he has!

BENITO (*glumly*)
Francesco is a good man.

DELANO    As long as you've known him,
he's been a worthy fellow, hasn't he?
Tell me, I am particularly curious to know.

5. The governing body, created by the National Assembly in 1792, which abolished
the monarchy and set up the First Republic.

BENITO    Francesco is a good man.

DELANO    I'm glad to hear it, I am glad to hear it!
You refute the saying of a planter friend of mine.
He said, "When a mulatto has a regular European face,
look out for him, he is a devil."

BENITO    I've heard your planter's remark applied
to intermixtures of Spaniards and Indians;
I know nothing about mulattoes.

DELANO    No, no, my friend's refuted;
if we're so proud of our white blood,
surely a little added to the blacks improves their breed.
I congratulate you on your servants, Sir.

BABU    We've heard that Jefferson, the King of your Republic,
would like to free his slaves.

DELANO    Jefferson has read too many books, boy,
but you can trust him. He's a gentleman and an American!
He's not lifting a finger to free his slaves.

BABU    We hear you have a new capital modelled on Paris,[6]
and that your President is going to set up
a guillotine on the Capitol steps.

DELANO    Oh, Paris! I told you you could trust Mr. Jefferson,
boy,
he stands for law and order like your mulatto.
Have you been to Paris, Don Benito?

BENITO    I'm afraid I'm just a provincial Spaniard, Captain.

DELANO    Let me tell you about Paris.
You know what French women are like—
nine parts sex and one part logic.
Well, one of them in Paris heard
that my ship was the *President Adams*. She said,
"You are descended from Adam, Captain,
you must know everything,
tell me how Adam and Eve learned to sleep together."
Do you know what I said?

BENITO    No, Captain.

DELANO    I said, "I guess Eve was a Frenchwoman,
the first Frenchwoman."

6. Pierre L'Enfant, the French-born engineer and architect, who drew up the first plans for Washington, was much influenced by the way Versailles was laid out, but that is not exactly what Babu has in mind.

Do you know what she answered?

BENITO    No, Captain Delano.

DELANO    She said, "I was trying to provoke a philosophical
    discussion, Sir."

A philosophical discussion, ha, ha!

You look serious, Sir. You know, something troubles me.

BENITO    Something troubles you, Captain Delano?

DELANO    I still can't understand those calms,
    but let that go. The scurvy,
    why did it kill off three Spaniards in every four,
    and only half the blacks?

Negroes are human, but surely you couldn't have
    favored them
before your own flesh and blood!

BENITO    This is like the Inquisition, Captain Delano.

I have done the best I could.

*Babu dabs Benito's forehead with cider.*

BABU    Poor, poor Master; since Don Aranda died,
    he trusts no one except Babu.

DELANO    Your Babu is an uncommonly intelligent fellow;
    you are right to trust him, Sir.

Sometimes I think we overdo our talk of freedom.

If you looked into our hearts, we all want slaves.

BENITO    Disease is a mysterious thing;
    it takes one man, and leaves his friend.

Only the unfortunate can understand misfortune.

DELANO    I must return to my bosun;
    he's pretty green to be left alone here.

Before I go I want to propose a last toast to you!

*A good master deserves good servants!*

*He gets up. As he walks back to Perkins, the scrim curtain falls,
concealing Benito and Babu.*

That captain must have jaundice,

I wish he kept better order.

I don't like hitting menials.

PERKINS    I've done some looking around, Sir. I've used my
    eyes.

DELANO    That's what they're for, I guess. You have to watch
      your step,
    this hulk, this rotten piece of finery,
    will fall apart. This old world needs new blood
    and Yankee gunnery to hold it up.
    You shouldn't mess around, though, it's their ship;
    you're breaking all the laws of the sea.

PERKINS    Do you see that man-shaped thing in canvas?

DELANO    I see it.

PERKINS    Behind the cloth, there's a real skeleton,
    a man dressed up like Don Benito.

DELANO    They're Catholics, and worship bones.

PERKINS    There's writing on its coat. It says,
    "I am Don Aranda" and "Follow your leader."

DELANO    Follow your leader?

PERKINS    I saw two blacks unfurling a flag,
    a black skull and crossbones on white silk.

DELANO    That's piracy. We've been ordered
    to sink any ship that flies that flag.
    Perhaps they were playing.

PERKINS    I saw King Atufal throw away his chains,
    He called for food, the Spaniards served him two pieces
      of pumpkin,
    and a whole bottle of your cider.

DELANO    Don Benito has the only key to Atufal's padlock.
    My cider was for the captain's table.

PERKINS    Atufal pointed to the cabin where you were dining,
    and drew a finger across his throat.

DELANO    Who could want to kill Amasa Delano?

PERKINS    I warned our men to be ready for an emergency.

DELANO    You're a mind reader,
    I couldn't have said better myself;
    but we're at peace with Spain.

PERKINS    I told them to return with loaded muskets
    and fixed bayonets.

DELANO    Here comes Benito. Watch how I'll humor him
    and sound him out.

*Babu brings out Benito's chair. Benito sits in it.*

It's good to have you back on deck, Captain.
Feel the breeze! It holds and will increase.
My ship is moving nearer. Soon we will be together.
We have seen you through your troubles.

BENITO   Remember, I warned you about the yellow fever.
I am surprised you haven't felt afraid.

DELANO   Oh, that will blow away.
Everything is going to go better and better;
the wind's increasing, soon you'll have no cares.
After the long voyage, the anchor drops into the harbor.
It's a great weight lifted from the captain's heart.
We are getting to be friends, Don Benito.
My ship's in sight, the *President Adams!*
How the wind braces a man up!
I have a small invitation to issue to you.

BENITO   An invitation?

DELANO   I want you to take a cup of coffee
with me on my quarter deck tonight.
The Sultan of Turkey never tasted such coffee
as my old steward makes. What do you say, Don Benito?

BENITO   I cannot leave my ship.

DELANO   Come, come, you need a change of climate.
The sky is suddenly blue, Sir,
my coffee will make a man of you.

BENITO   I cannot leave my ship.
Even now, I don't think you understand my position here.

DELANO   I want to speak to you alone.

BENITO   I am alone, as much as I ever am.

DELANO   In America, we don't talk about money
in front of servants and children.

BENITO   Babu is not my servant.
You spoke of money—since the yellow fever,
he has had a better head for figures than I have.

DELANO   You embarrass me, Captain,
but since circumstances are rather special here,
I will proceed.

BENITO   Babu takes an interest in all our expenses.

DELANO   Yes, I am going to talk to you about your expenses.
I am responsible to my owners for all
the sails, ropes, food and carpentry I give you.

You will need a complete rerigging, almost a new ship,
   in fact,
You shall have our services at cost.

BENITO   I know, you are a merchant.
   I suppose I ought to pay you for our lives.

DELANO   I envy you, Captain. You are the only owner
of the *San Domingo*, since Don Aranda died.
I am just an employee. Our owners would sack me,
if I followed my better instincts.

BENITO   You can give your figures to Babu, Captain.

DELANO   You are very offhand about money, Sir;
   I don't think you realize the damage that has been done
      to your ship.
   Ah, you smile. I'm glad you're loosening up.
   Look, the water gurgles merrily, the wind is high,
   a mild light is shining. I sometimes think
   such a tropical light as this must have shone
   on the tents of Abraham and Isaac.
   It seems as if Providence were watching over us.

PERKINS   There are things that need explaining here, Sir.

DELANO   Yes, Captain, Perkins saw some of your men
unfurling an unlawful flag,
a black skull and crossbones.

BENITO   You know my only flag is the Lion and Castle of
   Spain.

DELANO   No, Perkins says he saw a skull and crossbones.
   That's piracy. I trust Perkins.
   You've heard about how my government blew
   the bowels out of the pirates at Tripoli?

BENITO   Perhaps my Negroes . . .

DELANO   My government doesn't intend
   to let you play at piracy!

BENITO   Perhaps my Negroes were playing.
   When you take away their chains . . .

DELANO   I'll see that you are all put back in chains,
   if you start playing pirates!

PERKINS   There's something else he can explain, Sir.

DELANO   Yes, Perkins saw Atufal throw off his chains
   and order dinner.

BABU   Master has the key, Yankee Master.

BENITO    I have the key.

You can't imagine how my position exhausts me, Captain.

DELANO    I can imagine. Atufal's chains are fakes.

You and he are in cahoots, Sir!

PERKINS    They don't intend to pay for our sails and service.
They think America is Santa Claus.

DELANO    The United States are death on pirates and debtors.

PERKINS    There's one more thing for him to explain, Sir.

DELANO    Do you see that man-shaped thing covered with
black cloth, Don Benito?

BENITO    I always see it.

DELANO    Take away the cloth. I order you to take away the
cloth!

BENITO    I cannot. Oh, Santa Maria, have mercy!

DELANO    Of course, you can't. It's no Virgin Mary.

You have done something terrible to your friend,
Don Aranda.

Take away the cloth, Perkins!

*As Perkins moves forward, Atufal suddenly stands unchained and
with folded arms, blocking his way.*

BABU (*dancing up and down and beside himself*)

Let them see it! Let them see it!

I can't stand any more of their insolence;
the Americans treat us like their slaves!

*Babu and Perkins meet at the man-shaped object and start pulling
away the cloth. Benito rushes between them, and throws them back and
sprawling on the deck. Babu and Perkins rise, and stand hunched like
wrestlers, about to close in on Benito, who draws his sword with a
great gesture. It is only a hilt. He runs at Babu and knocks him down.
Atufal throws off his chains and signals to the Hatchet-Cleaners. They
stand behind Benito with raised hatchets. The Negroes shout
ironically, "Evviva Benito!"*

You too, Yankee Captain!

If you shoot, we'll kill you.

DELANO    If a single American life is lost,

I will send this ship to the bottom,

and all Peru after it.

Do you hear me, Don Benito?

BENITO   Don't you understand? I am as powerless as you are!

BABU   He is as powerless as you are.

BENITO   Don't you understand? He has been holding a knife
at my back.

I have been talking all day to save your life.

BABU (*holding a whip*)

Do you see this whip? When Don Aranda was out
of temper,

he used to snap pieces of flesh off us with it.

Now I hold the whip.

When I snap it, Don Benito jumps!

*Snaps the whip. Don Benito flinches.*

DELANO (*beginning to understand*)

It's easy to terrorize the defenseless.

BABU   That's what we thought when Don Aranda held the
whip.

DELANO   You'll find I am made of tougher stuff than your
Spaniards.

ATUFAL   We want to kill you.

NEGROES   We want to kill you, Yankee Captain.

DELANO   Who could want to kill Amasa Delano?

BABU   Of course. We want to keep you alive.

We want you to sail us back to Africa.

Has anyone told you how much you are worth, Captain?

DELANO   I have another course in mind.

BENITO   Yes, there's another course if you don't like Africa,
there's another course.

King Atufal, show the Yankee captain

the crew that took the other course!

*Three dead Spanish sailors are brought on stage.*

ATUFAL   Look at Don Aranda?

BABU   Yes, you are hot-tempered and discourteous, Captain.

I am going to introduce you to Don Aranda.

You have a new command, Captain. You must meet your
new owner.

*The black cloth is taken from the man-shaped object and shows a
chalk-white skeleton dressed like Don Benito.*

Don Amasa, Don Aranda!
You can see that Don Aranda was a white man like you,
because his bones are white.

NEGROES   He is a white because his bones are white!
He is a white because his bones are white!

ATUFAL (*pointing to the ribbon on the skeleton's chest*)
Do you see that ribbon?
It says, "Follow the leader."
We wrote it in his blood.

BABU   He was a white man
even though his blood was red as ours.

NEGROES   He is white because his bones are white!

BABU   Don Aranda is our figurehead,
we are going to chain him to the bow of our ship
to scare off devils.

ATUFAL   This is the day of Jubilee,
I am raising the flag of freedom!

NEGROES   Freedom! Freedom! Freedom!

*The black skull and crossbones is raised on two poles. The Negroes
form two lines, leading up to the flag, and leave an aisle. Each man is
armed with some sort of weapon.*

BABU   Spread out the Spanish flag!

*The Lion and Castle of Spain is spread out on the deck in front of the
skull and crossbones.*

The Spanish flag is the road to freedom.
Don Benito mustn't hurt his white feet on the splinters.

*Kneeling in front of Benito.*

Your foot, Master!

*Benito holds out his foot. Babu takes off Benito's shoes.*

Give Don Benito back his sword!

*The sword-hilt is fastened back in Benito's scabbard.*

Load him with chains!

*Two heavy chains are draped on Benito's neck. The cane and ball are
handed to him.*

Former Captain Benito Cereno, kneel!
Ask pardon of man!

BENITO (*kneeling*)
I ask pardon for having been born a Spaniard.
I ask pardon for having enslaved my fellow man.

BABU    Strike off the oppressor's chain!

*One of Benito's chains is knocked off, then handed to Atufal, who dashes it to the deck.*

Former Captain Benito Cereno,
you must kiss the flag of freedom.

*Points to Don Aranda.*

Kiss the mouth of the skull!

*Benito walks barefoot over the Spanish flag and kisses the mouth of Don Aranda.*

NEGROES    *Evviva Benito! Evviva Benito!*

*Sounds are heard from Perkins, whose head is still covered with the sack.*[7]

ATUFAL    The bosun wants to kiss the mouth of freedom.
BABU    March over the Spanish flag, Bosun.

*Perkins starts forward.*

DELANO    You are dishonoring your nation, Perkins!
Don't you stand for anything?
PERKINS    I only have one life, Sir.

*Walks over the Spanish flag and kisses the mouth of the skull.*

NEGROES    *Evviva* Bosun! *Evviva* Bosun!
DELANO    You are no longer an American, Perkins!
BABU    He was free to choose freedom, Captain.
ATUFAL    Captain Delano wants to kiss the mouth of freedom.
BABU    He is jealous of the bosun.
ATUFAL    In the United States, all men are created equal.
BABU    Don't you want to kiss the mouth of freedom, Captain?

7. Lowell neglects to put Perkins in a sack. A stage direction in the early, *Show* magazine version of the play indicates that a Negro bags and ties the bosun during the scene in which Benito makes his gesture of defiance with the sword hilt, p. 128.

DELANO (*lifting his pocket and pointing the pistol*)
Do you see what I have in my hand?
BABU   A pistol.
DELANO   I am unable to miss at this distance.
BABU   You must take your time, Yankee Master.
You must take your time.
DELANO   I am unable to miss.
BABU   You can stand there like a block of wood
as long as you want to, Yankee Master.
You will drop asleep, then we will tie you up,
and make you sail us back to Africa.

*General laughter. Suddenly, there's a roar of gunfire. Several Negroes,
mostly women, fall. American Seamen in spotless blue and white throw
themselves in a lying position on deck. More kneel above them, then
More stand above these. All have muskets and fixed bayonets. The
First Row fires. More Negroes fall. They start to retreat. The Second
Row fires. More Negroes fall. They retreat further. The Third Row
fires. The Three American Lines march forward, but all the Negroes
are either dead or in retreat. Don Benito has been wounded. He
staggers over to Delano and shakes his hand.*

BENITO   You have saved my life.
I thank you for my life.
DELANO   A man can only do what he can,
We have saved American lives.
PERKINS (*pointing to Atufal's body*)
We have killed King Atufal,
we have killed their ringleader.

*Babu jumps up. He is unwounded.*

BABU   I was the King. Babu, not Atufal
was the king, who planned, dared and carried out
the seizure of this ship, the *San Domingo.*
Untouched by blood myself, I had all
the most dangerous and useless Spaniards killed.
I freed my people from their Egyptian bondage.
The heartless Spaniards slaved for me like slaves.

*Babu steps back, and quickly picks up a crown from the litter.*

This is my crown.

*Puts crown on his head. He snatches Benito's rattan cane.*

This is my rod.

*Picks up silver ball.*

This is the earth.

*Holds the ball out with one hand and raises the cane.*

This is the arm of the angry God.

*Smashes the ball.*

PERKINS   Let him surrender. Let him surrender.
We want to save someone.
BENITO   My God how little these people understand!
BABU (*holding a white handkerchief and raising both his hands*)
Yankee Master understand me. The future is with us.
DELANO (*raising his pistol*)
This is your future.

*Babu falls and lies still. Delano pauses, then slowly empties the five remaining barrels of his pistol into the body. Lights dim.*

# The Queen and the Rebels (1949)*

## Ugo Betti (1892-1953)

*The Queen and the Rebels* was one of the last plays of Ugo
Betti, who died in 1953. Written in 1949, it was first produced
on January 5, 1951, by the Compagnia Pagnani-Cervi at the
Teatro Eliseo, Rome; Alessandro Blasetti directed.

*The Queen* was one of three Betti plays that Henry Reed
translated during the 1950's for the Third Program, that part
of the British Broadcasting Corporation devoted to providing
entertainment to an audience which, by media standards, is
comparatively limited in size but not in its cultural interests.
The play was first broadcast on October 17, 1954, under the
direction of Donald McWhinnie. Revised for the stage, Reed's
translation, under Frank Hauser's direction, opened at the
Haymarket Theatre, London, on October 26, 1955. Irene
Worth played Argia in both productions.

Although a number of Ugo Betti plays have been
produced commercially in the United States and one of them,
*Corruption in the Palace of Justice* (1944), had a respectable run
off-Broadway in 1963, his work has never been very successful
here. One reason, perhaps, is that the American theater has
never been particularly congenial to the kind of philosophic
theater, much more popular in Europe, that Betti represents.
Although there have been regional and university productions
of *The Queen*, the play has yet to be done in New York.

---

* From *Three Plays* by Ugo Betti. Reprinted by permission of Grove Press, Inc., and Curtis Brown Ltd.:
Translated by Henry Reed, Copyright © 1956 by Adreina Betti.

# THE QUEEN AND THE REBELS
## (*La Regina e gli Insorti*)
### *A Play in Four Acts*

### Ugo Betti
#### TRANSLATED BY HENRY REED

### CHARACTERS

| | |
|---|---|
| ARGIA | THE PORTER |
| ELISABETTA | MAUPA |
| AMOS | AN ENGINEER |
| BIANTE | A PEASANT |
| RAIM | A PEASANT WOMAN |

*And a number of travelers, soldiers, and peasants, who do not speak.*

*The time is the present day.*

## ACT ONE

*The scene, which is the same throughout the play, represents a large hall in the main public building in a hill-side village. There are signs of disorder and neglect.*

*The stage is empty when the curtain rises. The time is sunset. After a moment the Hall Porter comes in. He is humble and apologetic in manner.*

THE PORTER (*to someone behind him*)  Will you come this way, please?

*A group of men and women come silently into the room. They are all carrying traveling bags and cases.*

THE PORTER  You can all wait in here for the time being.

ONE OF THE TRAVELERS (*cautiously*)  We could wait just as well outside.

THE PORTER  Yes, but you can sit down in here. You'll find everything you want. This used to be the town hall.

THE TRAVELER   But we don't want to sit down. We want to get on. We're several hours late as it is.

THE PORTER   I'm sorry, sir. But you'll be all right in here. There are plenty of rooms, even if you have to stay the night.

THE TRAVELER   Well, let's hope we don't have to stay the night! They told us we'd only be here half-an-hour, while the engine was cooling down.

THE PORTER   Yes, it's a stiff climb up here. The roads up those hills are very steep.

THE TRAVELER   This is the third time they've stopped us to look at our papers. (*After a pause.*) I'm a district engineer. I . . . (*dropping his voice*) Do you think they've some special reason for stopping us?

THE PORTER   No, no. They'll let you go on directly.

THE ENGINEER   Yes, but what are we waiting for?

THE PORTER   Sir, I . . . I really don't know what to say. I'm only the hall porter here. That's to say, I *was* the hall porter. Since the trouble began, I've been alone here. I have to look after everything. Anyway, will you all make yourselves comfortable?

THE ENGINEER   Is it possible to telegraph from here? Or telephone?

THE PORTER   All the lines are down. We're cut off from the world. And we're very out of the way here, in any case. I'll go and see if I can find you some blankets. (*A pause.*)

THE ENGINEER   Look here: I can only speak for myself, of course, but I dare say these other ladies and gentlemen feel much the same as I do about this. You surely realize that nobody's going to travel about just now unless they have to. Every one of us here has some important business or other to attend to. We've all been given permits to travel. Otherwise we wouldn't have come up here at a time like this. We aren't political people; we're just ordinary peaceful travelers. We've all had to pay very large sums of money for a wretched little seat in that lorry out there. And we've all had to get permission from——

THE PORTER (*clearly unconvinced by his own words*)   But you'll see, sir: they'll let you go on directly. (*A pause.*)

THE ENGINEER   Do you know who's in charge here?

THE PORTER    *I* don't, no, sir. I just take orders from everybody else.

THE ENGINEER    Is there anybody we can speak to?

THE PORTER    The trouble is they keep coming and going the whole time. They say there's a general expected here this evening; and a commissar.

THE ENGINEER    Then there's no one here now that we can speak to?

THE PORTER    The N.C.O.s are a bit rough-spoken, sir. The only one would be the interpreter. But no one takes much notice of him either, I'm afraid.

THE ENGINEER    Interpreter? What do they need an interpreter for?

THE PORTER    Oh, he's just an interpreter. He's an educated young man.

THE ENGINEER    Very well, then: fetch the interpreter.

THE PORTER    I'll get him, sir.

*He goes out. The travelers sit down silently, here and there.*

THE ENGINEER    I don't suppose it's anything to worry about. I saw some other people outside. They'd been held up too. It's obviously only another examination because we're so near the frontier. My own papers are all in order. But if there *is* anyone here who's . . . traveling irregularly . . . It might perhaps be as well if they had the courage to speak up straight away, and say so; before they get us all into trouble.

ANOTHER TRAVELER (*as though speaking to himself*)    The large number of spies about the place doesn't exactly inspire people with much desire to "speak up," as you call it. In any case, it's obvious no one here is traveling irregularly. That would have been a little too simple-minded; or so I should have thought?

THE ENGINEER    Well, if that's the case, we ought to be on our way again in half-an-hour or so.

THE TRAVELER    I can't say I share your optimism. It's been rather an odd journey, all along. Why did they make us come round this way in the first place? This village wasn't on our route at all. And the engine didn't need to cool down either. And why do we have all these inspections anyway?

The only reasonable explanation is that they're looking for someone.

THE ENGINEER   One of us?

THE TRAVELER   Though it's just as likely that they're simply being stupid and awkward, as usual. That's about all nine-tenths of the revolution comes to.

THE ENGINEER   I . . . think we'd better change the subject, if you don't mind. There's no point in . . .

THE TRAVELER   In what?

THE ENGINEER   Well, after all, this upheaval has very great possibilities, when all's said and done.

THE TRAVELER   You really think so?

THE ENGINEER   Yes. Yes, I do. Quite sincerely.

THE TRAVELER   Couldn't you . . . spare yourself this extreme cautiousness? It looks rather as if the extremists aren't doing too well at the moment. You didn't notice, as we came along the road?

THE ENGINEER   Notice what?

THE TRAVELER   Over towards the mountains. That faint crackling sound every now and then.

THE ENGINEER   What was it?

THE TRAVELER   Rifle fire. They're fighting near here, on the far slope. Everything's hanging by a thread at the moment. It's possible the Unitary Government won't last the week out.

THE ENGINEER   A week. It doesn't take a week to shoot anybody. (*He drops his voice.*) I didn't notice the noises; I was too busy noticing the smell. Did you . . . catch that smell every now and then?

THE TRAVELER   It's the smell of history.

THE ENGINEER   They don't even take the trouble to bury them.

*The Porter comes in. Raim, the interpreter, follows him, blustering and bombastic. He pretends not to deign to glance at the group of travelers.*

THE PORTER (*as he enters*)   The interpreter's just coming.

RAIM (*off*)   Where are they? Foreign slaves and spies, that's what they'll be. (*Entering.*) Where are the reactionary traitors?

THE ENGINEER (*amiably*)  You can see that we are not reactionaries. We are nothing of the kind.

RAIM  Then you must be filthy loyalists; a lot of monarchist swine.

THE ENGINEER  I assure you you're mistaken.

RAIM  You're enemies of the people. What have you come up here for? We fight and die, up here! Have you come up here to spy on us? Are you trying to smuggle currency across the frontier?

THE ENGINEER  We are ordinary peaceful travelers. Our papers have been inspected and stamped over and over again. I must ask you once again to rest assured that we are all sympathizers with the League of Councils.

RAIM (*satirically*)  Oh, yes, I knew you'd say that. You're a lot of exploiters, all of you. (*He drops his voice a little.*) And stuffed to the neck with money, I'll bet.

THE ENGINEER  No, sir.

RAIM  Poor little things. No money. We shall see about that.

THE ENGINEER  Not one of us has any money above the permitted amount.

RAIM  Gold, then? Valuables.

THE ENGINEER  No, sir. We all have permission to travel. We merely wish to be allowed to proceed on our way. On the lorry.

RAIM  I'm afraid you'll find that lorry's been requisitioned.

*A silence.*

THE ENGINEER  Shall we . . . be able to go on . . . by any other means?

RAIM  The road's blocked. In any case the bridges have all been blown up.

*A silence.*

THE ENGINEER  In that case, will you allow us to go back again to our families?

RAIM  Oh, yes, *I'm* sure! You people, you come up here, and poke your noses into everything, and then go back home and tell tales. I've a pretty shrewd suspicion you'll have to wait here.

THE TRAVELER  And what shall we be waiting for?

RAIM   The requisite inspections.

THE TRAVELER   Has anyone authorized you to speak in this way?

RAIM   Has anyone authorized you to poke your nose in?

THE TRAVELER   On what precise powers do you base your right to interfere with our movements?

RAIM   My powers are my duties as a good citizen of the republic. I act for the republic. And you? What are you waiting for? Show me your hands. Come on.

*The Traveler holds out his hands.*

RAIM   Proper priest's hands, aren't they just? *You've* never worked for your living. A bishop at least, I should say.

THE TRAVELER   Your own hands seem to be very well kept ones too.

RAIM   Thanks, your reverence, very clever, aren't you? Yes: a great pianist's hands, mine are. A pity I can't play. (*He laughs, and turns to the Porter.*) Orazio, collect these people's documents.

*The Porter begins to collect the documents.*

THE TRAVELER   Will *you* be examining them?

RAIM   They'll be inspected by Commissar Amos. We're expecting him any minute. Or better still, General Biante. He'll be here as well, very soon. Yes! Amos and Biante! Are those gigantic figures big enough for you?

THE TRAVELER   Quite.

RAIM   In the meanwhile, let me hear you say very clearly the word: purchase.

THE TRAVELER   Purchase.

RAIM   Center.

THE TRAVELER   Center.

RAIM   Now say: January.

THE TRAVELER   January.

RAIM   Can't say I like your accent very much. You wouldn't be a dirty refugee, by any chance?

THE TRAVELER   Your own accent isn't particularly good either, if I may say so.

RAIM   Ah, but I'm the interpreter, your reverence. I'm unfortunately obliged to soil my lips with foreign expressions. See? Give me this man's papers, Orazio. (*After a pause.*) You claim to have been born in the High Redon, I see.

THE TRAVELER   Yes.

RAIM   Are you a Slav?

THE TRAVELER   No.

RAIM   Your surname looks like an alien's to me. Are you a Catholic?

THE TRAVELER   No.

RAIM   Orthodox? Protestant? Jew?

THE TRAVELER   I haven't decided yet.

RAIM   Good: but I shouldn't take too long about it. Do you live on investments?

THE TRAVELER   No.

RAIM   Do you own large estates?

THE TRAVELER   No.

RAIM   Gold?

THE TRAVELER   No.

RAIM   Bonds?

THE TRAVELER   No.

RAIM   What are your political opinions?

THE TRAVELER   I cannot deny that I feel a certain concern for the Queen.

*A silence. Everyone has turned to look at him.*

RAIM   The Queen?

THE TRAVELER   The Queen.

RAIM   Good. We'll see how you like trying to be funny when Biante and Amos get here. (*Rudely, to another of the travelers.*) You. Show me your hands. (*To another.*) You.

*The person in front of him is a timid, shabbily dressed peasant woman. She puts out her hands, at which he glances in disgust.*

RAIM   Peasant. (*Turning to the Porter.*) Even peasants can travel all over the place, these days! (*Turning back to the travelers, with his finger pointing.*) You.

*He stands there speechless, with his finger still pointing. He is facing a rather attractive woman, with crumpled but not unpretentious clothes, and badly dyed hair. She has hitherto remained hidden among the other travelers. She stares at him and slowly puts out her hands.*

ARGIA (*in quiet tones, half-teasing and half-defiant*)  I have never done a stroke of work in my life. I have always had a very large number of servants at my disposal.

*They have all turned to look at her. Raim stands there embarrassed, and seeking some way out of his embarrassment. He turns abruptly to the Traveler.*

RAIM  You, sir: *You*, I mean!

THE TRAVELER (*politely*)  Yes? Is there something else I can . . . ?

RAIM  I've been thinking: I didn't like the way you . . . your manner of . . .

THE TRAVELER  Yes?

RAIM (*still trying to recover his self-possession*)  I'm afraid this . . . this casual manner of yours demands closer attention. And the rest of you too: I shall have to go into things in more detail. We must get these things straight. Orazio, you'll bring these people into my room . . . in small groups . . . or better perhaps, one by one, separately. Yes. These things have to be dealt with quietly, calmly. (*He has gone over to the door. Turning back.*) I'd like you all to understand me. You mustn't think I'm doing all this out of spite. On the contrary, you'll find I'm really a friend. It's a devil's cauldron up here: everything in a state of confusion. All sorts of different people . . . different races and languages, infiltrators, priests with beards, priests without; everything you can think of: this spot here's a picture of the whole world in its small way. There's too much friction everywhere. Why shouldn't we all try to help one another? Rich and poor, poor and rich. What I mean is, I should be very happy if I could . . . assist any of you. Orazio, send them all in to me. (*He goes out.*)

THE PORTER (*after a very brief pause*)  Well, come on. You first . . . and you.

*He points first to one, then to another of the travelers. They follow Raim.*

THE ENGINEER  Well, it's just as I said: another inspection.

THE PORTER (*with a quick glance at Argia*)  Yes. They've been tightening things up since this morning.

ARGIA (*lighting a cigarette*)  But are they really looking for somebody?

THE PORTER  Well . . . there's a lot of gossip flying about. (*He casts another furtive glance at her.*)

ARGIA  Is it . . . the so-called "Queen" they're after?

THE PORTER (*evasively*)  That's what people are saying.

THE ENGINEER  My dear fellow, all this talk about the woman they all call the Queen, just goes to show what a ridiculous race of people we are.

ARGIA (*smoking*)  I thought the clever lady died, five years ago?

THE TRAVELER (*intervening*)  Yes, so it's said. But the ordinary people still maintain that in the cellar at Bielovice the body of the woman was never found.

THE PORTER  They were all of them in that cellar to begin with: when they were alive: ministers, generals, and so on.

ARGIA  And was she there too?

THE TRAVELER (*to Argia, with detachment*)  Yes, she was. Haven't you ever heard about it? It's quite a story. It's claimed that when the soldiers poured their machine-gun fire down through the barred windows, they instinctively omitted to aim at the woman. So that after the job was finished, under all those bloody corpses . . .

THE ENGINEER (*sarcastically*)  . . . the cause of all the trouble was unharmed.

THE TRAVELER (*to Argia, as before*)  There were four soldiers on guard at the Nistria bridge, up in the mountains. In the evening a woman appeared. She was covered in blood from head to foot. The soldiers said: "Where are you going?" She looked at them, and said: "Are you sure you have any right to ask me that?" The soldiers said they had orders to stop everyone, especially women. She said: "Are you looking for the Queen?" "Yes," they said. She looked at them again, and said: "I am the Queen. What are my crimes?"

ARGIA  She wasn't lacking in courage.

THE TRAVELER  No. She spoke with such calmness, and went on her way with such dignity, that the soldiers didn't recover till the woman had disappeared into the woods.

THE ENGINEER  Very moving. And from then on, according to you, in a country like this, with more traitors than there are leaves on the trees, that woman has been able to stay in hiding for five years?

THE TRAVELER  Very few people actually knew her. She always remained in the background.

THE ENGINEER (*ironically*)  It's a pretty little tale. In any case what reasons would such a woman have now for springing up out of the ground? Events have passed her by. All the parties either hate her or have forgotten her, which is worse. And why do you call her the Queen? She was never that. Even her most slavish accomplices never flattered her to that extent.

THE TRAVELER (*gently*)  All the same, the common people have taken to calling her by that name.

THE ENGINEER  The common people have always been fascinated by the major gangsters. Especially blue-blooded ones. That great lady was not only the blazoned aristocratic wife of a usurper; she was the real usurper and intriguer herself. She was the evil genius behind everything, the Egeria,[1] the secret inspirer of all this country's disasters.

THE PORTER (*suddenly, in an unjustifiably sharp voice, to two more of the travelers*)  The next two, please, go along, in there. What are you waiting for?

*The two travelers go out. Only the Porter, the Engineer, the Traveler, Argia, and the Peasant Woman are left.*

THE PORTER (*to the Engineer*)  I . . . I hate that woman, too, of course. I hate her more than you do.

THE TRAVELER (*as though to himself*)  All the same, she must have had *some* sort of sway over people.

THE PORTER  People who talk about her say she . . . did seem very proud and haughty, but at the same time . . . sincere. They say people could never bring themselves to tell lies to her.

THE TRAVELER (*with detachment*)  The only human needs she ever seems to have acknowledged were the ones that can be reconciled with a dignified and honorable idea of the world. Everything she did and said was, as it were, essential and

---

1. He may mean simply "woman counselor" or that, like the mythical Egeria advising the legendary King Numa on Rome's religious laws, the Queen was particularly persuasive.

refined. It must be costing her a great deal to stay in hiding.

THE ENGINEER   Forgive my asking: but did any of you ever see her in those days? (*To Orazio.*) Did you?

THE PORTER   No.

THE ENGINEER   Have you ever spoken to anybody who'd ever seen her?

THE PORTER   No.

THE ENGINEER   You see, then? It's all popular ignorance: a spirit of opposition prepared to raise even a ghost against the idea of progress, if it can.

THE TRAVELER   It's a very remarkable ghost, then. (*A pause.*) I'd like to meet it.

*Raim bursts into the room.*

RAIM   I'd like to know what you all think you're doing? You take all this very calmly, don't you? The general has been sighted.

THE TRAVELER (*calmly*)   Indeed?

RAIM (*to the Porter*)   You, quick, take all these people in there; try and fix them up in there somehow . . . (*To Argia.*) No, not you. You wait in here. There are some things I have to ask you.

*The Engineer, the Traveler and the Peasant Woman go out into the next room, at a sign from the Porter. The Porter picks up their documents, which have been left on a table.*

RAIM (*severely, to Argia*)   And in particular I should like to know what are the exact and precise reasons . . . the, ah, the reasons why you have undertaken this journey up here.

ARGIA (*adopting the same official tone*)   Personal reasons.

*The Porter is on his way out of the room.*

RAIM   What were they? I may as well say that it will be as well for you if you explain them in detail.

*The door closes behind the Porter.*

ARGIA (*slowly dropping the official tone*)   The reasons in detail were as follows: I was getting horribly miserable down in Rosad, my darling, and I didn't know what to do.

RAIM   I suppose you think it's very clever, coming up here?

ARGIA    They told me you were up in the mountains.

RAIM    What do you want with me?

ARGIA    So now you've joined up with the Unitary Party, Raim? Clever boy. Are you fighting? Shooting people?

RAIM    I asked you what you'd come for.

ARGIA    Nothing. You should have seen your face when you saw me. I could have died laughing. Have I upset you?

RAIM (*harshly*)    Not at all, I was very glad to see you.

ARGIA    I wonder what your present bosses would say if anyone told them who the ones before were.

RAIM    That's not the sort of thing *you* can feel particularly easy about. When did you leave?

ARGIA    Yesterday.

RAIM    Have you any money?

ARGIA    . . . A certain amount.

RAIM (*sarcastically*)    Yes, I dare say.

ARGIA    I sold everything I had. Not that it fetched much.

RAIM    My dear girl, this is the very last place you should have come to. I only managed to get fixed up here by a miracle. I've had to tell them the most incredible tales. You needn't think I'm going to start running any risks, now.

ARGIA    I will make you run risks, Raim.

RAIM    No, my dear, we're a bit too near Rosad for that. I've enough risks of my own to run; too many. You're a woman, you always get along somehow. But these bloody fools up here, they suspect everybody. The slightest thing, and they're foaming at the mouth. I want to come through all this mess alive. And rich. Yes. What you want up here is a good memory: for afterwards. That's all you want: it'll be a good investment. One side's going to come out on top after all this; and if you've been robbing and betraying and murdering on that side you'll be a hero; if you've done the same for the other you'll be ruined. And there are so many people living in fear and trembling, I've decided to be one of the landed gentry in my old age. If it's anyhow possible you and I can meet up again in the spring. May I ask why you came up here to find me? (*Sarcastically.*) Do you love me? Did you miss me down there?

ARGIA    Raim, I really didn't know what to do. The other day, the police arrested me.

RAIM   Why?

ARGIA   They were just rounding people up. I hadn't done anything. I was in a cafe on one of the avenues. It's difficult now, being a woman on your own.

RAIM   So what?

ARGIA   Oh, nothing. I was actually rather a success at the police station. I had to stay the night there to start with; but the superintendent was quite kind to me in the morning. He told me to ring up someone who'd vouch for me. Raim: it was then I realized something for the first time: I don't really know anybody. I know people: but they're only Christian names or nicknames, as a rule. I hardly know anybody by their surname. And now, with all this confusion, so-and-so run away, so-and-so dead . . . There I was, with the telephone book, turning over the pages . . . and I could think of no one.

RAIM   So what?

ARGIA   They questioned me about my means of subsistence. The result was I was given repatriation notice. The superintendent told me I had to be decentralized, whatever that is. He said they'd send me away the next day with a military escort. "All right," I said, "but I'll have to pack my bags." They sent me home with a guard. I gave the guard my watch, and he pretended to lose me in the crowd. There were no trams, of course; the streets were all blocked; soldiers everywhere; "no stopping here." And so on. Finally, I managed to get a seat on a lorry; the price was sheer robbery. It was raining, my feet were hurting, my clothes were soaking wet; do you know what I felt like, Raim? A rat, a drowned rat. Then at Bled they made us detour, then again at Nova. Inspections. And then more inspections; hold-ups; bayonets. At Sestan they stole my coat. It hasn't been easy getting up here. I'm lucky I've found you so soon. *(She has seated herself on his knee.)*

RAIM   *(getting up)* I'm sorry, my dear, but the people here mustn't know I know you. I'm speaking for your own good as well as mine.

ARGIA   Raim, I couldn't stay down there. I was frightened; can't you understand? Not that they can really charge me with anything. But everywhere you go . . . *(with a sudden cry, which she quickly suppresses*) you see the gallows, Raim. Just because of stray accusations . . . or vague resemblances, rows of people have been hanged. . . .

RAIM   And you think that's going to encourage me to keep you here? I've as much cause to be worried as you have. It would be madness just to slap our worries together. No, Argia, no: everyone has to look after himself; I want to finish this war above ground, not underneath.

ARGIA   (*after a pause, with an effort to make it seem unimportant*) Raim: what if I told you . . . that I'd really . . . missed you?

RAIM   That's what I said. You love me. I've bewitched you.

ARGIA   Oh, I know you're quite right to laugh at me. (*Lightly imploring him.*) But . . . when we're both together I feel . . . a bit safer. . . . I was happy, when I saw you; don't you understand?

RAIM   Well, I wasn't, see? I wasn't.

ARGIA   Raim. . . .

RAIM   My dear . . . I've no intention of burdening myself with you. Besides, you'll be sure to find a way out, I know you. (*Shrugging his shoulders.*) There aren't many women round here. They're in great demand.

ARGIA   (*lowers her eyes for a moment; then looks at him and says, in low quiet tones*)   What a disgusting creature you are, aren't you, Raim? I sometimes think you must be the nastiest person in the world.

RAIM   Ah, now you're talking sense. You go away and leave me, my dear; I'm not worthy of you. I'd feel guilty at keeping you here.

ARGIA   And to think that *I* am running after somebody like *you*, begging . . . from *you*. It's enough to make one weep; or laugh.

RAIM   Well, you laugh, then, my dear. Let's both have a good laugh, and say good-bye. You'd be wasted on me. You know, Argia, one of the reasons you don't attract me is your silly games of make believe the whole time. You've always tried to act so very grand. With me! The superior lady, always disgusted, so easily offended. You of all people! Always behaving as though dirt was something that only belonged to other people.

ARGIA (*her eyes lowered*)  No, Raim, that's not true.

RAIM  While the truth is that if ever there was a filthy creature in the world, you're it.

ARGIA  I'm sorry, Raim, if I spoke like that . . . It's only because deep down I love you, and want to . . .

RAIM  You let me finish. I'm not angry; not at all. But you may as well get this straight. You see, Argia: you're not only a dead weight on me. . . . It's not only that. You've begun to get rather too many wrinkles for my liking. . . .

ARGIA (*trying to turn the whole thing into a jest*)  Really, Raim? A few minutes ago, when they were all talking about the Queen, did you know they all looked at me? They half thought I was the Queen.

RAIM  You! The Queen? They've only got to look at you to see what *you* are. The Queen. There isn't a square inch about you that's decent.

ARGIA (*with another hoarse effort at playfulness*)  Be quiet, Raim, if you don't, I'll bite you! (*She takes his hand.*)

RAIM (*freeing himself with a brutal jerk which makes her stagger backwards*)  You leave me alone. Don't try and pretend I'm joking. What you ought to do, my dear, is to go and stand in front of your looking glass and say to yourself as often as you can: "I'm a cheap, low, dirty slut." You've never done a decent thing in your whole life. (*Deliberately.*) Smell of the bed. Cigarette smoke. Wandering about the room with nothing on, whistling. That's you. And there have been one or two unsavory episodes which even suggest that the secret police made use of you. Oh, make no mistake, I'm not the kind of man who's easily prejudiced. But you, Argia, quite apart from everything else, you're cheap. The little bogus middle-class girlie, who's read a few books. Even in your intrigues you're small and petty: the little tart with the furnished rooms and the pawnshop tickets: I've been getting fed up with you now for quite a long time, see? Well: it's over. I'm not going through all that again.

ARGIA (*her eyes lowered; and with a faint wail*)  Raim, I've nowhere to go.

RAIM  Then go to hell. It's the one place . . . (*His voice suddenly reassumes its official tone. He has heard footsteps coming.*) It's absolutely necessary for . . . for political reasons. And even if you have to stay here tonight, it's no great disaster. You and the other woman, that peasant woman, can stay in here. The other passengers in the other rooms. It'll be all right. I'll see about finding some blankets for you. Political and military necessities, unfortunately. It isn't my fault.

*It is the Traveler who has come in. Raim has turned to him on his last words. The Traveler approaches amiably.*

THE TRAVELER    Nor ours either. I seem to get the impression that you, too, regard these . . . these military and political necessities, with a certain amount of skepticism.

RAIM (*looks at him for a moment: and then says, also amiably*)    Bless my soul, that's exactly what I was saying to . . . (*To Argia, sharply.*) You may withdraw, madam. Go in there with the others.

*Argia goes out.*

RAIM (*amiably but cautiously*)    Yes, I was just saying that . . . well, of course, I'm a good revolutionary and all that (we all are, of course), but I . . . understand things. I know how to put myself in another man's place. Unfortunate travelers . . . perhaps even important men, well-to-do, plenty of money and so on, suddenly finding themselves . . .

THE TRAVELER    Reduced to hoping for a blanket!

RAIM (*carefully feeling his way*)    I'm afraid I may have seemed a little bit . . . official with you just now. I had to be, of course. You understand.

THE TRAVELER    I have the feeling that you too understand. . . .

RAIM    Oh, at once, my dear friend, straight away. I'll be happy to be of any help, if it's at all possible. . . .

THE TRAVELER    The secret is to regard these things with a certain amount of detachment; don't you agree?

RAIM    Definitely. You know, I got the impression, when we were talking here a few minutes ago, that you too . . . feel a certain distaste for some of the excesses that . . .

THE TRAVELER    Ah, you noticed that, did you?

RAIM    Oh, but of course! I'm a man . . . who doesn't feel so very bitter as all that towards your *own* ideals, you know, sir.

THE TRAVELER    Is that so? I'm delighted to hear it.

RAIM (*mysteriously*)  I'm too much in contact with the new chiefs the whole time, of course.

THE TRAVELER (*shaking his head*)  And they . . .

RAIM (*laughing*)  . . . aren't so terribly different from the old ones.

THE TRAVELER  That was to be expected.

RAIM  Once you ignore the individual differences of character, you find they raise their voices, ring the bell, upset people and shoot 'em . . .

THE TRAVELER  . . . in exactly the same way as the others. Yes. I assume you were also in the habit of hobnobbing with the former high-ups?

RAIM  Oh, no, God forbid. I had to put up with them. And now I have to put up with these. "Put up!" It's all very sad.

THE TRAVELER  Especially for men of intelligence. (*As though speaking to himself.*) Who really ought to be looking after themselves.

RAIM (*warmly*)  Exactly! That's just what I say. These disturbances ought to be a godsend for people with any imagination . . . ! (*He has taken a bottle out of its hiding place and is pouring out a drink for himself and the Traveler.*) "Ought to be looking after themselves." Yes. As you say. Look after yourself, what? You know, I have a theory about all these things.

THE TRAVELER  I'd like to hear it.

RAIM  There are two kinds of people in this world: the people who eat beefsteaks and the people who eat potatoes. Whose fault is it? Because it's certainly not true that the millionaire eats a hundred thousand beefsteaks.

THE TRAVELER (*drinking*)  He'd soon have indigestion if he did.

RAIM (*also drinking*)  He eats half a beefsteak and helps it down with a dose of bicarbonate. Yes. Then why do all these other poor devils have to make do with potatoes? It's simple. There aren't enough beefsteaks to go round. The limitation on the number of beefsteaks in the world is a profound inconvenience on which social reforms have not the slightest influence. Not the slightest. Now, it follows from this that whatever regime you're under, the number of eaters of beefsteak . . .

THE TRAVELER  Remains constant.

RAIM   Exactly. And the wonderful thing is that the beefsteak
eaters are always the same people. They may *look* different,
of course. But who are they?

THE TRAVELER   The bosses . . .

RAIM   . . . and the wide-boys.[2] It's always the same act; the
palaces and the armchairs are always there, and it's always
by virtue of the people and the potatoes that the high-ups
can sit in the palaces eating their beefsteaks. That being
agreed, what's the logical thing to do? It's to belong,
whatever happens, to . . .

THE TRAVELER   The beefsteak party.

RAIM   It's not for everybody, of course. It requires intelligence
. . . intuition. (*With sudden firmness.*) You'll forgive me, sir,
but I don't believe in equality; except over toothpicks. It's
only by climbing up and down that we keep fit. (*Gently.*) I
believe in money.

THE TRAVELER   You're not the only one.

RAIM   If man had never developed that great vision of having
a bank account, he'd never have emerged from cave life.

THE TRAVELER (*solemnly*)   Progress. Progress.

RAIM   A little bit of salt on the tail.[3] Just think what a colossal
bore it'd all be otherwise. Everybody stuck there as though
in a morgue. A row of coffins. If a man's a hunchback, he's
always a hunchback. We all know that. If a man's ugly, he's
ugly. If he's a fool, he's a fool. But at any rate, however
common and unfortunate a man may be, he can always
hope to get rich, little by little. Rich. Which means he won't
be ugly any more, nor a fool . . .

THE TRAVELER   Nor even a hunchback.

RAIM   That's your *real* democracy; your real progress. Yes,
that's why it's the duty, the absolute duty of every intelligent man . . . (*his voice changes once more and becomes peremptory
and severe; footsteps are approaching*) to fight and to strive! To

2. Men living by their wits. Reed's use of English slang here to translate *furbi*
(cheats, rogues) is unusual in a play that is mostly in conventional English. We might
say "con men" in American slang.

3. The line suggests the old mock advice about catching a bird by sprinkling salt on
its tail, but the allusion seems inappropriate in this context. Perhaps Reed wanted a
seasoning equivalent to the Italian original, *"Un po' di pepe nel sedere"* (a little pepper on
the seat). What the line means, however, is that money is an incentive. Perhaps "a
little spice in life" comes closer.

fight and strive in the service of our flag and our republic!
(*He turns to see who is coming in and is at once thrown into great
agitation.*) Good God, it's you, General Biante, forgive me, I
never saw you come in! (*He runs to the door.*) How are you?
Are you feeling a little better?

*Biante has entered, supported by an armed guard, Maupa, who at once
helps him to sit down. Biante is a hirsute man in civilian clothes. His
shoulders, neck, and one arm are voluminously bandaged, and compel
him to move stiffly. He looks first at Raim, then at the Traveler, and
then turns back to Raim.*

BIANTE (*his voice is low and hoarse*)   What are you doing?

RAIM (*eagerly*)   Nothing, general, I was just interrogating a
traveler.

BIANTE   Oh. Good. And what did the traveler have to say to
you?

THE TRAVELER (*sweetly*)   We were discussing some rather
curious offers of help he'd just been making to me.

RAIM   I? General Biante! (*He sniggers.*) I was just holding out a
little bait, just wriggling a little hook about. I ought to say
that this gentleman seems to me a very suspicious character.
I think we should do well to point him out to Commissar
Amos . . .

BIANTE (*between his teeth, not amused*)   Don't be a bloody fool.

RAIM   . . . the minute the commissar arrives.

THE TRAVELER (*calmly, to Raim*)   I arrived an hour ago. I am
Commissar Amos. How are you, Biante?

BIANTE   Haven't you managed to get me a doctor?

AMOS   Not yet.

BIANTE   I'd be damned glad of one. I come through the whole
war safely, and what do I have to be wiped out by? A stray
bullet. Amos, I'm swollen right up to the neck; my fingers
feel like sausages. I wouldn't like to die, Amos. I'd like to
live and see the new age in. Do you think I'm getting
gangrene?

AMOS (*calmly*)   Let's hope not.

BIANTE (*suddenly to Raim, hysterically*)   Go and find a doctor, for
Christ's sake! You filthy bastard, go and find a doctor! And
send all those people in here!

*Raim rushes out.*

BIANTE (*breathing laboriously*)  The Queen's here! Somewhere: in our midst. Nobody's doing anything, nobody knows anything. And yet they're all saying it! The Queen's here!

AMOS (*calmly*)  Yes, I'd heard for certain she was.

BIANTE  Good God. Who from?

AMOS  They stopped a man on the road from Bled. He was coming up here to meet her.

BIANTE  Where is he?

AMOS  He was too quick for us. While they were bringing him here. He poisoned himself. So as not to have to acknowledge his accomplice.

BIANTE (*almost a whisper*)  The Queen's here! Alive!

MAUPA (*suddenly, from the background, without moving, in a kind of ecstasy*)  We want to see the color of the Queen's entrails.

*Raim is escorting the travelers into the room.*

MAUPA (*continuing without pause*)  All our troubles come from the Queen. If our sick are covered with wounds, if our children grow up crippled and our daughters shameless, the Queen's to blame, no one else. (*His voice gets gradually louder.*) If she falls into my hands, I'll keep her dying slowly for three whole days. I'll make them hear her screams from the mountain tops. I'll slit her up bit by bit till she lies there wide open like a peach. The thought that the Queen is near makes my hair stand on end like a wild boar's. We must find her.

AMOS (*calmly*)  She will be found soon enough. The road up here has been blocked since this morning, but the number of road passengers they've stopped hasn't been very large. This very night we shall begin to go over them methodically.

BIANTE (*turning to the others, who are standing huddled together in the background*)  Yes, you there! It's you we're talking about! (*Shouting and getting up from his chair.*) I'm here: General Biante. I assume full powers . . . together with Commissar Amos here. . . . Is there anybody here who's a doctor? No? Blast you. (*Brief pause.*) You're all under arrest! No one's to move an inch from where you are now.

AMOS  The exits are all guarded; the guards have orders to shoot.

BIANTE  You'll all be questioned. So look out! You'll be detained here till further orders! (*Pointing.*) The women in there; the men in here. Get on with it, everyone to his proper place. (*He moves towards the door.*)

AMOS (*calmly, for the pleasure of contradicting him*)  The men will go in there; the women will stay in here.

*Biante casts a sharp glance at Amos, and goes out, supported by Maupa.*

*The travelers have all gone out again except Argia and the Peasant Woman.*

AMOS (*also on his way out, turns in the doorway*)  Goodnight for the present. (*He goes out.*)

*Argia stands for a moment looking at the door, and then shrugs her shoulders.*

ARGIA  What a lot of stupid nonsense! The result is that we sleep in here. Let's hope the interpreter remembers to bring us some blankets. There was a sofa in that other room too. (*She points to the next room.*) I'm very tired, aren't you? (*She sits.*) What a lot of clowns they all are. Let's hope they let us sleep till tomorrow morning. (*She begins to fumble in her handbag, and brings out a small pot; she takes some cold cream on one finger and dabs it on her face. To the Peasant Woman, who is still seated in the background.*) I suppose in the country you don't go in for this sort of thing? I have to, every night: I'm not so young as I was, I've just been told; it would be asking for trouble if I didn't look after myself. (*She massages her face.*) I suppose I must look a sight with this grease all over my face? Sorry. (*She thinks for a moment.*) I find it rather humiliating being a woman. Even rather humiliating being alive. (*She massages her face.*) You spit in a blackguard's face, and even as you do it, you know perfectly well the only thing to do is to make him go to bed with you . . . I'm sorry: but we're both women, after all. I don't mean one really wants to, even. It's all so squalid and humiliating. (*She breaks off.*)

*Raim crosses the stage and goes out.*

ARGIA   I've come a long, long way just to go to bed with a man. (*Pause.*) Making a fuss of a man to try and find out if he's in a good mood or not. Very amusing. (*Pause.*) The trouble is having no money either. Let's hope after we're dead there'll be nothing of that to worry about. (*Turning to the Peasant Woman.*) Do you mind my asking, dear: I suppose you haven't a bit bigger mirror than this? What . . . what's the matter? Aren't you feeling all right?

THE PEASANT WOMAN (*almost inaudibly*)   Yes . . .

ARGIA (*going over to her*)   Why, you're covered with sweat. Do you feel ill? You look as if you're going to faint.

THE PEASANT WOMAN   No . . . no. . . . (*She sways.*)

ARGIA (*supporting her*)   Did what that brute in here said about the Queen frighten you? You mustn't take any notice of that, it's nothing to do with us . . .

*She breaks off; lets the woman go; and stares at her. The woman stares back at her with wide-open eyes; then she rises, slowly.*

ARGIA (*after a long pause, in a different voice*)   Is there anything you want?

THE PEASANT WOMAN   No . . . no. . . .

ARGIA   You could go and lie down in there, on the sofa. Where is your bag?

*The Peasant Woman grips her bag, as though frightened by Argia's words.*

ARGIA   What have you got in there?

THE PEASANT WOMAN   Some bread. . . .

ARGIA   Well, my dear, you go in there. Lie down. You'll soon feel better.

*Argia helps the woman into the next room. After a moment she returns, and walks about for a moment or two, perplexed and thoughtful. Suddenly she runs to the other door, opens it and calls in a stifled whisper.*

ARGIA   Raim! Raim! (*She comes back, and waits.*)

RAIM (*enters: in a whisper*)   What d'you want? Are you mad?

ARGIA (*whispers*)   I'm rich, Raim. I'm worth marrying now. Look at me: I'm a splendid match.

RAIM   What's the matter?

ARGIA  Rich, Raim. Rich. We'll be able to stay in the grandest hotels.

RAIM  What do you mean?

ARGIA  I've discovered the Queen. (*She points towards the next room.*)

RAIM  But there's only that peasant woman in there.

*Argia nods.*

CURTAIN


## ACT TWO

*Only a few moments have passed since the end of the preceding scene. Argia and Raim are speaking rapidly, in low voices.*

RAIM  (*sweating and agitated*)  God damn the day I ever met you! You're the cause of all my troubles. This is a frightful thing . . . it's terribly dangerous.

ARGIA  (*mockingly*)  Well, why not go to Amos and Biante, then, and tell *them* about it? Tell them the Queen's here; with a heavy bag.

RAIM  Yes, and you know what they'll do? Kill me; and you too. So that they can have the credit . . . and the bag as well. It's a murder factory up here. Their only aim here is to kill people. Yes: accidentally; for amusement.

ARGIA  Then we'd better forget about it, that's all.

RAIM  I could box your ears! This is the first piece of luck I've ever had in the whole of my life. It's my big chance. I shall go mad if I have to let this slip through my fingers.

ARGIA  Well, don't let it, then.

RAIM  God, I'm frightened of this. A rifle can go off all by itself up here. Damn the whole bloody world! But are you sure about this, Argia? You've always been half crazy; you imagine things the whole time.

ARGIA  I'm quite certain. We looked at one another. It was just a flicker. And then I saw. And she saw that I saw. She was almost fainting.

RAIM  The devil is there's not a minute to lose. What was this bag like?

ARGIA  Small; but quite heavy.

RAIM  Gold; diamonds. It'll kill me. You couldn't get a needle out of this place. Bury it; come back later: some hopes! They're more likely to bury *me*. (*In a burst of anger.*) I'm the one who's in danger, can't you see?

ARGIA  But I can help you. I can do it for you.

RAIM  Yes. You're a woman, of course. You know her . . . You've already been talking to her  . . . But, mind, it would have to look as if it were your own idea. Something you'd thought of yourself. How did she seem?

ARGIA  Terrified.

RAIM  Yes, that's the way to go about it, obviously. Try and frighten her. She'll give you the bag herself, without even being asked.

ARGIA  We mustn't bother too much about the bag, Raim.

RAIM  Why not?

ARGIA  We couldn't be seen with it; and it would be difficult to take it away, or bury it.

RAIM  Well, what, then?

ARGIA  The names.

RAIM  What do you mean, for God's sake, what names?

ARGIA  The names: of her friends. There's sure to be a whole gang round her. Big, important people.

RAIM  By God! You clever piece! (*He kisses her.*) Do you think she'd talk?

ARGIA  We can try and persuade her to. Her life's in our hands.

RAIM  You could manage that all right, if you frightened her. But what then?

ARGIA  We won't take the bag away with us. We'll take the names. In our heads.

RAIM  Yes, but surely we could try and get the bag as well? And what if we got the names?

ARGIA  Well, from then on there'd be quite a number of people who might be feeling extremely uneasy . . .

RAIM  (*completing the sentence*)  . . . and every so often the tax collector would drop in and see them. Yes. Me. "Excuse me, your Excellency, you won't forget the usual donation, will you? Though only, of course, if you're interested in surviving a little longer . . . Yes?" My God, what a game! No.

No. No! It's too dangerous. It's a good idea, but sooner or later, they'd have me done in. Don't you see? (*With bitter nastiness.*) The bastards would soon be sparing *me* the afflictions of old age, don't worry! No, no, Argia, we must try and grab what we can out of it, quickly. Jewels, rubies, and so on . . . (*He suddenly lowers his voice.*) God, here she is. Go on: see what you can do.

*The Queen has opened the door, and stands looking, as though hypnotized, at Argia; Raim casts a glance at her and goes out in silence.*

ARGIA  Did you want something?

THE QUEEN  (*breathing painfully*) No . . . no . . . I only wanted . . .

ARGIA  To come and talk to me for a bit? Is that it?

THE QUEEN  I . . . saw that perhaps . . . you have a kind heart . . .

ARGIA  Well . . . that always depends how God made us, doesn't it? Come over here, my dear. Come on. I wanted to talk to you as well. You're a country woman, aren't you?

THE QUEEN  (*almost inaudibly*)  Yes . . .

ARGIA  I'm fond of country people. Do you actually go out in the fields?

THE QUEEN  Yes . . .

ARGIA  What do you do there?

THE QUEEN  I work . . .

ARGIA  Digging? Hoeing?

*The Queen holds out her hands appealingly.*

ARGIA  Yes, they're real peasant's hands, aren't they? Good girl. It can't be easy to get your hands like that. It must take a long time. And a good deal of hard work. A good deal of digging and hoeing.

THE QUEEN  Yes . . .

ARGIA  Are you all by yourself?

THE QUEEN  Yes . . .

ARGIA  I can see you're very frightened; I think you've every reason to be. It was sensible of you to come to me. As a matter of fact, I could probably help you. And in return you could perhaps be kind enough to do something for me.

THE QUEEN  I . . . don't know what sort of thing . . . you mean.

ARGIA (*almost a whisper*)  My dear friend, your name isn't Elisabetta by any chance, I suppose?

*There is a long silence.*

THE QUEEN (*she can scarcely speak*)  No.

ARGIA  Odd. I thought it was, somehow . . . However. (*She raises her voice slightly.*) You're quite sure your name is not Elisabetta?

THE QUEEN  No . . . no . . . no . . . (*She again holds out her hands.*)

ARGIA (*a little louder still*)  You insist on denying that your name is . . .

THE QUEEN (*interrupting her with a gesture*)  My bag is in there. You can have it. I thought you'd want it. (*She points.*) I've hidden it. You can take it whenever you want to.

ARGIA  Hidden it where?

THE QUEEN  In there. Up above the rafters, in the corner.

ARGIA  Is there much in it?

THE QUEEN  Only what I have left. It's hidden in the bread. There are three little loaves.

ARGIA  It's not really much of a sacrifice for you, is it? If you ever come to the top again, it'll be a mere trifle to you. And if you don't, it's all up with you anyway. But it would be a godsend to me. You see, I'm poor; I'm hag-ridden with debts . . . (*She breaks off.*)

RAIM (*coming in quickly*)  Excuse me, ladies! I've just remembered about the blankets . . . I came to see if . . . (*He goes up to Argia, and speaks to her under his breath, almost with fury.*) I've been thinking. I want the names as well. I want everything. (*Retreating.*) I'll bring you the blankets, in half a minute. (*He goes out.*)

ARGIA  Yes, you've shown a good deal of common sense. Well, you'll have to show a little more now. The situation is very simple. I can either go out of that door and call a soldier. Or I can keep my mouth shut, and help you. I've a friend here; you just saw him. But I'm afraid it means sharing things out, your majesty. We're sisters now. Everything in common. I'd be a fool to be satisfied with the leavings in the middle of three small loaves, wouldn't I?

THE QUEEN (*almost inaudibly*)  I've nothing else.

ARGIA  For year after year you used to walk on marble and sleep in silk. I've not had quite such a good time. The moment's come to level things up.

THE QUEEN  I swear to you I've nothing else.

ARGIA  That's not true. You still have friends. People working for you. I want them to be my friends as well. I want them to help me. *I* want people I can rely on, too. Do you see what I mean?

THE QUEEN  Yes . . .

ARGIA  In any case, the people I mean are hard-boiled enough. They're the people who've shoved you into all this mess. It was they who drove you out of your hiding place.

THE QUEEN  No, no, there wasn't anybody.

ARGIA  Your friends.

THE QUEEN  I haven't any.

ARGIA  Come, come, you won't be doing *them* any harm. The only trouble they'll have is helping me a little in these hard times. Your friends.

THE QUEEN (*imploring*)  They're all dead, they've all been killed. I'm alone now.

ARGIA  Your majesty, you used to sweep down red-carpeted staircases; the ones I had to climb weren't half so pretty. But even they taught me things. I learned . . . a good deal. You'll be very silly if you try to fool *me*.

THE QUEEN  Oh, please have pity. . . .

ARGIA  I'm hardened, your majesty. I'm indifferent even to my own misfortunes by now; you can imagine how I feel about yours. (*Almost shouting.*) Come on, tell me who they are: who are your friends? Who are they? (*She breaks off.*)

*The Queen has taken from her bosom a piece of paper; she offers it to Argia.*

ARGIA (*before taking it*)  They're there?

THE QUEEN  Yes.

ARGIA (*taking the paper*)  A good many stories about you are going the rounds. I thought I should have to insist much harder. You're rather meek and mild, for a Queen, aren't you? (*She looks at the paper.*) Darling, you must take me for an idiot. A list of them, all ready? Just like that?

THE QUEEN    Yes.

ARGIA    You've been carrying it about on you?

THE QUEEN    Yes.

ARGIA (*sarcastically condescending*)    Why, my dear, why?

THE QUEEN    Because I'm frightened.

ARGIA    Of what?

THE QUEEN (*desperately*)    Of being tortured. I've heard of them doing . . . terrible . . . dreadful things . . . And I'm frightened; don't you understand? (*Overcome for a moment.*) The thought of it is driving me insane! (*Controlling herself.*) I'd have been bound to tell them in the end just the same . . . And if there was this paper . . . They'd have found it on me; it would all have been simple. Oh, please believe me, I beg of you, please. It's the truth.

ARGIA (*looks at the paper*)    So these are the ones? Your faithful friends. The people who are risking their lives for you.

THE QUEEN    Yes.

ARGIA (*dropping her voice*)    But are you really the "Queen"?

THE QUEEN    Yes . . . Except that I . . . lost whatever courage I had, in that cellar, at Bielovice. Please: I've nothing else to give you now. I hope you'll save me . . . I hope you and your friend will help me to escape . . .

*Raim enters quickly with a couple of blankets.*

RAIM    Here you are, ladies, the blankets! (*He throws them on a chair; to the Queen.*) Do you mind? (*He takes the paper from Argia's hand, and draws her aside. He looks at the card, and says quietly.*) It's so stupid and childish it's bound to be true. (*He stares at the paper hard; then puts it under Argia's eyes.*) You fix these four names in your head as well.

ARGIA    Yes.

RAIM    Good. Have you got them? You're sure?

ARGIA    Yes.

RAIM    So have I. (*He lights a match and sets the paper alight; to the Queen.*) Madam, we have to think of our safety as well, though our methods may be a bit different. (*He stamps on the ashes hysterically.*)

ARGIA (*a whisper*)    Do you think it's possible to get her away?

RAIM (*a whisper*)  It's not only possible, it's indispensable. And it's not only indispensable, it's not enough. Escape isn't enough. There's something else as well.

ARGIA  What?

RAIM (*rapidly*)  If she gets across the mountains and gets in touch with those people (*he points to the ashes*) it'll go very hard with us. And if she doesn't, it'll be even worse: they'll catch her; and she'll tell everything. And if we leave her here, when they question her tomorrow, she'll talk just the same. She'll give us away. I'd be a madman to risk my life—and yours—on a damn silly thing like that.

ARGIA  What then?

RAIM  We've got to make *sure* she keeps her mouth shut.

ARGIA (*has understood*)  No!

RAIM  It's the best thing for her too, in a way. If those two in there find her, her last minutes aren't going to be very enviable. She's finished now, either way. Better for her it should all be over quickly without frightening her.

ARGIA  No, no.

RAIM (*in an excited whisper*)  Do you think I like it? Our lives depend on this. We can't back out now, it's too late. We oughtn't to have started it. Darling, it's got to be done.

ARGIA (*horrified*)  Got to? And do you think *I* . . .

RAIM  It's always you, isn't it? Whose idea was it? Yours. You got me into this danger. You arranged it all. And now it's not nice enough for you. You're worse than anybody. No, my dear. It's got to be done. And we're in it together.

ARGIA (*with horrified resignation*)  Have you thought . . . how?

RAIM  I'm thinking now. (*Moving away and speaking louder.*) I'll be back in a few minutes, madam. We're looking after you. (*He goes out.*)

THE QUEEN  Does he intend to help me?

ARGIA (*without looking at her*)  Yes.

THE QUEEN  Your friend will get me away?

ARGIA  Yes.

THE QUEEN (*suddenly, torn with anguish*)  For pity's sake, don't let them hurt me, don't betray me, for pity's sake . . . (*She darts forward and takes Argia's hand as though to kiss it.*)

ARGIA (*almost angrily, tearing her hand away*)  What are you doing? What's the matter with you?

THE QUEEN (*desperately*)  Oh, my God, you're deceiving me, everybody deceives me . . . Everybody plays with me like a cat with a mouse . . . I can't go on any longer; oh, God, I'd rather die now . . . I don't want to think any more; call them, call the soldiers, I'll call them myself, kill me, kill me, straight away . . .

ARGIA (*shaking her*)  Stop it, stop it, you silly woman.

*The Queen has fallen to her knees and remains there gasping for breath.*

ARGIA (*exasperated*)  You'll dirty your knees, your majesty. Yes, of course, you'll be saved, you'll be got away. It's important to us as well, isn't it? (*With gloomy hostility.*) In any case, it's dishonorable, it's unfair, to lose your dignity like this. It's against the rules of the game; it embarrasses people. A chambermaid would behave better. I would myself, my dear; I've never squealed like that: like a mouse under a peasant's foot. And I'm not a queen . . . far from it. When you used to give your orders, with the flag flying over the palace, down below, underneath all the people who were obeying you and giving your orders to other people, down below all of them, right down on the pavement, there was I. I didn't drive in a landau; and they'd made a woman of me by the time I was eleven. Your majesty, there were some days when I used to feel as if the whole world had wiped their feet on my face. And now you come and slobber all over my hands. No, no, my dear: the silk clothes and the box at the Opera have to be paid for. You heard a few minutes ago, in here, what the people think of you. Your hands have not always been rough. And they've signed a lot of papers in their time.

THE QUEEN  No.

ARGIA  What do you mean: no?

THE QUEEN  I've never done any harm to any one. It was never left to me to decide anything. Nothing they say of me is true. (*She shudders with horror.*) The only thing that's true is that at Bielovice I was covered with dead bodies and blood. I could feel them dying, on top of me! Since then I've been in perpetual flight. It isn't true that I met the soldiers on the bridge at Nistria. If I had, I should have fainted at their feet. I've not had a single moment free from terror for five years. They've killed almost every one of my friends; but unfortunately not all of them. Every so often one or other of them manages to track me down. I'm running away from my friends even more than from my enemies. What can they want of me any more? I can't do anything, I don't want to do anything, the only thing I know now is fear; I sleep in fear, I dream in fear. I'll never, never do anything again either for anyone or against anyone. I only want to escape, and never see or know anything again. I want to stop being afraid. Nobody can have anything to fear from me. I'll give up everything, rights, titles, I'll forget everything.

ARGIA (*with sombre irony*)   It almost looks as if I'd done you a service in taking your jewels off you. You are abdicating. There are some people who'd be extremely disillusioned if they could hear you.

THE QUEEN   I have nothing and I no longer want anything.

ARGIA   Then why are you making so much fuss? What *do* you want?

THE QUEEN   To be left alive. Nothing else. Unknown; far away. And to sleep, night after night, in peace.

*The two women turn round. Raim has entered, slowly. He bows slightly to the Queen, and beckons Argia aside.*

RAIM (*whispers*)   The job's going to be taken off our hands. I've found a way out. It's quite respectable, too. This building has two exits: this one, and that one over there. The guard on this one, across the courtyard, will be me. The one on the other, on the wall, is Maupa, that soldier you saw in here. He's a real brute. (*To the Queen.*) Yes, this is for you, madam. We are preparing a way out for you. (*To Argia once more.*) It was easy to persuade that swine that the revolution demanded that he should fire; often; at sight; the first squeak of a door or movement in the shadows. Even me, if I tried to: if I opened that door, I'd be opening my own way to hell. But that I shan't do. In a few minutes' time you'll hear a signal: the hoot of an owl. The Queen will say good-bye to you, and come out through this door. Our hands will be as white as snow.

ARGIA (*horrified*)   And if the shot doesn't kill her?

RAIM (*gloomy, subdued*)   In that case, I . . . (*He breaks off.*) It would be just reckless cowardice to leave the thing half-done. What should I get out of that? The only profit there, would be for my dead bones, because it's obvious the Queen would talk and I'd lose my life. But if a dead man's bones know nothing about profit and loss, do you think stupidity and superstition are going to hold my hand back? Why light candles if your prayers mean nothing? (*He blows to left and right as though to put out two imaginary candles burning before a nonexistent shrine.*) They're all wolves: why should I be a lamb? Plenty of good people are dying in these hard times, one more or less makes no odds. They say the Bible stories prophesy a bath of blood for the earth. But in practice it needs gallons, especially when you see how much the earth soaks up. Besides, I suffer from poor health; I've got to make sure of some sort of a future. (*He returns to the subject.*) So if anything goes wrong . . . Oh, why does this woman get people into such a mess instead of doing away with herself? Her life's useless and wretched and short, anyway. Better for her to finish here than run about, being smelt out like a hare the whole time, always in fear and trembling. (*To Argia.*) If anything does go wrong, as soon as I hear the shots, I shall run round through the courtyard . . . and if the soldier's shots haven't been enough . . . I'll finish it off myself . . . Let's hope it won't be necessary. Quickly, now. I shall be glad when it's all over. (*He makes a slight bow to the Queen and goes out.*)

ARGIA (*avoids looking at the Queen*)   Madam, you must be very brave now, this is going to be very dangerous for all of us. But I think you'll be all right.

THE QUEEN   I am ready.

ARGIA (*breathing heavily*)   What has to be done, has to. That's true, isn't it? If you want to escape . . .

THE QUEEN   Go on.

ARGIA   They've found a man who's willing to accompany you up the hidden paths as far as the frontier. In a few minutes we shall hear a signal. Then you'll go out, through that door over there. Outside, you'll find the man who's willing to take you on your way. You'll have nothing more to worry about.

THE QUEEN (*her hands clasped*)  Oh, my dear. Your sweet face and your gentle voice will stay in my heart till the last day of my life, and beyond. Yes, surely beyond; so that when I meet you again in heaven, I can run to you, crying . . . (*She takes Argia's hands.*) "Bright soul! My dear, dear sister! Do you remember me? It is I. And now we are together because on that day we had to part so soon."

*Argia tries to push her away.*

THE QUEEN  Don't push me away from you; oh, please let me stay like this for a moment. (*She laughs.*) Treat me like a frightened animal who has sought refuge in your lap. That does happen sometimes. Hold me and stroke me. (*She clasps Argia tightly.*) What is your name?

ARGIA  Argia.

THE QUEEN  I feel as if I were being re-born, here, in your arms. (*She starts.*) What's that? Was it the signal?

ARGIA  No, not yet.

THE QUEEN  But please tell me: are you sure the man who is going to come with me up the mountain is really to be trusted? Can I really be sure of him? When we get to one of those dark gullies in the hills, he won't leap at me and cut my throat, will he?

ARGIA  No. No.

THE QUEEN  Don't, don't think I don't trust you. It's only that it is so difficult to shake off the terror. Through the whole of these years I've been haunted by only one single thought: the horrible tortures they do . . . My God, they put people to inhuman horrors: did you know that? I have a poison with me . . . but I can never be sure if I shall be able to swallow it in time. I always used to imagine that dreadful moment: a man looking at me . . . turning round to look at me . . . then a glint in his eye . . . and I was recognized . . . lost. That's why I've . . . oh, dearest Argia, please forgive me! But you said yourself we were women together . . . (*Whispers.*) Sometimes a man has stared hard at me . . . a peasant, or a herdsman, or a woodman . . . I've given myself to him! Given myself! I'm no longer either a queen or a woman. (*Weeping and laughing.*) I'm like a terrified animal running this way and that. Argia: I've had a baby too, up in the mountains. You're the first person I've ever told.

ARGIA  Is that why you're going? You want to see the baby again?

THE QUEEN  Oh no! No! No! Why should I want to see him? Why should I love him? No, no, he only pursues me like all the rest. I'm running away from him as well. I don't want to see him. He can only be another threat to me. Let him stay where he is, and grow up in peace. (*She bursts into sobs.*) And may God forgive all of us.

ARGIA  Don't shake like that, my dear. Try and be calm. You'll be all right.

THE QUEEN (*whispering and laughing*)  Argia, I even think I'm . . . pregnant again. I keep feeling so hungry the whole time.

ARGIA (*looks at her, and gently strokes her face*)  You're covered in sweat. Wipe your face.

*The hoot of an owl is heard outside.*

THE QUEEN (*starting*)  That's the signal, isn't it? And now I have to go.

ARGIA  Wait a moment.

*The signal is heard again.*

THE QUEEN  Yes, it's the signal. Good-bye, Argia. Let me kiss you. (*She kisses Argia and gets ready to go to the door.*)

ARGIA  Wait.

THE QUEEN  Why do you say wait?

ARGIA  I didn't explain properly. That's not the way you must go out. They'll shoot you, if you go through that door.

THE QUEEN  What then?

ARGIA  It's through this other door. You must go through here. I've thought of a better plan.

THE QUEEN  How?

ARGIA  I'll push the door open on this side . . . oh, there won't be any danger. All I'll have to do is to push the door; they're such fools, they'll fire at once. The men on guard over that side will run round as soon as they hear the noise.

That other door will be unprotected. You must seize the moment, and get away.

THE QUEEN    Shall I find the man there—the man who's to go with me?

ARGIA    No. Make for the mountains by yourself. You were probably right, it's safer that way.

*The signal is heard again.*

ARGIA (*pointing*)    Stand ready, over there. Quietly.

*The Queen fumbles for a moment, and gives Argia a ring.*

THE QUEEN    This was the last burden I had . . .

ARGIA (*putting it on*)    It's tight on me. So I shan't lose it.

*The Queen goes and stands ready near one of the doors. Argia puts out the lamp; takes a pole, makes a sign of encouragement to the Queen, and goes cautiously over to the other door. She moves the door with the pole, and suddenly throws it wide open. A deafening burst of machine-gun fire splinters the door. Argia laughs silently. She makes a sign to the Queen.*

ARGIA    Now! Go . . . Good-bye.

*The Queen slips out. Argia stands waiting.*

VOICES (*outside*)    On guard! On guard, there! Look out!

MAUPA (*coming in with his gun in his hands: to Argia*)    Don't you move!

ARGIA    You're irresistible.

MAUPA    And don't speak.

ARGIA    Oh, I wouldn't know what to say to you, anyway.

VOICES (*distant*)    On guard! On guard!

ANOTHER VOICE    On guard!

RAIM (*enters breathlessly*)    What's the matter?

MAUPA    This woman was trying to escape.

RAIM    My dear fellow . . . haven't you made a mistake?

MAUPA    I tell you she tried to get away! Perhaps you doubt my word?

RAIM    No, no. I'm sure you're right.

MAUPA    You watch her. I'll go and call the others. (*He goes out.*)

RAIM (*greatly agitated*)    What's happened? Where is she?

ARGIA   Gone.

RAIM   What have you done, you fool? And what are you going to tell them now?

ARGIA   I shall think up something; don't worry.

RAIM   Just you see you don't bring me into it . . . You needn't count on me . . . You'll get yourself out of it, I don't doubt . . . (*He breaks off at the sound of footsteps; turns to the newcomers; and says with emphasis.*) Sir, this woman was trying to run away.

AMOS   (*has entered, followed by Maupa. He turns quietly to him*) Friend, will you please point that gun downwards? We've no need of it.

*Maupa does so.*

AMOS   (*to Raim*)   And you, will you give the lady a seat?

*Raim does so.*

AMOS   (*politely to Argia*)   Will you please sit down, madam? You wanted to go out?

ARGIA   I was thirsty.

AMOS   Ah, that explains it. You'll forgive us. At all events the incident has one good side to it. It offers us (*he points to Biante, who is coming in supported by the Porter*) an opportunity of asking you to be good enough to grant us an interview . . . which I hope will be quiet and friendly. It's an opportunity I was looking for during the whole of our journey.

BIANTE   (*coming forward and shouting*)   Light! Light! We might as well be in a cave! Bring some candles and lamps! Give us some illumination worthy of our cause.

*Raim, Maupa, and the Porter have already rushed out to fetch lights from the neighboring rooms. The first to return is the Porter, with a strong lamp. Its light falls on Argia. There is a moment of curious silence.*

AMOS   (*to Argia*)   Madam: what is your name?

CURTAIN

# ACT THREE

*Only a few seconds have gone by. Raim, Maupa, and the Porter are still bringing in lamps, and arranging the room. Then they all sit. Argia is standing in the midst of them.*

AMOS  Well?

ARGIA  (*with hostile indifference*)  You will find my name, and everything else about me, in my documents. I have already been questioned once this evening, with the other travelers. Is this extra honor reserved for me alone?

AMOS  Madam: we have to ask you for a little further information.

ARGIA  There is no need to address me as madam. I'm only one of those very common plants you naturally find growing on the manure heap of three wars.

AMOS  What is your nationality?

ARGIA  I was born in this country. And from that day to this, people like you have done nothing but repatriate me, expel me, deport me, search me, give me notice to quit; and so forth.

AMOS  (*coldly polite*)  You sound as though you considered *us* responsible for all that.

ARGIA  Well, what are you doing now, if not giving orders? There are a great number of people in the world who've made it their job to decide what the rest of us have to do. Congratulations. You might tell me what it feels like.

AMOS  Have you never known what it feels like?

ARGIA  I? (*She pauses a moment, surprised.*) I? (*With a shrug.*) I've always been one of the people who take orders, not give them. It's my job to be here submitting to them, at this time of night; when I'm dropping with fatigue.

AMOS  Political necessities.

ARGIA  Ah, yes, political necessities: they're the reason we're forbidden to eat what we choose, every other day; the reason we're forbidden to go to bed when we're tired, or to light the fire when we're cold. "Every time is the decisive time." And how brazen you all are about it! It's been going on since Adam. Political necessities.

AMOS  Have you never used those words on your own behalf?

ARGIA (*surprised*)  I? My dear friend—you will forgive the expression—I've already told you that I've never done anything very useful or respectable in the whole of my life. Satisfied?

AMOS  What occupations have you followed up till now?

ARGIA  Oh, various ones. What I could pick up. You, and others like you, have always been so busy shouting that I've never had much chance to think about my own condition. There have been times when I've not been sorry if I could find someone willing to pay for my lunch or my dinner.

AMOS  Can you prove that?

ARGIA  Witnesses? Certainly, darling, certainly. Lots of men know me. I can prove it whenever I like.

BIANTE (*sneering: his voice is like a death rattle*)  Have you any distinguishing marks on your body to prove your identity? Little things . . . that might have struck the attention of the men who paid for your lunches and dinners?

ARGIA (*after a pause; in a low voice*)  Yes. Men like you, and men even more repellent than you, if possible, have seen me and made use of me. That is what I am.

AMOS (*quieting Biante with a gesture*)  You don't seem to like us very much. Is there any special reason for that?

ARGIA  Yes: I always dislike the authorities: people who walk over our faces the whole time; and have rather a heavy tread.

AMOS (*still politely*)  Madam: I should perhaps convey to you some idea of the impression you are creating.

ARGIA  Well?

AMOS  The sharpness of your answers is in rather striking contrast with the humble condition you declare yourself to be in. And the bluntness you attempt to give those answers is in equally striking contrast with your obvious refinement and breeding.

ARGIA (*after a pause*)  Refinement and breeding? In me? You think I look . . . ? (*She laughs.*) How nice. You're trying to make love to me.

AMOS  I also have the impression that the liveliness of your behavior is largely due to your need to conceal a certain amount of fear.

ARGIA  Fear? I?

AMOS   Yes.

ARGIA   Fear of whom? Of you? I realize that the contempt people feel for you makes you try and console yourselves with the idea that everyone's frightened of you. But I'm not frightened of you; why should I be? I've told you what I am. And I can prove it, whenever I choose.

BIANTE   Why not now?

ARGIA   Because just at the moment, I happen to be enjoying myself. Yes, it's odd, isn't it? I'm actually enjoying myself.

BIANTE   Let's hope you go on enjoying yourself.

AMOS (*imperturbably*)   If your insolence fails to conceal your fear, your fear seems to be equally unsuccessful in curbing your insolence.

ARGIA (*ironically*)   I wonder why?

AMOS   Pride.

ARGIA   You think I'm proud, do you?

AMOS   Yes: with a pride which won't even listen to your own common sense when it warns you. You are scarcely even taking the trouble to lie successfully. What you would really like at this moment is to tell us you despise us.

ARGIA (*taking out a cigarette*)   As a matter of fact, it does strike me as slightly unnatural that people like you should give yourselves airs.

BIANTE   You'd better be careful, my dear; he was trained for the priesthood.

AMOS   An ancient pride which has soaked right through to your veins. Footsteps, used to the echo of surroundings where the press of the crowd is unknown. Hands, accustomed always to holding bright and precious objects; a voice that never had any need to raise itself in order to call for silence.

ARGIA (*after a moment's reflection*)   And that's what your intuition tells you about me, is it? All that?

AMOS   Madam, you are doing yourself a great deal of harm by lying to us. Suppose you come down to earth? Where were you born?

ARGIA (*is silent for a moment; then she laughs, and shrugging her shoulders, says with insulting sarcasm*)   I was born in one of the finest mansions in the city. I won't say whether it was on the first floor, or in the porter's lodge. In my room, when I woke, I always saw nymphs on the walls. The tapestries had hung there for five hundred years. Yes, you are right: I did, indeed, grow up among people who were silent the minute I indicated that I was about to speak. And when they answered me, it was always in pleasant voices, saying pleasant things. (*Mockingly.*) I walked on carpets as large as a village square! The doors were always opened for me! The rooms were always heated; I have always been sensitive to the cold. The food was excellent; I have always been rather greedy. My dear friend, you should have seen the table-cloths, and the silver! The crystal goblets I used to drink from!

AMOS    And all this good fortune cost *you* very little trouble.

ARGIA (*in satirically affected tones*)    We don't ask the rose what trouble it has taken: we ask it simply to be a rose: and to be as different as it can from an artichoke. They used to bring me whatever I wanted on beautiful carved trays; then they would bow and retire, always turning at the door and bowing once again before they went out. (*Indicating her cigarette.*) Do you mind?

AMOS (*going across and lighting it*)    And why did you insist on their doing all that?

ARGIA    I didn't insist. They wanted to. And you know, I think you too, if I were to smile at you, would also wag your tails. But no, the price would be too high: for me, I mean. Your arrogance is simply your way of bolstering yourselves up. And I . . . (*She breaks off.*)

AMOS (*in lighting the cigarette, has noticed the ring*)    That's a very beautiful ring you have there.

ARGIA (*tries to remove it, but cannot*)    It won't come off. (*Lightly*) I've been wearing it too long. It's a family heirloom. (*She looks for a moment at them all; then laughs, with mocking bitterness.*) Yes; in my time, I've been a proud woman . . . rich . . . highly respected, elegant, happy . . . fortunate . . .

AMOS (*coldly*)    And your political opinions?

ARGIA    I'm not interested in politics.

AMOS    But at least you prefer one party to the other?

ARGIA    Do you?

AMOS    Yes.

ARGIA    Then I prefer the opposite one.

AMOS   Why?

ARGIA   For the simple reason that I don't like the way you behave. You strut about a great deal too much. (*With derisive affectation.*) You see, ever since I was a child I have been brought up to respect people of a very different sort from you. People who washed properly, and wore clean-smelling linen. Perhaps there's some political significance in that? I can't believe that an unpleasant smell gives people special rights. Or perhaps the revolution has a smell?

BIANTE   The smell of bitter soup in the people's tenements.

ARGIA   (*affectedly*)   I'm sorry. I have never smelt it. I think you probably give yourselves too much work to do; you smell of sweat.

AMOS   The stonebreakers and the poor who follow us have less delicate nostrils.

ARGIA   That must be very sad for them.

BIANTE   (*with painful vehemence*)   Tomorrow we shall have no stonebreakers and no poor!

ARGIA   (*insolently*)   We shall have other troubles. Otherwise what would *you* do? You canalize people's miseries. You turn them first into envy, then into fury. The thick rind of bad temper on the world has grown a great deal thicker since you began to cultivate it. The number of the dead has grown too. And all your great ideas don't prevent a distinct smell of blood rising from you.

BIANTE   Amos, for God's sake!

AMOS   (*cutting him short*)   Do you realize where all these questions are leading?

ARGIA   Yes.

AMOS   Is there anyone here who can identify you?

ARGIA   Certainly. Otherwise I would hardly be taking such risks.

AMOS   Who is it?

ARGIA   I'll tell you later. The night is long . . . and so is the mountain road. Provided *you* have the time to spare . . .

*A Soldier has entered, and has whispered something into Biante's ear.*

ARGIA   . . . though they do say that gunfire can be heard round about. Bad news? Is that what's worrying you?

AMOS   Don't hope for miracles; they don't happen any more.

BIANTE  Stop it, Amos, make her talk, for God's sake! Make her talk, I'm in a hurry! My body's burning as if it would set the whole bloody world on fire.

ARGIA  (*insolently*)  Moderate your voice, please. (*Suddenly and passionately.*) If I were the Queen . . . If I were the Queen, do you know what I would say to you at this moment? (*In a manner not devoid of majesty.*) I'd say: "Gentlemen." (*She drops back into a more normal tone, but soon returns to her former manner.*) "Gentlemen, you are angry with me; but I am not angry with you. Neither the power you have usurped, nor your threats, are capable of disturbing me. We are far apart. It is that that makes you boil with rage; and keeps me calm."

AMOS  If you're not the Queen, I'm bound to say you give a very good imitation of the haughty way in which she'd behave on an occasion like this.

ARGIA  The reason is that I've been rehearsing this role for a very long time. Every time any one has been rude to me—and that can happen to anyone, can't it?—every time I've come away with my cheeks still burning, what scathing retorts, what tremendous, noble answers I've always imagined! I know everything a woman of spirit can say to put the insolent in their places. . . .

*The noise of hoarse voices begins to be heard outside.*

ARGIA  (*continues passionately*)  And if I were the Queen I'd say to you: "It's true, gentlemen, there was no mob round me, there was space. The echo used to carry my words on high and purify them . . . make them lonely; and calm. The echo used to liberate them . . . (*Slightly intoxicated by her own words, she plays with the echo.*) Re . . . gi . . . na . . . It made them mount upward . . . up . . . on high . . . high . . . high . . . it wanted them to be calm and just . . . Re . . . gi . . . na . . ."

*They have all, one after another, stood up; they stand listening to that echo, and to the distant voices.*

BIANTE  (*suddenly*)  What's happening? What's the matter, out there? Who are those people coming up the road? Why are we wasting time? My fever's getting worse; I'm burning all over. What are our weapons for? Yes, we do need dead people! What are we waiting for? Are you waiting till I'm dead here in the middle of them? (*To the Porter.*) What's going on out there?

THE PORTER (*has been out; and now re-enters, distressed*) General Biante and Commissar Amos! Something's happening. The road out there is black with people.

BIANTE  Who are they?

THE PORTER  The people living in the upper valley. They must have got to hear about this woman, they must have heard she'd been caught, and they've come down under cover of the dark.

ARGIA  I told you, did I not, that your power was only provisional?

*Biante is already hobbling quickly out. Amos, Raim and Maupa follow him.*

THE PORTER (*remains alone with Argia. He looks at her; and suddenly, with impulsive reverence, takes off his cap; he is at once ashamed of himself, and pretends to be looking at a sheet of paper on the table beside him. As though reading from the paper: in a low voice*) There are a great many cowards in this world, who are so frightened that they hide their true feelings; and I am the lowest and most cowardly of them all. But for us, more than for others, what comfort and healing it brings, to know that there is someone . . . (*his eyes do not move from the sheet of paper, but his voice rises slightly*) . . . there is someone who is still unafraid, and can stand alone against all the rest! What consolation, for us in our shame, to think that in a soul shaped like our own, everything that in us is ruined, stays faithful and untarnished! To know that such a creature has drawn breath in this world! I believe that even God Himself, hearing her speak, is proud of her. And whoever shall think of her, though it be a thousand years from now, shall feel once more upon his face a look of dignity. (*His voice has become louder, but his eyes have never once raised themselves from the sheet of paper.*)

*Maupa and Raim come in, holding the door open for Biante.*

BIANTE (*goes up to Argia, and suddenly bursts into a laugh*) Hahaha! Your Majesty! Yes, your famous name has

brought a lot of people down from the mountains to meet
you. Do you know what sort of help they're bringing you?
Do you know what they want? (*Almost casually.*) To see you
condemned to death and hanged.

MAUPA (*with quiet ecstasy*)   We want to see the color of the
Queen's entrails.

AMOS (*entering and raising his hand*)   There will be a proper trial.
Otherwise we should be showing very little trust in our own
purpose.

BIANTE (*shouting*)   Proper trial! Formal procedure! To hell
with this chattering. I've no time to waste. I can't feel my
own hands any more; I can hardly keep my eyes open.

AMOS   A jury will sit. (*To Maupa.*) You: Go and bring some of
those people in here.

BIANTE (*to Maupa, as he goes out*)   And choose people who look
sensible, and keep their eyes on the ground!

AMOS   Peasants merely: but now they have authority: opti-
mists, and the world is full of them; in revolutions they are
manna dropped from heaven. Every one of them believes
that the sickle will cut the whole meadow but will stop a
quarter of an inch short of his own throat.

BIANTE   And the jury ought to have a few beggars on it as
well . . .

AMOS   . . . a few people who are stupid and lazy, and
imagine that a change in the insignia over the doors will
give them the reward of the industrious and the intelligent . . .

*A number of peasants, men and women, have entered. The Engineer is
among them.*

BIANTE (*to the newcomers*)   Come in, my friends! Sit down. You
already know that I have taken over the command. That
means that everybody can kill a man, but I can do it with a
roll of drums, like an acrobat making a difficult leap. The
republic has conquered. (*He beats his fist on the table.*) Well
then, I preside! (*To Amos.*) You shall be the accuser! (*To
Raim.*) You shall write. (*To the newcomers.*) You shall judge!
(*Lowering his voice.*) And after that, I, as president, if I'm still
alive, shall carry out the sentence. You can begin, Amos.

*Amos has already risen: he speaks in the tones of a chancellor reading out an act.*

AMOS   The accusation charges this woman with having concealed her identity, and falsified her papers.

ARGIA   Gentlemen! Please, please listen to me. I came up here . . .

AMOS   . . . with the intention of fleeing the country? Or to try to discover the whereabouts of your son? Yes, madam, we are fully informed about that also. Your son. (*His voice slightly rising.*) She is also accused of having formerly exercised a secret and illicit influence on the heads of the state, inducing them to enact factious and oppressive laws. . . .

BIANTE   Oh, get on with it, Amos! You're cold, you've got no guts! You're just being cruel!

AMOS   (*louder*)   . . . of inciting to massacre and persecution . . .

ARGIA   But I have never done anything of the kind!

AMOS   . . . of having fomented conspiracies aimed at undermining the authority of the state. . . .

ARGIA   But that's what you've done! And you blame it on the Queen! *You* were the sowers of discord.

AMOS   (*louder*)   . . . to the point of inducing a number of fanatics to take up arms against their country.

ARGIA   But I . . .

AMOS   This woman is accused of having herself unloosed the present conflict; of having herself driven it to atrocious excesses. She herself summoned to this country foreign armed forces, herself lit the fires that now smoke from every point of the horizon, herself disfigured the dead along the roads. . . .

ARGIA   But I tell you I . . .

AMOS   . . . didn't know? Didn't want it?

ARGIA   I tell you that my hands . . .

AMOS   Are clean? Is that it? That only shows how cunning you've been. It deprives you of extenuating circumstances, if there ever were any.

THE ENGINEER   (*suddenly and violently*)   I was walking in the street one day; there was a cordon of soldiers; and they said to me: "Not this way, the Queen will be coming down here." I went round another way, and they told me: "You can't come through here." Everywhere I went, it was the same. Madam, you were always in the way.

ARGIA    Friends, friends, but I was there too, with you: on your side of the cordon, not the other.

A PEASANT WOMAN (*suddenly bursting into sobs*)    The shirt I washed for my son, he said it was shabby. He said the soup I cooked for him tasted nasty. And now they've told me that he's lying out there, in the fields, with his arms wide-open, covered with ants. It's all the Queen's fault.

ARGIA    You stone that woman now, only because you one day fawned on her!

A PEASANT (*violently*)    When our children are old enough to play games, they're not allowed to play the same games as rich men's children. That's a terrible thing! That's what poisons their minds!

THE PEASANT WOMAN    My son hated the earthen crockery; he hated the smell of our home; he hated his own life!

THE PEASANT    My daughter went away with the soldiers, and I haven't heard a word of her since. That was your fault!

THE WOMAN    It was your fault!

BIANTE    All of you! All of you! Bear witness, all of you!

THE ENGINEER    It was her fault!

MAUPA    It was her fault!

OTHERS    Her fault! It was her fault!

BIANTE    And what about you? That porter over there! Are you the only one with nothing to say?

*A silence.*

THE PORTER    Yes . . . everything she did . . . humiliated us.

ARGIA (*rebelliously, to the Porter*)    And who was it who taught you humiliation and envy? Who was it who let your rancor loose?

AMOS (*with sudden intensity*)    You, the apex of privilege, the symbol of prerogative; you, the emblem of those distinctions from which humiliation and rivalry were born. Your whole authority is based and built upon inequality. It is in you that injustice is personified, it is in you she finds her arrogant features, her scornful voice, her contemptuous answers, her sumptuous clothes, and her unsoiled hands. Your name of Queen is of itself enough to make men see that they are unequal: on one side vast revenues, on the other, vast burdens. You are the hook from which the great act of tyranny hangs. The world will be a less unhappy place when you have vanished from it.

ARGIA (*remains for a long moment with her head bent*)    Forgive me. I have been play-acting a little: perhaps too much. Now I will tell you the truth. I can prove that I am not the Queen, and I can prove it at once. There is someone here who can witness for me.

BIANTE    Who is it?

ARGIA    That man over there, your interpreter. Stop, Raim, don't run away. He knows me only too well. He knows I'm not a queen. I'm the sort of woman who has to smile at lodging-house keepers, and traffic in pawn tickets.

RAIM (*comes forward slowly, in silence*)    There must be some misunderstanding. This woman must be mad. I've never seen her before in my life.

ARGIA    Look at me, Raim.

RAIM    I am looking at you. (*To Amos.*) I've never seen her before.

ARGIA (*turning to the others*)    My friend is frightened things may have gone too far. Whether I'm the Queen or not, or he's my friend or not, he's afraid you just have to have a certain number of people to shoot, up here. He just wants to stay alive, that's all.

RAIM    I knew you'd say that. But I must insist that I do not know you.

ARGIA    Gentlemen! I and this man, who "doesn't know" me, kept each other warm all through one whole winter!

RAIM    Rubbish!

ARGIA    I came up here solely to look for him. There are people here who saw us talking.

RAIM (*to the others*)    Of course they did. I tried to approach her: because I thought she looked suspicious. I don't know who she is. I'm sorry, madam, but I can't help you.

*He moves away, disappearing among the others. Argia stands for a moment in silence.*

ARGIA (*almost absently*)  Perhaps it's true. Perhaps that man and I never did know one another. But, even so, gentlemen, that doesn't give you the right to make stupid mistakes. If you have to have a corpse to show people, when you tell them the Queen's dead, you might at least look for a corpse a bit more like her. You fools! I, the Queen? Is mine the voice of a queen . . . ? Has my life been the life of a queen . . . ? (*Suddenly calling.*) Raim! Raim! Call him back!

AMOS  I'd like to bet that your friend is far away by now; and making for the mountains like a hare.

ARGIA (*bewildered*)  Gentlemen, there is someone else who can witness for me. There were two women travelers in this room. I . . . and another woman.

AMOS (*amiably*)  Yes. (*He makes a sign to one of the soldiers, who at once goes out.*)

ARGIA  . . . a peasant woman.

AMOS (*amiably*)  Yes. And where is she now?

ARGIA  She ran away. But she can't be far off. That woman . . . can tell you . . . that I'm not what you think. And you will have what you want, just the same. Send out and look for her.

AMOS  Up in the mountains?

ARGIA  Yes.

AMOS  All you can say of your witnesses, is that one is fleeing and the other has fled. (*A pause.*) Madam, we have a surprise for you. (*A pause.*) Your peasant woman is here. She didn't get very far. Here she is.

*In a great silence the Queen appears, escorted by the soldier. The Queen, pale and rather stiff, looks round her. Amos points to Argia. The Queen comes forward to Argia; and speaks to her with a slight stammer.*

THE QUEEN  Forgive me, my dear . . . it was all no use . . . I knew they'd have caught me . . . The moment I was so frightened of . . . arrived . . . But I don't think . . . they've caught me in time . . . to hurt me. I managed to fool them . . . you know how . . . I prefer it . . . to be all over at once. Good-bye, my dearest friend. I was so afraid . . . but not so much, now. (*She sways, and sinks slowly to the ground.*)

BIANTE  What's the matter?

ARGIA (*kneels down beside the Queen, and takes her hand. After a while she looks up, and says, as though lost in thought*) She carried poison with her. (*A pause.*) You have killed her.

AMOS (*cutting her short*) You are now completely without accomplices. Say something, why don't you?

BIANTE (*shouting*) You've no-one left now!

AMOS  It's all over with you, your majesty! Answer us! You are the Queen!

ARGIA (*rises slowly*) Not every eye shall look to the ground. There shall still be someone to stand before you. Yes. I am the Queen!

*A silence.*

BIANTE  She's confessed, Amos. Quick, make your speech for the prosecution.

AMOS (*rises, and thinks for a moment*) If friction is to be stopped, the only way is to remove the cause; if disturbances are to be brought to an end, the only way is to eliminate the disturber. I see only one way to make such eliminations final.

*The witnesses, perturbed by the decision by which they are to be faced, rise cautiously, first one, then another, trying to efface themselves.*

AMOS  No other method is known whereby revolutions may be at once prudent and rapid; nor any other argument that makes them so persuasive; nor any procedure which more effectively seals dangerous lips and more finally immobilizes enemy hands.

*The witnesses have cautiously moved towards the door, but at this point Amos's look arrests them.*

AMOS (*continuing*) Such a method serves also, among other things, to identify the weak pillars; in fact, you will notice that some of our jurymen who have divined the responsibility that is about to face them are cautiously trying to slip away one by one: they do not realize that, in the course of time, that may render them also liable to furnish proofs of the excellence of the method. It is quite true that the importance of a revolution is in proportion to the number of dead it produces. Biante, it is your duty to pronounce sentence.

BIANTE *(exhausted and swaying, rises, supported by Maupa)* The revolution has decided that the Queen must die. I order . . . I order . . . *(He cannot go on, he has come to the end: Maupa lifts him back into his chair.)*

AMOS You are no longer in a position to give orders. Your post is vacant. *(He turns to the others.)* The revolution has decided that the Queen must die. The sentence will be carried out during the course of the night.

CURTAIN

## ACT FOUR

*A short time has elapsed since the previous act. Argia is dozing. In the background, a soldier is asleep on a wooden chair. Amos comes in: he shakes the soldier, and sends him away. Then he wakes Argia.*

AMOS I've come to inform you that the sentence must be carried out very shortly. The messenger who is to take the news of the execution to my government must leave during the night. In fact, we all have to leave this area before morning, for unexpected military reasons.

ARGIA *(half-absently)* Yes.

AMOS I also have to tell you that you can discount any possibility of rescue. Any move on the part of the Coalitionists would be ineffective: arrangements have already been made to carry out the sentence at the first alarm.

ARGIA Was this the only reason you came to see me?

AMOS No. On the contrary. There is a much more important reason. In fact, you may regard everything that has happened so far tonight as a mere preamble to what I have to tell you now.

ARGIA Well?

AMOS Do you really think the revolution would have given so much of its time to your frivolities this evening, and taken so much trouble to give an appearance of legality to the trial, if we had no precise aim in mind?

ARGIA Well: what is it?

AMOS   The revolution intends to be irreproachable right to the end. I have come to tell you that you are free to ask for pardon.

ARGIA   From whom?

AMOS   From us. Will you ask for it?

ARGIA   (*after a pause*)   I will ask for it.

AMOS   Good. The coldness of the night seems to have brought you to your senses. (*He sits.*) Naturally the pardon is dependent on certain conditions.

ARGIA   What are they?

AMOS   Formal ones. Futile even. Before I disclose them to you, I would like you to realize exactly what would happen to you in the event of the pardon being refused. The human mind often seeks refuge in vagueness. However: outside this building is a stone platform. On it, when you went out, you would see six armed soldiers. You would then go and stand in front of them. You would fall. A short while after, the sunrise would illuminate a universe in all respects as usual, except that you would not be there. That is all.

ARGIA   The conditions.

AMOS   The signing of a list of declarations concerning the events of the last few years. The witnesses are ready. (*He turns to the door.*) Come in.

*The Porter and Maupa come in and remain in the background.*

ARGIA   What sort of declarations?

AMOS   Saying that you acknowledge that you have conspired, etcetera, have summoned foreign help against your country, etcetera, and confess yourself guilty of illegal actions, dishonorable conduct, etcetera.

ARGIA   (*almost indifferently*)   They sound like lies to me.

AMOS   You will also be required to give us certain information. But that we can go into later.

ARGIA   Is the paper ready?

AMOS   Here it is.

*He makes a sign, and the Porter approaches Argia with a paper in his hand. She turns, and sees him; she has stretched out her hand; now she withdraws it. The Porter puts the paper in her hand.*

AMOS   I forgot to give you one other piece of news. The flight of your accomplice—the so-called interpreter, I mean—was unsuccessful. They had to fire at him; I am afraid he was seriously wounded. In the hope of surviving and winning our clemency, he employed his last moments in betraying you even more comprehensively than he had done before. He confirmed all the allegations made in that document.

ARGIA (*thoughtfully*) Poor Raim. His eyes were a nice color; it was pleasant to look into them. How terribly concerned he was to keep them open on the world. In vain, apparently. Good-bye, Raim. This wind is carrying all the leaves away.

AMOS Yes, madam. It's the time of year. Whole gatherings of people who yesterday sat in gilded halls, could today reassemble in hell with no one missing. Your other accomplice, the peasant woman, was at least able to say good-bye to you.

ARGIA (*thoughtfully*) She was so terrified; so very unpractical. She wanted to sleep, night after night, in peace. Good-bye.

AMOS I mean that you are now alone. But alive, luckily for you. Try and remain so. In times like these, and at so small a cost (*pointing to the paper*), it's a good bargain.

ARGIA To tell you the truth, I scarcely know any longer whether I want to make a good bargain or not. (*She takes an uncertain step forward; sees the Porter staring at her; and stands still again.*) But, Commissar Amos, you must really think me very simple, if you imagine you can deceive me so easily. No, I know as well as you do that there is no way out of this. (*She gives back the paper to Amos.*) To survive and to be able to describe such things would be hard enough, even for your witnesses. And think who the chief character is. No. It wouldn't be a very clever move on your part to allow the Queen to go free, so that the common people could come and kiss the hem of her garments while she described to them how you forced her signature from her.

AMOS A reasonable objection. We had thought of it already. It also explains your courage earlier this evening . . . (*with a faint suggestion of bitterness*) a courage which would have been a very humiliating slap in the face for us, if we hadn't been aware how gratuitous and false and easy it was: as courage usually is, in my opinion. Madam: you thought then that everything was lost already; so your fine gestures cost you nothing. Very well. I've come to tell you that in fact nothing is lost, so far as you're concerned. The revolution has an interest in keeping you alive. (*A pause.*) Alive, and in circulation. Alive . . . (*almost casually*) and in disgrace. Confess. And first you'll be despised; then ignored. And then: no longer a queen, but a woman: a woman, no longer walking on fine soft carpets, but huddled on the hard floor of an all-night bar, learning the pleading smiles of poverty . . .

ARGIA (*lost in her recollections*) . . . listening to the cheap jokes of the bar-man, with an anxious smile on her face; soothing and flattering the bad-tempered taxi driver . . . (*The eye of the Porter is on her.*) But who, who on earth, could ever conceive that a woman of such birth and spirit, stainless and honorable, could foul herself by signing such a document? They'll never be willing to believe that.

AMOS They will have to believe it. We shall give them the proof. I've already told you that you will furnish us with certain information, information you alone possess. On that information we shall act. And the world will be compelled to realize that it was you who gave it to us.

ARGIA (*with melancholy indifference*) . . . And so . . . poor Queen in disgrace . . . you spare her, and the others cut her throat; her friends.

AMOS At least it would be time gained. Unless—and this is the point—some of the others, your friends, I mean . . . (*Breaking off: to Maupa.*) You go outside.

*Maupa goes out.*

AMOS (*to the Porter*) You wait over there. (*He turns back to Argia.*) I was speaking about the others, your friends: in order that we can take steps to protect you and save you from them, (*dropping his voice*) you will tell us their names. (*With a sudden cry, pointing a finger at her.*) Yes! You know them! I saw it! I read it there, in your eyes! They glinted. You've seen the way to save yourself. And you know you have it there at your disposal: inside your head. (*Persuasively.*) Well, then, first: it's clearly in the interest of the revolution to keep you alive so that respect for you shall die out. Secondly: it's indispensable that the revolution shall know the names of your accomplices. The two things fit together; and save you. Your disclosures will be the beginning of a great clean-up. There are cold-blooded vipers lying curled up in our very beds. Illustrious personages and obscure imbeciles. Even here, a short time ago; it was quite clear that your fine speeches were directed to someone's ears. They will all be rendered permanently harmless. (*His voice drops to a whisper.*) Who are they? Where are they? What are their names? Quickly: tell me their names.

ARGIA (*stands for a moment with bent head*)  Your voice went very quiet when you asked me for them, didn't it? If it made you feel sick to ask for them, what do you suppose I should feel if I were to divulge them? (*With a wan smile.*) It's obviously not a thing to be very proud of. And unfortunately, I don't know any names.

AMOS  You not only know them; you've already wisely decided to disclose them to me. However, you will no doubt make me wait a little for them; that was to be expected, and I shall not refuse to indulge you. It's a due one has to pay to the concept of honor. You merely want to be persuaded.

ARGIA (*with a wan smile*)  The men you want me to hand over to you certainly never expected this as their reward.

AMOS  Those men have simply staked everything on one card. In their complete selfishness, they were prepared to make use of you. Do you know any of them personally; or feel affection for any of them? No. Bonds of gratitude? No. (*Ironically.*) Is it for some political ideal that you are prepared to sacrifice yourself?

ARGIA (*almost absently*)  I know very little about such things; I've told you that before.

AMOS  Or perhaps the thought of your good name is holding you back? The little plaster figure of your reputation crashing in pieces? Madam: don't take any notice of cant-phrases; follow nature: which fears death, and knows nothing else. Only thus will you be sincere, and therefore honorable. After all, the finest reputation in the world is very little comfort to a corpse.

ARGIA (*thoughtfully*)  Yes.

AMOS  Good. (*Although the room is almost empty, and the silence in it is absolute.*) Well, then, gentlemen, silence! The Queen is deciding.

*A silence.*

ARGIA   So my decisions can actually make people hold their breath. Messengers are getting ready to announce them beyond the mountains.

AMOS   That does not, however, give you one minute's extra time. (*He calls.*) Maupa!

MAUPA (*appearing in the doorway*)   Everything is ready.

AMOS (*dismissing him with a wave*)   Good. Tell them to wait.

ARGIA   I am a person who can make people wait. It's the first time that's ever happened to me. I can say yes: I can say no.

AMOS   You have very little time left, madam.

ARGIA   Do not try to hurry the Queen. The Queen. I am only just beginning to realize what it means to be one.

AMOS   It means obeying a few flatterers in order to rule over many subjects.

ARGIA   Not at all. To be a queen really means: to be alone. It means: to have gone on ahead, to have left everyone else behind. Enemies, friends: all gone. A great simplicity. This room is indeed a palace; your aversion from me is only a form of respect; you are only a rebel subject. I can say yes; I can say no.

AMOS   At a price, however.

ARGIA   It is the only one I can pay. (*She suddenly shivers with cold.*) And suppose I decide to pay it? I am free: to say yes, or no. And no one in the world can do anything about it. I am the one who decides. It's beautiful; to be able to talk to you like this; to look about me like this . . . and to feel my breathing so free, and the beating of my heart so peaceful.

*Amos has taken up the cloak left by the soldier, and places it round her shoulders.*

AMOS   You are shivering.

ARGIA   It is the cold that announces the dawn. The only thing I am afraid of is getting tired; it's been a wearing night. (*A pause.*) I don't even feel dislike towards you.

AMOS   The technique of pride, is it not? The technique of pride. (*With sudden anger.*) But pride is not flesh and blood, madam! The chosen creature's superiority with which you think you can even now keep us at a distance! But it's not your flesh and blood! It's a shell! A crust, that's all. Born of habit. Like the hardness of the hands of a peasant. But you haven't earned it by digging. It's come to you from the bowings and scrapings of a whole palace all round you since the day you were born! Give me those names. Firmness, honor, eyes that never lower themselves, the technique of pride: I'd like to know what would be left of all that, if you'd had to live in some of the places I've known, and cooked yourself an egg over a spirit lamp, and gone out of an evening in a greasy overcoat, with a nice smile ready to try and soften the man at the dairy. Yes, yes, our eyes can't look at people as yours do . . . even our thoughts, here inside us, are a bit grubby, and shabby, and common, and bruised by rubbing shoulders with the crowd . . . But don't try to imagine they are so very different from your own. Just lift the curtain a little. Come on, give me the names. If I were to twist your wrist, you'd scream like the rest of us! Your majesty, have you ever seen the little white grubs in rotten meat? They suddenly spurt out, and writhe about furiously. Minute as they are, they want to live; to feed; to reproduce; they do exactly what we do: you: everyone: and in exactly the same way. The proud boast of being a person, a will, someone distinguished, is no more than a matter of fine linen. Take people's clothes away from them; and that's exactly what they'll be. All naked, equal grubs, wriggling about as best they can. The slightest planetary disturbance could quietly wipe everything out. And instead of wriggling as equals, do we have to give one man heaven and another man hell? Come down from your tin-pot throne. Get used to these things. Get used to being reasonable. Let your own instincts win; and be afraid: it's your way of wriggling. Give me those names.

ARGIA (*her teeth chattering*) What you're saying, in fact, is that if there were here, in my place, some less fortunate woman than I, someone who'd had to cook herself an egg in her room, you're saying that there'd be some real merit in *her*, if she were courageous at this moment? Commissar Amos, there was once a woman whom they played a joke on. I was

told about it. One Sunday, this woman went to the seaside.
And the bathing attendants, for a joke, knowing the sort of
woman she was, got out for her a bathing costume of the
kind that becomes almost transparent in the water. There
was a good deal of merriment. And all of a sudden, the
woman noticed that everyone was looking at her, and that
there was rather a row going on.

AMOS  Come on: the names.

ARGIA  And at last that woman saw that she was standing
there almost naked! Alone and naked. She stood there
bewildered. And suddenly, do you know what she did? She
tried to laugh, with them. (*Controlling herself, and shrugging her
shoulders.*) And after all what did they see? That she was a
woman. We know what a woman is. A man comes up to her
. . . cheerful, with his big, sweaty hands, and says: "Do this
. . . go like this . . . do that . . . (*louder*) . . . go on . . ."
(*Suddenly, with a real cry of anguish and protest.*) Well, do you
know what I think! I think there comes a time when the
only thing to do is to stand up and say . . . (*as though actually
turning on someone*) "Why do you insult me like this? And, my
God, why have I allowed you to? Get away from me! Go
away! Go away! Leave me alone! You take advantage of an
immense mistake, a monstrous delusion! Respect me! Show
me respect! Respect . . . because I am . . . the Queen! The
Queen, and destined for other things than this." (*With a
change of voice.*) What I want to do is to go out of doors, as if it
were a fine morning, and as if I had seen down there, at the
end of the street, the cool fresh color of the sea, a color that
makes the heart leap! And someone stops me, and then
someone else, and someone else, with the usual rudenesses.
But this morning I don't even hear them. I'm not afraid any
longer. My face expresses dignity. I am as I would always
have wished to be. And it would have been simple after all.
It would have been enough to want to be. Palaces have
nothing to do with it. It was my own fault.

AMOS  (*after a long pause*)  Am I to take this to mean that you
still refuse? (*Almost with melancholy.*) Very well; in that case,
your troubles are not yet over. Madam: you are forcing me
to do this, remember.

*He goes to the door, and makes a sign to someone outside. Maupa enters slowly, leading by the hand a small boy about three years old, dressed in peasant-boy's clothes.*

AMOS    You can go, now, Maupa. So can you, porter.

*Maupa and the Porter go out. The boy is left standing alone in the middle of the room.*

ARGIA (*shaken*)    Who is he?

AMOS (*with the same melancholy, moving to the child's side*)    It is the person who will persuade you.

ARGIA (*desperately*)    I don't know who he is!

AMOS    I know of course that you don't actually recognize him. We ourselves had a great deal of trouble in tracing him.

ARGIA (*cries out*)    I swear to you! I swear . . . that he isn't my son! I'm not his mother!

AMOS    He's a fine child. He'll be able to live and grow up as an unknowing peasant . . . so long as the protection you are according to a few seditious men doesn't force us to eliminate in him any pretext for sedition in the future. In such an orgy of blood, the scales won't be upset by a few drops more . . . Well, that is what you wanted: to choose: now you can do so.

ARGIA (*instinctively clutching her face*)    He isn't mine! I tell you he isn't mine.

AMOS    It is in your power to choose. The weight of this tiny little boy puts an end to your flights of fancy, and brings you back to earth. Even the wolves in the woods up here love their young. Yes: that's a real thing: the rest is smoke. Make your choice: make it according to nature: no one will condemn you.

ARGIA (*astounded*)    And if I don't, you're capable of a crime like this?

AMOS (*with a lofty sadness*)    Madam: I shall do everything that is necessary. Common reproaches should be reserved for common occasions. The blood that your disclosures will make flow may be a great deal, but it will be far away. There is only a little here. But it is warm. And it is your own.

ARGIA   Oh God, how can a human mind have so much hate in it?

AMOS (*with painful intensity*)   It is not hate. But it is too late to argue now. I also made my choice once upon a time. However a stone rolls, the one who has dislodged it rolls down with it.

ARGIA   My God, how can you . . . break laws so sacred . . . ? I tell you he isn't mine! Did you keep me alive only to save me for this? I swear to you he isn't mine, take him away, take him away . . . Oh God, oh God, how can you think you've the power to . . . (*Crying out.*) In what name, by what right, do you dare to do this?

AMOS (*shouting her down*)   In what name! By what right! (*Suddenly controlling himself.*) Listen to me: I want to tell *you* something also. When we overthrew the October republic, I was in the palace too. An agreement had been reached; our victory was total and peaceful. There had been no bloodshed. All the same, we were in the palace rooms; we wanted to pull down the coats-of-arms. We began to unnail them. A man was fetching great blows at one of the trophies. And I noticed that little by little something seemed to dawn in his face. Down below in the street the crowds were yelling. Suddenly this man, as soon as he'd knocked the trophy off the wall, turned round. He was covered in sweat. And he hurled his axe at one of the mirrors! The others followed suit. Then they began to smash everything. And their faces were furious, they were intoxicated, they were beautiful, they were holy. The smoke was already appearing! And the fire followed! (*Controlling himself suddenly.*) But it would have been contemptible if the aim of it all was merely to take a few pence from the hand of a fat dead man and put them in the hand of a thin living man. So much noise simply in order to modify a few tariffs and initiate a few austere apostles into the pleasures of wearing silk shirts? But this fury, which spouts up like a fountain of black oil, comes from deep down, madam, it's the distillation of a very different grief, the memory of a very different betrayal, it doesn't merely utter its "no" to your silks and satins and the farmer's hoard. (*He cries.*) It says "no" to everything there is!

It says rage towards everything, despair towards everything! What we hear coming towards us down there, is the thunder of the great waterfall! It's towards the great rapids that the boat is rushing! This fury says "no" to the whole world: it says (*with despairing weariness*) that the world is wrong, it's all absurdity; an immense, unchangeable quarry of despair, a grotesque, unchangeable labyrinth of injustice, an insensate clockwork, that one day compels you and me to say and do what we're saying and doing now. It says "no"; total sterilization; away with everything: the just and the unjust, loyalty and betrayal, worthiness, guilt, glory: (*He points to Argia.*) . . . everything that makes us grasping and boastful owners in life and in death, all this mass of falsehoods, this immense fraud! Tell me the names.

ARGIA (*staring at the child*)  The names? But you'll kill him whatever happens, I know you will. (*A brief pause.*) Oh, poor little child, in his little peasant's dress! No one wants him. His mother runs away from him. I've done nothing but say: "Take him away." Completely alone. (*She suddenly runs to the child, and hugs him tightly.*) Oh, what a lovely child you are, my darling. How healthy you are. And what pretty little teeth. My angel, your mother won't ever come and see if you're asleep, she'll never see you run, and say: "Look how he's grown." He isn't at all sleepy, is he, and not the tiniest bit afraid, is he? No, no, he's very well, he's in the warm . . . (*She is pressing him against her breast.*) . . . This is the right place for a little boy to be, isn't it? This is a little throne for a child . . . (*She turns to Amos.*) Sir, I've been deceiving myself. I thought that everything would be simple. Perhaps I should after all do as you say . . . I ought to tell you those names . . . I'm so confused . . . Wait a moment . . . those names . . . (*She stands there, with eyes wide open, looking before her; suddenly she laughs softly; and whispers.*) A miracle, sir. A miracle. I've forgotten them! Perhaps I have been too much upset, or perhaps I have been helped in some way; but that step has been spared me. (*She hugs the child tightly, hiding her face against him, and remains thus.*)

AMOS (*after a long pause*)  In that case the struggle between us is over. All that remains is to finish what was begun. (*A pause;*

*then, seriously and gently.*) If you believe in the survival of your soul, and desire a confessor, anyone you choose may hear you.

ARGIA   Yes, I do desire it. (*She rises without letting go the child.*) I have made sad and improvident use of my person, my words, my thoughts, and for the most part, of the whole of my life. I laid the blame for this upon others, when the blame was all my own. This I understood too late. I have often told lies; and even now.

AMOS   What is your real name?

ARGIA   I believe that the Lord, in a short time from now, will not be asking names of me; He will be asking what my profit has been. The only one I have had I have had this night. And so, not utterly bereft, but with a little coin I go before Him. (*She raises her head slightly, and her voice also.*) Only a little, but my own; not given to me, nor inherited; but mine. This is the profit that makes owners and possessors of us. I am sinning still; since of what I have done tonight I am a little proud: it is the single thing that I can tell about myself . . . (*Dropping her voice a little.*) I have great need that soon I shall meet someone who will listen to me. (*She turns.*)

*Maupa comes in, followed by the Porter.*

ARGIA   Now is it?
AMOS   Yes.

*Maupa goes over to take the child from her. Argia prevents him, hugging the child close.*

AMOS (*motioning Maupa to stand back*)   The child will return to where he has lived hitherto, and where no one is informed of who he is. (*He takes the child from Argia.*) The sentence will be carried out at once. Immediately afterwards, it will be announced that the woman known as the Queen is dead, and that therefore the Unitary Government has triumphed, the actions of our enemies being now deprived of their aim.

*Argia moves towards the door, preceded by Maupa.*

ARGIA   I believe that God . . . has intentionally made us, not docile, for that He would find useless . . . but different from Himself and a little too proud . . . so that we may . . .

stand against Him, thwart Him, amaze Him . . . Perhaps
that is His purpose. (*She takes another step forward.*) It is a long
struggle. Only at the end do we find reconciliation; and rest.
(*She looks at the child.*) I go away rich. I have acquired a son
. . . and memories . . . If even a little memory survives in
us, this night, for me, shall shine indeed. (*She shows her hand
to Amos.*) Tell them to leave this ring on my finger. (*She holds
out a hand to the child.*) Good-bye, my sweet.

*The child also puts a hand out towards her. Argia turns to go towards
the door; pauses in momentary bewilderment; extracts her lipstick, and
puts a little on her lips.*

ARGIA   My mouth was rather pale. (*She is now at the door.*) How
lovely and serene it is over the mountains; and the star
Diana[1] is still there in the sky. Unquestionably, this is a seat
for kings, and in it we must try to live regally.

*She goes out. There is a silence. Suddenly the Porter runs out after her.
Amos, listening, puts his hands over the child's ears. A burst of gun
fire is heard. Argia is dead.*

---

1. It is interesting that the morning star is called "star Diana" (*stella Diana* instead
of *stella del mattino*). After all, the mythical Egeria (see p. 145) is supposed to have been
turned into a spring when, lamenting the death of Numa, she interrupted the rites of
Diana. I am not sure what, if anything, one is to make of that in the context of this
play.

# The Tragedy of
# Coriolanus   (1607 ?)

## *William Shakespeare*   *(1564-1616)*

It was not until the publication of the First Folio in 1623 that *Coriolanus* found its way into print. It is generally assumed, primarily on the basis of style, that the play was written in 1607 or early in 1608, and the first production is presumed to have taken place in 1608. There are a number of references, internal and external, that help to date the play, if one is willing to accept the significance that scholars attach to them. One of the conjectures is particularly interesting in the context of this volume. Shakespeare's primary source for the play is Sir Thomas North's translation of Plutarch's *Lives* (1595), but E. C. Pettet, writing in *Shakespeare Survey* (1950), examines changes in emphasis in Shakespeare's use of the original and suggests that the playwright's version of the incipient Roman revolution owes something to the peasant insurrection that took place in the Midlands in 1607. According to Pettet, not only was that rebellion triggered by a shortage of corn, but it was the first of the rural riots of the period that was entirely a popular movement, hence, a genuine class struggle such as the plebeian-patrician conflict in the play.

*Coriolanus* has never been as popular a play as Shakespeare's more celebrated tragedies, but it has been performed fairly regularly in England. Richard Burton was Coriolanus at the Old Vic in 1954, and Laurence Olivier, who first played the part at the Old Vic in 1938, did it again at Stratford in 1959. It was again at Stratford in 1972, as part of the Royal Shakespeare Company's season of Roman plays. Until recently, the play was put on so infrequently in the United States that it was an astonishing event when, in 1954, the Phoenix Theatre revived the play in New York with Robert

Ryan in the lead. In recent years, however, the political implications of the play seem to have made it a more likely choice for contemporary audiences. In 1965, for instance, there were four professional productions in the United States —in San Diego, Princeton, New York, and Stratford, Connecticut. This sudden popularity may owe something to the most famous recent recreation of the play—Bertolt Brecht's adaptation. His version of the play was written in 1952–53, but it was not until after his death in 1956 that the Berliner Ensemble brought it to the stage. Readers of this anthology might want to have a look at Günter Grass's *The Plebeians Rehearse the Uprising* (1966), a play in which a character, modeled on Brecht, insists on rehearsing his actors in *Coriolanus* while the East Berlin uprising of 1953 is going on in the streets.

There is a recording of the play (Shakespeare Recording Society 226) with Richard Burton as Coriolanus and Jessica Tandy as Volumnia.

The text is that of the First Folio, quietly doctored according to the guesses of later editors. The original edition was unusual in that it included fairly extensive stage directions, which has led some critics (see Harley Granville-Barker's *Prefaces to Shakespeare*, II) to guess that Shakespeare may have been back home in Stratford when the play was first presented in London, trying to control the production at a distance. In any case, the Folio directions are presented here either without marks or in parentheses; those added by later editors are in brackets. Although the Folio divided the play into acts, there was no designation of scenes; the act-scene breakdown here is the one conventionally used in modern editions of Shakespeare.

# THE TRAGEDY OF CORIOLANUS

## William Shakespeare

### [CHARACTERS

CAIUS MARCIUS, *afterwards Caius Marcius Coriolanus*
TITUS LARTIUS *Generals against the Volscians*
COMINIUS
MENENIUS AGRIPPA, *friend to Coriolanus*
SICINIUS VELUTUS, *Tribunes of the People*
JUNIUS BRUTUS
YOUNG MARCIUS, *son to Coriolanus*
A ROMAN HERALD
NICANOR, *a Roman*
ADRIAN, *a Volscian*
TULLUS AUFIDIUS, *General of the Volscians*

LIEUTENANT TO AUFIDIUS
CONSPIRATORS WITH AUFIDIUS
A CITIZEN OF ANTIUM
TWO VOLSCIAN GUARDS
VOLUMNIA, *mother to Coriolanus*
VIRGILIA, *wife to Coriolanus*
VALERIA, *friend to Virgilia*
GENTLEWOMAN, *attending on Virgilia*
ROMAN *and* VOLSCIAN SENATORS, PATRICIANS, ÆDILES, LICTORS, SOLDIERS, CITIZENS, MESSENGERS, SERVANTS TO AUFIDIUS, *and other* ATTENDANTS

*Scene: Rome and the neighborhood; Corioles and the neighborhood; Antium*]

## ACT ONE

### Scene 1

*Enter a company of mutinous Citizens, with staves, clubs, and other weapons.*

FIRST CITIZEN   Before we proceed any further, hear me speak.
ALL   Speak, speak.
FIRST CITIZEN   You are all resolved rather to die than to famish?
ALL   Resolved, resolved.

FIRST CITIZEN    First, you know Caius Marcius is chief enemy to the people.

ALL    We know't, we know't.

FIRST CITIZEN    Let us kill him, and we'll have corn at our own price. Is't a verdict?

ALL    No more talking on't! Let it be done! Away, away!

SECOND CITIZEN    One word, good citizens.

FIRST CITIZEN    We are accounted poor citizens, the patricians good.[1] What authority surfeits on would relieve us. If they would yield us but the superfluity while it were wholesome, we might guess they relieved us humanely; but they think we are too dear. The leanness that afflicts us, the object[2] of our misery, is as an inventory to particularize their abundance; our sufferance is a gain to them. Let us revenge this with our pikes ere we become rakes; for the gods know I speak this in hunger for bread, not in thirst for revenge.

SECOND CITIZEN    Would you proceed especially against Caius Marcius?

FIRST CITIZEN    Against him first. He's a very dog to the commonalty.

SECOND CITIZEN    Consider you what services he has done for his country?

FIRST CITIZEN    Very well, and could be content to give him good report for't, but that he pays himself with being proud.

SECOND CITIZEN    Nay, but speak not maliciously.

FIRST CITIZEN    I say unto you, what he hath done famously, he did it to that end. Though soft-conscienced men can be content to say it was for his country, he did it to please his mother and to be partly proud, which he is, even to the altitude of his virtue.

SECOND CITIZEN    What he cannot help in his nature, you account a vice in him. You must in no way say he is covetous.

FIRST CITIZEN    If I must not, I need not be barren of accusations. He hath faults, with surplus, to tire in repetition.

1. Well-to-do.
2. Spectacle.

*Shouts within.*

What shouts are these? The other side o' th' city is risen.
Why stay we prating here? To the Capitol! [3]
ALL   Come, come!
FIRST CITIZEN   Soft! who comes here?

*Enter Menenius Agrippa.*

SECOND CITIZEN   Worthy Menenius Agrippa, one that hath
   always loved the people.
FIRST CITIZEN   He's one honest enough. Would all the rest
   were so!
MENENIUS   What work's, my countrymen, in hand? Where go
   you
   With bats and clubs? The matter? Speak, I pray you.
FIRST CITIZEN   Our business is not unknown to th' Senate.
   They have had inkling this fortnight what we intend to
   do, which now we'll show 'em in deeds. They say poor
   suitors have strong breaths; they shall know we have
   strong arms too.
MENENIUS   Why, masters, my good friends, mine honest
   neighbors,
   Will you undo yourselves?
FIRST CITIZEN   We cannot, sir, we are undone already.
MENENIUS   I tell you, friends, most charitable care
   Have the patricians of you. For your wants,
   Your suffering in this dearth, you may as well
   Strike at the heaven with your staves as lift them
   Against the Roman state, whose course will on
   The way it takes, cracking ten thousand curbs
   Of more strong link asunder than can ever
   Appear in your impediment. For the dearth,
   The gods, not the patricians, make it, and
   Your knees to them, not arms, must help. Alack,
   You are transported by calamity
   Thither where more attends you, and you slander
   The helms o' th' state, who care for you like fathers,
   When you curse them as enemies.
FIRST CITIZEN   Care for us? True, indeed! They ne'er cared for

3. Capitoline Hill, site of the senatorial palace.

us yet: suffer us to famish, and their storehouses crammed with grain; make edicts for usury, to support usurers; repeal daily any wholesome act established against the rich, and provide more piercing statutes daily to chain up and restrain the poor. If the wars eat us not up, they will; and there's all the love they bear us.

MENENIUS   Either you must
Confess yourselves wondrous malicious,
Or be accused of folly. I shall tell you
A pretty tale. It may be you have heard it;
But, since it serves my purpose, I will venture
To stale't[4] a little more.

FIRST CITIZEN   Well, I'll hear it, sir; yet you must not think to fob off our disgrace with a tale. But, an't please you, deliver.

MENENIUS   There was a time when all the body's members
Rebelled against the belly, thus accused it:
That only like a gulf it did remain
I' th' midst o' th' body, idle and unactive,
Still cupboarding the viand, never bearing
Like labor with the rest, where th' other instruments
Did see and hear, devise, instruct, walk, feel,
And, mutually participate, did minister
Unto the appetite and affection common
Of the whole body. The belly answered—

FIRST CITIZEN   Well, sir, what answer made the belly?

MENENIUS   Sir, I shall tell you. With a kind of smile,
Which ne'er came from the lungs, but even thus—
For, look you, I may make the belly smile
As well as speak—it tauntingly replied
To th' discontented members, the mutinous parts
That envied his receipt; even so most fitly
As you malign our senators, for that
They are not such as you.

FIRST CITIZEN                  Your belly's answer? What?
The kingly crowned head, the vigilant eye,
The counsellor heart, the arm our soldier,
Our steed the leg, the tongue our trumpeter,
With other muniments and petty helps

---

4. Make it stale, i.e., by repetition. But *stale* also means *urinate,* and Menenius is not above that kind of double entendre.

In this our fabric, if that they—
MENENIUS                                    What then?
'Fore me, this fellow speaks! What then? what then?
FIRST CITIZEN    Should by the cormorant belly be restrained,
Who is the sink o' th' body—
MENENIUS                              Well, what then?
FIRST CITIZEN    The former agents, if they did complain,
What could the belly answer?
MENENIUS                                I will tell you;
If you'll bestow a small—of what you have little—
Patience awhile, you'st hear the belly's answer.
FIRST CITIZEN    Y' are long about it.
MENENIUS                                    Note me this, good friend;
Your most grave belly was deliberate,
Not rash like his accusers, and thus answered:
'True is it, my incorporate friends,' quoth he,
'That I receive the general food at first,
Which you do live upon; and fit it is,
Because I am the storehouse and the shop
Of the whole body. But, if you do remember,
I send it through the rivers of your blood
Even to the court, the heart, to th' seat o' th' brain;
And, through the cranks and offices[5] of man,
The strongest nerves and small inferior veins
From me receive that natural competency
Whereby they live. And though that all at once'—
You, my good friends! This says the belly. Mark me.
FIRST CITIZEN    Ay, sir, well, well.
MENENIUS                                'Though all at once cannot
See what I do deliver out to each,
Yet I can make my audit up, that all
From me do back receive the flour of all,
And leave me but the bran.' What say you to't?
FIRST CITIZEN    It was an answer. How apply you this?
MENENIUS    The senators of Rome are this good belly,
And you the mutinous members. For examine
Their counsels and their cares, digest things rightly

5. Winding passages and outlying, modest rooms in a house. The next phrase might be defining the metaphorical "cranks and offices of man," except that grammatically the phrase is not in apposition.

Touching the weal o' th' common, you shall find
No public benefit which you receive
But it proceeds or comes from them to you,
And no way from yourselves. What do you think,
You, the great toe of this assembly?

FIRST CITIZEN   I the great toe! Why the great toe?

MENENIUS   For that, being one o' th' lowest, basest, poorest
Of this most wise rebellion, thou goest foremost.
Thou rascal, that art worst in blood to run,
Lead'st first to win some vantage.[6]
But make you ready your stiff bats and clubs.
Rome and her rats are at the point of battle;
The one side must have bale.

*Enter Caius Marcius.*

                              Hail, noble Marcius!

MARCIUS   Thanks. What's the matter, you dissentious rogues,
That, rubbing the poor itch of your opinion,
Make yourselves scabs?

FIRST CITIZEN                  We have ever your good word.

MARCIUS   He that will give good words to thee will flatter
Beneath abhorring. What would you have, you curs,
That like nor peace nor war? The one affrights you,
The other makes you proud. He that trusts to you,
Where he should find you lions, finds you hares;
Where foxes, geese. You are no surer, no,
Than is the coal of fire upon the ice,
Or hailstone in the sun. Your virtue is
To make him worthy whose offense subdues him
And curse that justice did it. Who deserves greatness
Deserves your hate; and your affections are
A sick man's appetite, who desires most that
Which would increase his evil. He that depends
Upon your favors swims with fins of lead
And hews down oaks with rushes. Hang ye! Trust ye?
With every minute you do change a mind,

6. This sentence has been glossed in a variety of ways, one popular one having to do with an out-of-condition deer. The one that makes most sense is the hunting metaphor in which a hound of inferior breed ("rascal . . . worst in blood") leads the pack when there is something to be gained by it.

And call him noble that was now your hate,
Him vile that was your garland. What's the matter,
That in these several places of the city
You cry against the noble Senate, who,
Under the gods, keep you in awe, which else
Would feed on one another? What's their seeking?
MENENIUS  For corn at their own rates, whereof they say
  The city is well stored.
MARCIUS                  Hang 'em! They say?
  They'll sit by th' fire and presume to know
  What's done i' th' Capitol, who's like to rise,
  Who thrives and who declines; side factions and give out
  Conjectural marriages, making parties strong
  And feebling such as stand not in their liking
  Below their cobbled shoes. They say there's grain enough?
  Would the nobility lay aside their ruth,
  And let me use my sword, I'd make a quarry[7]
  With thousands of these quartered slaves as high
  As I could pick[8] my lance.
MENENIUS  Nay, these are almost thoroughly persuaded;
  For though abundantly they lack discretion,
  Yet are they passing cowardly. But, I beseech you,
  What says the other troop?
MARCIUS              They are dissolved. Hang 'em!
  They said they were anhungry, sighed forth proverbs—
  That hunger broke stone walls, that dogs must eat,
  That meat was made for mouths, that the gods sent not
  Corn for the rich men only. With these shreds
  They vented their complainings, which being answered
  And a petition granted them, a strange one,
  To break the heart of generosity,[9]
  And make bold power look pale, they threw their caps
  As they would hang them on the horns o' th' moon,
  Shouting their emulation.
MENENIUS          What is granted them?
MARCIUS  Five tribunes to defend their vulgar wisdoms,
  Of their own choice. One's Junius Brutus,

7. Pile of dead (used for deer).
8. Pitch.
9. The aristocracy.

Sicinius Velutus, and I know not—'Sdeath!
The rabble should have first unroofed the city
Ere so prevailed with me; it will in time
Win upon power, and throw forth greater themes
For insurrection's arguing.

MENENIUS            This is strange.

MARCIUS    Go, get you home, you fragments!

*Enter a Messenger hastily.*

MESSENGER    Where's Caius Marcius?

MARCIUS           Here. What's the matter?

MESSENGER    The news is, sir, the Volsces are in arms.

MARCIUS    I'm glad on't. Then we shall ha' means to vent
Our musty superfluity. See, our best elders.

*Enter Sicinius Velutus, Junius Brutus, Cominius, Titus Lartius, with
other Senators.*

FIRST SENATOR    Marcius, 'tis true that you have lately told us:
The Volsces are in arms.

MARCIUS         They have a leader,
Tullus Aufidius, that will put you to't.
I sin in envying his nobility;
And were I any thing but what I am,
I would wish me only he.

COMINIUS         You have fought together?

MARCIUS    Were half to half the world by th' ears and he
Upon my party, I'd revolt, to make
Only my wars with him. He is a lion
That I am proud to hunt.

FIRST SENATOR        Then, worthy Marcius,
Attend upon Cominius to these wars.

COMINIUS    It is your former promise.

MARCIUS         Sir, it is,
And I am constant. Titus Lartius, thou
Shalt see me once more strike at Tullus' face.
What, art thou stiff? Stand'st out?

TITUS         No, Caius Marcius,
I'll lean upon one crutch and fight with t' other,
Ere stay behind this business.

MENENIUS        O, true-bred!

FIRST SENATOR    Your company to th' Capitol, where I know
  Our greatest friends attend us.
TITUS                                  [*to Cominius*] Lead you on.
  [*To Marcius*] Follow Cominius. We must follow you.
  Right worthy you priority.
COMINIUS                    Noble Marcius!
FIRST SENATOR [*to the Citizens*]    Hence to your homes, be gone!
MARCIUS                            Nay, let them follow.
  The Volsces have much corn. Take these rats thither
  To gnaw their garners. Worshipful mutineers,
  Your valor puts well forth. Pray follow.

*Exeunt. Citizens steal away. Manent Sicinius and Brutus.*

SICINIUS    Was ever man so proud as is this Marcius?
BRUTUS    He has no equal.
SICINIUS    When we were chosen tribunes for the people—
BRUTUS    Marked you his lip and eyes?
SICINIUS                            Nay, but his taunts.
BRUTUS    Being moved, he will not spare to gird the gods.
SICINIUS    Bemock the modest moon.
BRUTUS    The present wars devour him. He is grown
  Too proud to be so valiant.
SICINIUS                    Such a nature,
  Tickled with good success, disdains the shadow
  Which he treads on at noon. But I do wonder
  His insolence can brook to be commanded
  Under Cominius.
BRUTUS                Fame, at the which he aims,
  In whom already he's well graced, cannot
  Better be held nor more attained than by
  A place below the first; for what miscarries
  Shall be the general's fault, though he perform
  To th' utmost of a man, and giddy censure
  Will then cry out of Marcius, 'O, if he
  Had borne the business!'
SICINIUS                    Besides, if things go well,
  Opinion, that so sticks on Marcius, shall
  Of his demerits rob Cominius.
BRUTUS                        Come.

Half all Cominius' honors are to Marcius,
Though Marcius earned them not; and all his faults
To Marcius shall be honors, though indeed
In aught he merit not.

SICINIUS                         Let's hence and hear
How the dispatch is made, and in what fashion,
More than his singularity, he goes
Upon this present action.

BRUTUS                         Let's along.

*Exeunt.*

*Scene 2*

*Enter Tullus Aufidius, with Senators of Corioles.*

FIRST SENATOR    So, your opinion is, Aufidius,
That they of Rome are entered in our counsels
And know how we proceed.

AUFIDIUS                         Is it not yours?
What ever have been thought on in this state,
That could be brought to bodily act ere Rome
Had circumvention? 'Tis not four days gone
Since I heard thence. These are the words. I think
I have the letter here. Yes, here it is:
'They have pressed a power, but it is not known
Whether for east or west. The dearth is great,
The people mutinous; and it is rumored,
Cominius, Marcius your old enemy,
Who is of Rome worse hated than of you,
And Titus Lartius, a most valiant Roman,
These three lead on this preparation
Whither 'tis bent. Most likely 'tis for you.
Consider of it.'

FIRST SENATOR    Our army's in the field.
We never yet made doubt but Rome was ready
To answer us.

AUFIDIUS           Nor did you think it folly
To keep your great pretenses veiled till when

They needs must show themselves, which in the hatching,
It seemed, appeared to Rome. By the discovery
We shall be shortened in our aim, which was
To take in many towns ere almost Rome
Should know we were afoot.

SECOND SENATOR                    Noble Aufidius,
Take your commission; hie you to your bands;
Let us alone to guard Corioles.
If they set down before's, for the remove
Bring up your army; but, I think, you'll find
Th' have not prepared for us.

AUFIDIUS                         O, doubt not that,
I speak from certainties. Nay more,
Some parcels of their power are forth already,
And only hitherward. I leave your honors.
If we and Caius Marcius chance to meet,
'Tis sworn between us we shall ever strike
Till one can do no more.

ALL                         The gods assist you!
AUFIDIUS   And keep your honors safe!
FIRST SENATOR                      Farewell.
SECOND SENATOR                            Farewell.
ALL   Farewell.

*Exeunt omnes.*


## Scene 3


*Enter Volumnia and Virgilia, mother and wife to Marcius.*
*They set them down on two low stools and sew.*

VOLUMNIA   I pray you, daughter, sing, or express yourself in a
more comfortable sort. If my son were my husband, I
should freelier rejoice in that absence wherein he won
honor than in the embracements of his bed where he
would show most love. When yet he was but tender-bod-
ied and the only son of my womb, when youth with
comeliness plucked all gaze his way, when for a day of
kings' entreaties a mother should not sell him an hour

from her beholding, I, considering how honor would become such a person, that it was no better than picture-like to hang by th' wall, if renown made it not stir, was pleased to let him seek danger where he was like to find fame. To a cruel war I sent him, from whence he returned, his brows bound with oak.[10] I tell thee, daughter, I sprang not more in joy at first hearing he was a man-child than now in first seeing he had proved himself a man.

VIRGILIA  But had he died in the business, madam, how then?

VOLUMNIA  Then his good report should have been my son; I therein would have found issue. Hear me profess sincerely: had I a dozen sons, each in my love alike, and none less dear than thine and my good Marcius, I had rather had eleven die nobly for their country than one voluptuously surfeit out of action.

*Enter a Gentlewoman.*

GENTLEWOMAN  Madam, the Lady Valeria is come to visit you.

VIRGILIA  Beseech you, give me leave to retire myself.

VOLUMNIA  Indeed, you shall not.
Methinks I hear hither your husband's drum;
See him pluck Aufidius down by the hair;
As children from a bear, the Volsces shunning him.
Methinks I see him stamp thus, and call thus:
'Come on, you cowards! You were got in fear,
Though you were born in Rome.' His bloody brow
With his mailed hand then wiping, forth he goes,
Like to a harvest-man that's tasked to mow
Or all or lose his hire.

VIRGILIA  His bloody brow? O Jupiter, no blood!

VOLUMNIA  Away, you fool! it more becomes a man
Than gilt his trophy. The breasts of Hecuba,

10. The oak was awarded to those who saved a comrade's life in battle, but Shakespeare seems to use it to mean battlefield honor in a more general sense. The "cruel war" is presumably the fight against the Tarquins, who were deposed as rulers of Rome some years before the action in this play is supposed to have taken place; it was in that struggle that Caius Marcius is said to have made his reputation as a warrior.

When she did suckle Hector, looked not lovelier
Than Hector's forehead when it spit forth blood
At Grecian sword, contemning. Tell Valeria,
We are fit to bid her welcome.

*Exit Gentlewoman.*

VIRGILIA    Heavens bless my lord from fell Aufidius!
VOLUMNIA    He'll beat Aufidius' head below his knee
And tread upon his neck.

*Enter Valeria, with an Usher and a Gentlewoman.*

VALERIA    My ladies both, good day to you.
VOLUMNIA    Sweet madam.
VIRGILIA    I am glad to see your ladyship.
VALERIA    How do you both? You are manifest house-keep-
ers.¹¹ What are you sewing here? A fine spot,¹² in good
faith. How does your little son?
VIRGILIA    I thank your ladyship; well, good madam.
VOLUMNIA    He had rather see the swords and hear a drum
than look upon his schoolmaster.
VALERIA    O' my word, the father's son! I'll swear 'tis a very
pretty boy. O' my troth, I looked upon him o' Wednesday
half an hour together: 'has such a confirmed counte-
nance! I saw him run after a gilded butterfly, and when
he caught it, he let it go again, and after it again, and
over and over he comes, and up again; catched it again;
or whether his fall enraged him, or how 'twas, he did so
set his teeth and tear it! O, I warrant, how he mam-
mocked it! ¹³
VOLUMNIA    One on's father's moods.
VALERIA    Indeed, la, 'tis a noble child.
VIRGILIA    A crack,¹⁴ madam.
VALERIA    Come, lay aside your stitchery. I must have you
play the idle housewife with me this afternoon.
VIRGILIA    No, good madam, I will not out of doors.

11. You are obviously settled down for work indoors.
12. Embroidery pattern.
13. Tore it to pieces.
14. Mischievous boy.

**VALERIA** Not out of doors?

**VOLUMNIA** She shall, she shall.

**VIRGILIA** Indeed, no, by your patience. I'll not over the threshold till my lord return from the wars.

**VALERIA** Fie, you confine yourself most unreasonably. Come, you must go visit the good lady that lies in.

**VIRGILIA** I will wish her speedy strength and visit her with my prayers, but I cannot go thither.

**VOLUMNIA** Why, I pray you?

**VIRGILIA** 'Tis not to save labor, nor that I want love.

**VALERIA** You would be another Penelope; yet they say all the yarn she spun in Ulysses' absence[15] did but fill Ithaca full of moths. Come; I would your cambric were sensible as your finger, that you might leave pricking it for pity. Come, you shall go with us.

**VIRGILIA** No, good madam, pardon me; indeed I will not forth.

**VALERIA** In truth, la, go with me, and I'll tell you excellent news of your husband.

**VIRGILIA** O, good madam, there can be none yet.

**VALERIA** Verily, I do not jest with you. There came news from him last night.

**VIRGILIA** Indeed, madam?

**VALERIA** In earnest, it's true; I heard a senator speak it. Thus it is: the Volsces have an army forth, against whom Cominius the general is gone, with one part of our Roman power. Your lord and Titus Lartius are set down before their city Corioles. They nothing doubt prevailing and to make it brief wars. This is true, on mine honor; and so, I pray, go with us.

**VIRGILIA** Give me excuse, good madam. I will obey you in everything hereafter.

**VOLUMNIA** Let her alone, lady. As she is now, she will but disease our better mirth.

**VALERIA** In troth, I think she would. Fare you well, then. Come, good sweet lady. Prithee, Virgilia, turn thy solemnness out o' door and go along with us.

15. While Ulysses was spending twenty years coming home from the Trojan War, his wife Penelope, beset by suitors to whom she had promised an answer as soon as she finished a robe she was working on, spent the days spinning yarn and the nights unraveling it.

VIRGILIA   No, at a word, madam. Indeed, I must not. I wish
you much mirth.
VALERIA   Well, then, farewell.

*Exeunt.*


## *Scene 4*


*Enter Marcius, Titus Lartius, with Drums and Colors, with Captains
and Soldiers, as before the city Corioles. To them a Messenger.*
MARCIUS   Yonder comes news. A wager they have met.
LARTIUS   My horse to yours, no.
MARCIUS                          'Tis done.
LARTIUS                                    Agreed.
MARCIUS   Say, has our general met the enemy?
MESSENGER   They lie in view, but have not spoke as yet.
LARTIUS   So, the good horse is mine.
MARCIUS                                    I'll buy him of you.
LARTIUS   No, I'll nor sell nor give him. Lend you him I will
For half a hundred years. Summon the town.
MARCIUS   How far off lie these armies?
MESSENGER                              Within this mile and half.
MARCIUS   Then shall we hear their 'larum, and they ours.
Now, Mars, I prithee, make us quick in work,
That we with smoking swords may march from hence,
To help our fielded friends! Come, blow thy blast.

*They sound a parley.*
*Enter two Senators, with others, on the walls of Corioles.*

Tullus Aufidius, is he within your walls?
FIRST SENATOR   No, nor a man that fears you less than he:
That's lesser than a little. (*Drums afar off.*) Hark! our drums
Are bringing forth our youth. We'll break our walls
Rather than they shall pound us up. Our gates,
Which yet seem shut, we have but pinned with rushes;
They'll open of themselves. (*Alarum afar off.*) Hark you, far
off!
There is Aufidius. List what work he makes

Amongst your cloven army.

MARCIUS                         O, they are at it!

LARTIUS   Their noise be our instruction. Ladders, ho!

*Enter the army of the Volsces.*

MARCIUS   They fear us not, but issue forth their city.
Now put your shields before your hearts, and fight
With hearts more proof than shields. Advance, brave Titus.
They do disdain us much beyond our thoughts,
Which makes me sweat with wrath. Come on, my fellows.
He that retires, I'll take him for a Volsce,
And he shall feel mine edge.

*Alarum. The Romans are beat back to their trenches.*
*Enter Marcius cursing.*

MARCIUS   All the contagion of the south[16] light on you,
You shames of Rome! you herd of—Boils and plagues
Plaster you o'er, that you may be abhorred
Farther than seen, and one infect another
Against the wind a mile! You souls of geese,
That bear the shapes of men, how have you run
From slaves that apes would beat! Pluto and hell!
All hurt behind! backs red, and faces pale
With flight and argued fear! Mend and charge home,
Or, by the fires of heaven, I'll leave the foe
And make my wars on you! Look to't. Come on!
If you'll stand fast, we'll beat them to their wives,
As they us to our trenches. Follow me!

*Another alarum and Marcius follows them to gates and is shut in.*[17]

So, now the gates are ope. Now prove good seconds.
'Tis for the followers fortune widens them,
Not for the fliers. Mark me, and do the like.

*Enter the gates.*

FIRST SOLDIER   Foolhardiness, not I.

SECOND SOLDIER                         Nor I.

16. Pestilence presumably. A northern writer's metaphor?
17. This stage direction provides the action encompassing the rest of Marcius's
speech, the next stage direction, and the lines of the soldiers.

FIRST SOLDIER    See, they have shut him in.

*Alarum continues.*

ALL                                      To th' pot,[18] I warrant him.

*Enter Titus Lartius.*

LARTIUS    What is become of Marcius?
ALL                                      Slain, sir, doubtless.
FIRST SOLDIER    Following the fliers at the very heels,
With them he enters, who upon the sudden
Clapped to their gates; he is himself alone,
To answer all the city.
LARTIUS                    O noble fellow!
Who sensibly outdares his senseless sword,[19]
And, when it bows, stand'st up. Thou art left, Marcius.
A carbuncle entire, as big as thou art,
Were not so rich a jewel. Thou wast a soldier
Even to Cato's wish, not fierce and terrible
Only in strokes; but with thy grim looks and
The thunder-like percussion of thy sounds,
Thou mad'st thine enemies shake, as if the world
Were feverous and did tremble.

*Enter Marcius, bleeding, assaulted by the Enemy.*

FIRST SOLDIER                        Look, sir.
LARTIUS                              O, 'tis Marcius!
Let's fetch him off, or make remain alike.[20]

*They fight, and all enter the City.*

## Scene 5

*Enter certain Romans, with spoils.*
FIRST ROMAN    This will I carry to Rome.

18. To destruction. A nice usage here, since the "shut him in" of the speech above
can work both realistically (in the town) and metaphorically (in the pot).
19. Who, although he feels pain, outdares his sword that feels nothing.
20. Stay with him, i.e., die with him.

SECOND ROMAN    And I this.

THIRD ROMAN    A murrain on't! I took this for silver.

*Alarum continues still afar off.*
*Enter Marcius and Titus Lartius, with a Trumpet.*[21]

MARCIUS    See here these movers that do prize their hours
At a cracked drachma! Cushions, leaden spoons,
Irons of a doit, doublets that hangmen would
Bury with those that wore them,[22] these base slaves,
Ere yet the fight be done, pack up. Down with them!
And hark, what noise the general makes! To him!
There is the man of my soul's hate, Aufidius,
Piercing our Romans. Then, valiant Titus, take
Convenient numbers to make good the city;
Whilst I, with those that have the spirit, will haste
To help Cominius.

LARTIUS                    Worthy sir, thou bleed'st.
Thy exercise hath been too violent
For a second course of fight.

MARCIUS                          Sir, praise[23] me not.
My work hath yet not warmed me. Fare you well.
The blood I drop is rather physical [24]
Than dangerous to me. To Aufidius thus
I will appear and fight.

LARTIUS                        Now the fair goddess Fortune
Fall deep in love with thee, and her great charms
Misguide thy opposers' swords! Bold gentleman,
Prosperity be thy page!

MARCIUS                        Thy friend no less
Than those she placeth highest. So, farewell.

LARTIUS    Thou worthiest Marcius! [*Exit Marcius.*]
Go sound thy trumpet in the market-place.
Call thither all the officers o' th' town,
Where they shall know our mind. Away!

*Exeunt.*

21. Trumpeter.
22. Worthless doublets. The hangman received the clothes of his victim as his perquisite.
23. Appraise.
24. Curative.

*Scene 6*

*Enter Cominius, as it were in retire, with Soldiers.*

COMINIUS   Breathe you, my friends. Well fought! We are
   come off
   Like Romans, neither foolish in our stands
   Nor cowardly in retire. Believe me, sirs,
   We shall be charged again. Whiles we have struck,
   By interims and conveying gusts[25] we have heard
   The charges of our friends. The Roman gods
   Lead their successes as we wish our own,
   That both our powers, with smiling fronts encountering,
   May give you thankful sacrifice.

*Enter a Messenger.*

                                    Thy news?
MESSENGER   The citizens of Corioles have issued,
   And given to Lartius and to Marcius battle.
   I saw our party to their trenches driven,
   And then I came away.
COMINIUS                         Though thou speakest truth,
   Methinks thou speak'st not well. How long is't since?
MESSENGER   Above an hour, my lord.
COMINIUS   'Tis not a mile; briefly we heard their drums.
   How couldst thou in a mile confound an hour,
   And bring thy news so late?
MESSENGER                         Spies of the Volsces
   Held me in chase, that I was forced to wheel
   Three or four miles about; else had I, sir,
   Half an hour since brought my report.
COMINIUS                                    Who's yonder,
   That does appear as he were flayed? O gods!
   He has the stamp of Marcius, and I have
   Beforetime seen him thus.

*Enter Marcius.*

25. At intervals, by winds carrying the sound.

MARCIUS                  Come I too late?

COMINIUS    The shepherd knows not thunder from a tabor
   More than I know the sound of Marcius' tongue
   From every meaner man.

MARCIUS                  Come I too late?

COMINIUS    Ay, if you come not in the blood of others,
   But mantled in your own.

MARCIUS                 O, let me clip ye
   In arms as sound as when I wooed, in heart
   As merry as when our nuptial day was done,
   And tapers burned to bedward!

COMINIUS              Flower of warriors!
   How is't with Titus Lartius?

MARCIUS    As with a man busied about decrees:
   Condemning some to death, and some to exile;
   Ransoming him or pitying, threatening th' other;
   Holding Corioles in the name of Rome,
   Even like a fawning greyhound in the leash,
   To let him slip at will.

COMINIUS          Where is that slave
   Which told me they had beat you to your trenches?
   Where is he? Call him hither.

MARCIUS          Let him alone.
   He did inform the truth. But for our gentlemen,
   The common file,—a plague! tribunes for them!—
   The mouse ne'er shunned the cat as they did budge
   From rascals worse than they.

COMINIUS          But how prevailed you?

MARCIUS    Will the time serve to tell? I do not think.
   Where is the enemy? Are you lords o' th' field?
   If not, why cease you till you are so?

COMINIUS          Marcius,
   We have at disadvantage fought and did
   Retire to win our purpose.

MARCIUS    How lies their battle? Know you on which side
   They have placed their men of trust?

COMINIUS          As I guess, Marcius,
   Their bands i' th' vaward are the Antiates,[26]

---

26. The troops from Antium, the chief Volscian city. The noun is sometimes used as a synonym for Volscian. See p. 266.

Of their best trust; o'er them Aufidius,
Their very heart of hope.

MARCIUS                              I do beseech you
By all the battles wherein we have fought,
By th' blood we have shed together, by the vows
We have made to endure friends, that you directly
Set me against Aufidius and his Antiates;
And that you not delay the present, but,
Filling the air with swords advanced and darts,
We prove this very hour.

COMINIUS                              Though I could wish
You were conducted to a gentle bath
And balms applied to you, yet dare I never
Deny your asking. Take your choice of those
That best can aid your action.

MARCIUS                              Those are they
That most are willing. If any such be here—
As it were sin to doubt—that love this painting
Wherein you see me smeared; if any fear
Lesser his person than an ill report;
If any think brave death outweighs bad life,
And that his country's dearer than himself;
Let him alone, or so many so minded,
Wave thus, to express his disposition,
And follow Marcius.

*They all shout and wave their swords, take him up in their arms, and
cast up their caps.*

O, me alone! Make you a sword of me?
If these shows be not outward, which of you
But is four Volsces? None of you but is
Able to bear against the great Aufidius
A shield as hard as his. A certain number,
Though thanks to all, must I select. The rest
Shall bear the business in some other fight,
As cause will be obeyed. Please you to march;
And four shall quickly draw out my command,
Which men are best inclined.

COMINIUS                              March on, my fellows.

Make good this ostentation, and you shall
Divide in all with us.

*Exeunt.*


## Scene 7


*Titus Lartius, having set a guard upon Corioles, going with Drum and
Trumpet toward Cominius and Caius Marcius, enters with a Lieutenant,
other Soldiers, and a Scout.*

LARTIUS So, let the ports be guarded. Keep your duties,
As I have set them down. If I do send, dispatch
Those centuries to our aid; the rest will serve
For a short holding. If we lose the field,
We cannot keep the town.

LIEUTENANT                          Fear not our care, sir.

LARTIUS Hence, and shut your gates upon's.
Our guider, come; to th' Roman camp conduct us.

*Exeunt.*


## Scene 8


*Alarum, as in battle. Enter Marcius and Aufidius at several doors.*[27]

MARCIUS I'll fight with none but thee, for I do hate thee
Worse than a promise-breaker.

AUFIDIUS                          We hate alike.
Not Afric owns a serpent I abhor
More than thy fame and envy.[28] Fix thy foot.

MARCIUS Let the first budger die the other's slave,
And the gods doom him after!

AUFIDIUS                          If I fly, Marcius,

27. By different entrances.
28. Reputation that I envy.

Hollo me like a hare.

MARCIUS                    Within these three hours, Tullus,
Alone I fought in your Corioles walls,
And made what work I pleased. 'Tis not my blood
Wherein thou seest me masked. For thy revenge
Wrench up thy power to th' highest.

AUFIDIUS                                    Wert thou the Hector
That was the whip of your bragged progeny,[29]
Thou shouldst not scape me here.

*Here they fight, and certain Volsces come in the aid of Aufidius.
Marcius fights till they be driven in breathless.*

Officious and not valiant, you have shamed me
In your condemned seconds.

*[Exeunt.]*

## Scene 9

*Flourish. Alarum. A retreat is sounded. Flourish. Enter, at one door,
Cominius, with the Romans; at another door, Marcius, with his arm in a
scarf.*

COMINIUS   If I should tell thee o'er this thy day's work,
Thou't not believe thy deeds. But I'll report it
Where senators shall mingle tears with smiles;
Where great patricians shall attend and shrug,
I' th' end admire; where ladies shall be frighted,
And, gladly quaked, hear more; where the dull tribunes,
That with the fusty plebeians hate thine honors,
Shall say against their hearts, 'We thank the gods
Our Rome hath such a soldier.'
Yet camest thou to a morsel of this feast,
Having fully dined before.

*Enter Titus Lartius, with his Power, from the pursuit.*

LARTIUS                    O general,

29. Ancestors. The Romans were supposed to be descended from the Trojans.

Here is the steed, we the caparison.
Hadst thou beheld—

MARCIUS               Pray now, no more. My mother,
Who has a charter to extol her blood,
When she does praise me grieves me. I have done
As you have done—that's what I can; induced
As you have been—that's for my country.
He that has but effected his good will
Hath overta'en mine act.

COMINIUS             You shall not be
The grave of your deserving. Rome must know
The value of her own. 'Twere a concealment
Worse than a theft, no less than a traducement,
To hide your doings and to silence that
Which, to the spire and top of praises vouched,
Would seem but modest. Therefore, I beseech you—
In sign of what you are, not to reward
What you have done—before our army hear me.

MARCIUS    I have some wounds upon me, and they smart
To hear themselves remembered.

COMINIUS             Should they not,
Well might they fester 'gainst ingratitude
And tent[30] themselves with death. Of all the horses,
Whereof we have ta'en good and good store, of all
The treasure in this field achieved and city,
We render you the tenth, to be ta'en forth
Before the common distribution at
Your only choice.

MARCIUS        I thank you, general,
But cannot make my heart consent to take
A bribe to pay my sword. I do refuse it,
And stand upon my common part with those
That have beheld the doing.

*A long flourish. They all cry, 'Marcius! Marcius!', cast up their caps and lances. Cominius and Lartius stand bare.*

MARCIUS    May these same instruments which you profane
Never sound more! When drums and trumpets shall

---

30. Cure. To tent a wound is to clean it by probing it.

I' th' field prove flatterers, let courts and cities be
Made all of false-faced soothing! When steel grows
Soft as the parasite's silk, let him be made
A coverture for th' wars. No more, I say!
For that I have not washed my nose that bled,
Or foiled some debile[31] wretch, which without note
Here's many else have done, you shout me forth
In acclamations hyperbolical,
As if I loved my little should be dieted
In praises sauced with lies.

COMINIUS                              Too modest are you,
More cruel to your good report than grateful
To us that give you truly. By your patience,
If 'gainst yourself you be incensed, we'll put you,
Like one that means his proper harm, in manacles,
Then reason safely with you. Therefore be it known,
As to us, to all the world, that Caius Marcius
Wears this war's garland; in token of the which,
My noble steed, known to the camp, I give him,
With all his trim belonging; and from this time,
For what he did before Corioles, call him,
With all th' applause and clamor of the host,
Caius Marcius Coriolanus. Bear
Th' addition nobly ever!

*Flourish. Trumpets sound, and drums.*

ALL   Caius Marcius Coriolanus!
CORIOLANUS   I will go wash;
And when my face is fair, you shall perceive
Whether I blush or no. Howbeit, I thank you.
I mean to stride your steed, and at all times
To undercrest your good addition
To th' fairness of my power.
COMINIUS                              So, to our tent,
Where, ere we do repose us, we will write
To Rome of our success. You, Titus Lartius,
Must to Corioles back. Send us to Rome
The best, with whom we may articulate,

31. Feeble.

For their own good and ours.

LARTIUS                                    I shall, my lord.

CORIOLANUS   The gods begin to mock me. I, that now
　　Refused most princely gifts, am bound to beg
　　Of my lord general.

COMINIUS                          Take't, 'tis yours. What is't?

CORIOLANUS   I sometime lay here in Corioles
　　At a poor man's house; he used me kindly.
　　He cried to me; I saw him prisoner;
　　But then Aufidius was within my view,
　　And wrath o'erwhelmed my pity. I request you
　　To give my poor host freedom.

COMINIUS                                O, well begged!
　　Were he the butcher of my son, he should
　　Be free as is the wind. Deliver him, Titus.

LARTIUS   Marcius, his name?

CORIOLANUS                          By Jupiter, forgot!
　　I am weary; yea, my memory is tired.
　　Have we no wine here?

COMINIUS                          Go we to our tent.
　　The blood upon your visage dries; 'tis time
　　It should be looked to. Come.

*Exeunt.*


*Scene 10*


*A flourish. Cornets. Enter Tullus Aufidius, bloody, with two or three Soldiers.*

AUFIDIUS   The town is ta'en.

FIRST SOLDIER   'Twill be delivered back on good condition.[32]

AUFIDIUS   Condition?
　　I would I were a Roman; for I cannot,
　　Being a Volsce, be that I am. Condition?
　　What good condition can a treaty find
　　I' th' part that is at mercy? Five times, Marcius,

32. On favorable terms.

I have fought with thee; so often hast thou beat me,
And wouldst do so, I think, should we encounter
As often as we eat. By th' elements,
If e'er again I meet him beard to beard,
He's mine or I am his. Mine emulation
Hath not that honor in't it had; for where
I thought to crush him in an equal force,
True sword to sword, I'll potch at him some way;
Or wrath or craft may get him.

FIRST SOLDIER                    He's the devil.

AUFIDIUS   Bolder, though not so subtle. My valor's poisoned
With only suffering stain by him; for him
Shall fly out of itself. Nor sleep nor sanctuary,
Being naked, sick, nor fane nor capitol,
The prayers of priests nor times of sacrifice,
Embargements all of fury, shall lift up
Their rotten privilege and custom 'gainst
My hate to Marcius. Where I find him, were it
At home, upon my brother's guard, even there,
Against the hospitable canon, would I
Wash my fierce hand in's heart. Go you to th' city.
Learn how 'tis held, and what they are that must
Be hostages for Rome.

FIRST SOLDIER              Will not you go?

AUFIDIUS   I am attended at the cypress grove: I pray you—
'Tis south the city mills—bring me word thither
How the world goes, that to the pace of it
I may spur on my journey.

FIRST SOLDIER                    I shall, sir.

[Exeunt.]


# ACT TWO

### Scene 1


*Enter Menenius, with the two Tribunes of the People, Sicinius and Brutus.*

MENENIUS   The augurer[1] tells me we shall have news to-night.

BRUTUS   Good or bad?

MENENIUS   Not according to the prayer of the people, for they love not Marcius.

SICINIUS   Nature teaches beasts to know their friends.

MENENIUS   Pray you, who does the wolf love?

SICINIUS   The lamb.

MENENIUS   Ay, to devour him, as the hungry plebeians would the noble Marcius.

BRUTUS   He's a lamb indeed, that baas like a bear.

MENENIUS   He's a bear indeed, that lives like a lamb. You two are old men: tell me one thing that I shall ask you.

BOTH   Well, sir.

MENENIUS   In what enormity is Marcius poor in, that you two have not in abundance?

BRUTUS   He's poor in no one fault, but stored with all.

SICINIUS   Especially in pride.

BRUTUS   And topping all others in boasting.

MENENIUS   This is strange now. Do you two know how you are censured here in the city, I mean of us o' th' right-hand file? Do you?

BOTH   Why, how are we censured?

MENENIUS   Because you talk of pride now—will you not be angry?

BOTH   Well, well, sir, well.

MENENIUS   Why, 'tis no great matter; for a very little thief of occasion will rob you of a great deal of patience. Give your dispositions the reins and be angry at your pleasures —at the least, if you take it as a pleasure to you in being so. You blame Marcius for being proud?

BRUTUS   We do it not alone, sir.

MENENIUS   I know you can do very little alone; for your helps are many, or else your actions would grow wondrous single.[2] Your abilities are too infant-like for doing much alone. You talk of pride: O that you could turn your eyes toward the napes of your necks, and make but an interior survey of your good selves! O that you could!

1. Soothsayer.
2. Feeble.

BRUTUS  What then, sir?

MENENIUS  Why, then you should discover a brace of unmerit-
ing, proud, violent, testy magistrates, alias fools, as any in
Rome.

SICINIUS  Menenius, you are known well enough too.

MENENIUS  I am known to be a humorous patrician, and one
that loves a cup of hot wine with not a drop of allaying
Tiber in't; said to be something imperfect in favoring the
first complaint; hasty and tinder-like upon too trivial
motion; one that converses more with the buttock of the
night than with the forehead of the morning. What I
think, I utter, and spend my malice in my breath.
Meeting two such wealsmen as you are,—I cannot call
you Lycurguses—if the drink you give me touch my
palate adversely, I make a crooked face at it. I cannot say
your worships have delivered the matter well, when I find
the ass in compound with the major part of your
syllables;[3] and though I must be content to bear with
those that say you are reverend grave men, yet they lie
deadly that tell you you have good faces. If you see this in
the map of my microcosm,[4] follows it that I am known
well enough too? What harm can your bisson conspectui-
ties[5] glean out of this character, if I be known well enough
too?

BRUTUS  Come, sir, come, we know you well enough.

MENENIUS  You know neither me, yourselves, nor anything.
You are ambitious for poor knaves' caps and legs. You
wear out a good wholesome forenoon in hearing a cause
between an orange-wife and a forset-seller, and then
rejourn the controversy of threepence to a second day of
audience. When you are hearing a matter between party
and party, if you chance to be pinched with the colic, you
make faces like mummers; set up the bloody flag against[6]
all patience; and, in roaring for a chamber-pot, dismiss
the controversy bleeding, the more entangled by your

3. Perhaps a joke about usage—"whereas," for instance—but hardly appropriate
since the tribunes are more demagogic than legalistic.
4. My face.
5. Blind eyes.
6. Make war.

hearing. All the peace you make in their cause is, calling both the parties knaves. You are a pair of strange ones.

BRUTUS Come, come, you are well understood to be a perfecter giber for the table than a necessary bencher in the Capitol.

MENENIUS Our very priests must become mockers, if they shall encounter such ridiculous subjects as you are. When you speak best unto the purpose, it is not worth the wagging of your beards; and your beards deserve not so honorable a grave as to stuff a botcher's cushion[7] or to be entombed in an ass's pack-saddle. Yet you must be saying Marcius is proud; who, in a cheap estimation, is worth all your predecessors since Deucalion, though per-adventure some of the best of 'em were hereditary hangmen. Good-e'en to your worships. More of your conversation would infect my brain, being the herdsmen of the beastly plebeians. I will be bold to take my leave of you.

*Brutus and Sicinius aside.*
*Enter Volumnia, Virgilia, and Valeria.*

How now, my as fair as noble ladies,—and the moon, were she earthly, no nobler—whither do you follow your eyes so fast?

VOLUMNIA Honorable Menenius, my boy Marcius ap-proaches. For the love of Juno, let's go.

MENENIUS Ha? Marcius coming home?

VOLUMNIA Ay, worthy Menenius, and with most prosperous approbation.

MENENIUS Take my cap, Jupiter, and I thank thee. Hoo! Marcius coming home!

TWO LADIES Nay, 'tis true.

VOLUMNIA Look, here's a letter from him. The state hath another, his wife another; and, I think, there's one at home for you.

---

7. Presumably the cushion that a cobbler or mender of old clothes sits on while working.

MENENIUS   I will make my very house reel to-night. A letter
  for me!

VIRGILIA   Yes, certain, there's a letter for you; I saw't.

MENENIUS   A letter for me! It gives me an estate of seven
  years' health, in which time I will make a lip[8] at the
  physician. The most sovereign prescription in Galen is
  but empiricutic[9] and, to this preservative, of no better
  report than a horse-drench. Is he not wounded? He was
  wont to come home wounded.

VIRGILIA   O, no, no, no.

VOLUMNIA   O, he is wounded; I thank the gods for't.

MENENIUS   So do I too, if it be not too much. Brings 'a victory
  in his pocket? The wounds become him.

VOLUMNIA   On's brows. Menenius, he comes the third time
  home with the oaken garland.

MENENIUS   Has he disciplined Aufidius soundly?

VOLUMNIA   Titus Lartius writes they fought together, but
  Aufidius got off.

MENENIUS   And 'twas time for him too, I'll warrant him that.
  An he had stayed by him, I would not have been so
  fidiused[10] for all the chests in Corioles and the gold that's
  in them. Is the Senate possessed of this?

VOLUMNIA   Good ladies, let's go. Yes, yes, yes! The Senate has
  letters from the general, wherein he gives my son the
  whole name of the war. He hath in this action outdone
  his former deeds doubly.

VALERIA   In troth, there's wondrous things spoke of him.

MENENIUS   Wondrous? Ay, I warrant you, and not without his
  true purchasing.

VIRGILIA   The gods grant them true!

VOLUMNIA   True? pow waw!

MENENIUS   True? I'll be sworn they are true. Where is he
  wounded? [*To the Tribunes.*] God save your good worships!
  Marcius is coming home. He has more cause to be
  proud.—Where is he wounded?

VOLUMNIA   I' th' shoulder and i' th' left arm. There will be
  large cicatrices to show the people, when he shall stand

8. Mock.
9. A quack's prescription.
10. Treated like Aufidius.

for his place.[11] He received in the repulse of Tarquin
seven hurts i' th' body.

MENENIUS  One i' th' neck and two i' th' thigh—there's nine
that I know.

VOLUMNIA  He had, before this last expedition, twenty-five
wounds upon him.

MENENIUS  Now it's twenty-seven. Every gash was an enemy's
grave. (*A shout and flourish.*) Hark! the trumpets.

VOLUMNIA  These are the ushers of Marcius. Before him he
carries noise, and behind him he leaves tears.
Death, that dark spirit, in's nervy arm doth lie;
Which, being advanced, declines, and then men die.

*A sennet. Trumpets sound. Enter Cominius the General and Titus
Lartius;[12] between them, Coriolanus, crowned with an oaken garland;
with Captains and Soldiers and a Herald.*

HERALD  Know, Rome, that all alone Marcius did fight
Within Corioles gates, where he hath won,
With fame, a name to Caius Marcius. These
In honor follows Coriolanus.
Welcome to Rome, renowned Coriolanus!

*Sound. Flourish.*

ALL  Welcome to Rome, renowned Coriolanus!

CORIOLANUS  No more of this; it does offend my heart.
Pray now, no more.

COMINIUS                     Look, sir, your mother!

CORIOLANUS                                        O,
You have, I know, petitioned all the gods
For my prosperity!

*Kneels.*

VOLUMNIA                     Nay, my good soldier, up.
My gentle Marcius, worthy Caius, and

11. Custom demanded that the candidate for consul (one of Rome's two chief
magistrates) show his scars to the people, presumably to prove his service to Rome.
See Act Two, Scene Three, and *passim* elsewhere in the play.
12. In Act One, Scene Nine (p. 225), Cominius leaves Titus Lartius in Corioles and
at the beginning of Act Three, Scene One, he appears to return to Rome for the first
time. Yet, Shakespeare sends him on stage at this point and Menenius's "You are
three" (p. 233) indicates that he belongs at this victory celebration.

By deed-achieving honor newly named—
What is it?—Coriolanus must I call thee?—
But, O, thy wife!

CORIOLANUS        My gracious silence, hail!
Wouldst thou have laughed had I come coffined home,
That weep'st to see me triumph? Ah, my dear,
Such eyes the widows in Corioles wear,
And mothers that lack sons.

MENENIUS                        Now, the gods crown thee!

CORIOLANUS   And live you yet? [*To Valeria.*] O my sweet lady,
    pardon.

VOLUMNIA   I know not where to turn. O, welcome home!
And welcome, General! and y' are welcome all!

MENENIUS   A hundred thousand welcomes! I could weep
And I could laugh; I am light and heavy. Welcome.
A curse begin at very root on's heart
That is not glad to see thee! You are three
That Rome should dote on; yet, by the faith of men,
We have some old crab-trees here at home that will not
Be grafted to your relish. Yet welcome, warriors!
We call a nettle but a nettle and
The faults of fools but folly.

COMINIUS                        Ever right.[13]

CORIOLANUS   Menenius, ever, ever.

HERALD   Give way there, and go on!

CORIOLANUS [*to Volumnia and Virgilia*]   Your hand, and yours.
Ere in our own house I do shade my head,
The good patricians must be visited;
From whom I have received not only greetings,
But with them change of honors.

VOLUMNIA                        I have lived
To see inherited my very wishes
And the buildings of my fancy. Only
There's one thing wanting, which I doubt not but
Our Rome will cast upon thee.

CORIOLANUS                        Know, good mother,
I had rather be their servant in my way,

---

13. He is either saying that Menenius is still the same or right as usual. A director
would have to decide whether they were showing simple fondness for the old man or
agreement with his words.

Than sway with them in theirs.

COMINIUS                                    On, to the Capitol!

*Flourish. Cornets. Exeunt in state, as before.*
*Brutus and Sicinius [come forward].*

BRUTUS   All tongues speak of him, and the bleared sights
Are spectacled to see him. Your prattling nurse
Into a rapture lets her baby cry,
While she chats him; the kitchen malkin pins
Her richest lockram[14] 'bout her reechy neck,
Clambering the walls to eye him. Stalls, bulks, windows
Are smothered up, leads filled, and ridges horsed[15]
With variable complexions, all agreeing
In earnestness to see him. Seld-shown flamens[16]
Do press among the popular throngs, and puff
To win a vulgar station. Our veiled dames
Commit the war of white and damask in
Their nicely-gawded cheeks to th' wanton spoil
Of Phoebus' burning kisses—such a pother
As if that whatsoever god who leads him
Were slily crept into his human powers
And gave him graceful posture.

SICINIUS                              On the sudden,
I warrant him consul.

BRUTUS                        Then our office may,
During his power, go sleep.

SICINIUS   He cannot temperately transport his honors
From where he should begin and end, but will
Lose those he hath won.

BRUTUS                          In that there's comfort.

SICINIUS                                          Doubt not
The commoners, for whom we stand, but they
Upon their ancient malice will forget
With the least cause these his new honors, which

14. The slovenly kitchen maid fastens her best scarf (made out of coarse linen)
around her dirty neck. And this from a people's tribune!
15. To see the returning hero, people climbed onto the frameworks in front of shops
(bulks), filled the roofs (leads: strips of lead were used as roofing) and mounted the
ridges atop buildings as though they were horses.
16. Priests who were seldom seen.

That he will give them make I as little question
As he is proud to do't.

BRUTUS                          I heard him swear,
Were he to stand for consul never would he
Appear i' th' market-place[17] nor on him put
The napless[18] vesture of humility;
Nor, showing, as the manner is, his wounds
To th' people, beg their stinking breaths.

SICINIUS                                    'Tis right.

BRUTUS  It was his word: O, he would miss it rather
Than carry it but by the suit of the gentry to him
And the desire of the nobles.

SICINIUS                          I wish no better
Than have him hold that purpose and to put it
In execution.

BRUTUS            'Tis most like he will.

SICINIUS  It shall be to him then as our good wills,
A sure destruction.

BRUTUS            So it must fall out
To him or our authorities for an end.
We must suggest the people in what hatred
He still hath held them; that to's power he would
Have made them mules, silenced their pleaders, and
Dispropertied their freedoms, holding them,
In human action and capacity,
Of no more soul nor fitness for the world
Than camels in their war, who have their provand
Only for bearing burthens, and sore blows
For sinking under them.

SICINIUS                          This, as you say, suggested
At some time when his soaring insolence
Shall touch the people—which time shall not want,
If he be put upon't, and that's as easy
As to set dogs on sheep—will be his fire
To kindle their dry stubble; and their blaze
Shall darken him for ever.

*Enter a Messenger.*

17. The Forum.
18. Threadbare.

BRUTUS                                What's the matter?

MESSENGER   You are sent for to th' Capitol. 'Tis thought
   That Marcius shall be consul.
   I have seen the dumb men throng to see him, and
   The blind to hear him speak. Matrons flung gloves,
   Ladies and maids their scarfs and handkerchers,
   Upon him as he passed. The nobles bended,
   As to Jove's statue, and the commons made
   A shower and thunder with their caps and shouts.
   I never saw the like.

BRUTUS                          Let's to the Capitol,
   And carry with us ears and eyes for th' time,
   But hearts for the event.[19]

SICINIUS                          Have with you.

   *Exeunt.*


## Scene 2


*Enter two Officers, to lay cushions, as it were in the Capitol.*

FIRST OFFICER   Come, come, they are almost here. How many
   stand for consulships?

SECOND OFFICER   Three, they say; but 'tis thought of every one
   Coriolanus will carry it.

FIRST OFFICER   That's a brave fellow; but he's vengeance
   proud, and loves not the common people.

SECOND OFFICER   Faith, there hath been many great men that
   have flattered the people, who ne'er loved them; and
   there be many that they have loved, they know not
   wherefore; so that, if they love they know not why, they
   hate upon no better a ground. Therefore, for Coriolanus
   neither to care whether they love or hate him manifests
   the true knowledge he has in their disposition, and out of
   his noble carelessness lets them plainly see't.

FIRST OFFICER   If he did not care whether he had their love or
   no, he waved indifferently 'twixt doing them neither good
   nor harm; but he seeks their hate with greater devotion

19. For what comes later.

than they can render it him, and leaves nothing undone
that may fully discover him their opposite. Now to seem
to affect the malice and displeasure of the people is as bad
as that which he dislikes—to flatter them for their love.

SECOND OFFICER   He hath deserved worthily of his country;
and his ascent is not by such easy degrees as those who,
having been supple and courteous to the people, bon-
neted,[20] without any further deed to have them at all into
their estimation and report. But he hath so planted his
honors in their eyes and his actions in their hearts that for
their tongues to be silent and not confess so much were a
kind of ingrateful injury; to report otherwise were a
malice that, giving itself the lie, would pluck reproof and
rebuke from every ear that heard it.

FIRST OFFICER   No more of him; he's a worthy man. Make
way, they are coming.

*A sennet. Enter the Patricians and the Tribunes of the People, Lictors
before them: Coriolanus, Menenius, Cominius the Consul. Sicinius and
Brutus take their places by themselves. Coriolanus stands.*

MENENIUS   Having determined of the Volsces and
To send for Titus Lartius, it remains,
As the main point of this our after-meeting,
To gratify his noble service that
Hath thus stood for his country. Therefore, please you,
Most reverend and grave elders, to desire
The present consul, and last general
In our well-found successes, to report
A little of that worthy work performed
By Caius Marcius Coriolanus, whom
We met here both to thank and to remember
With honors like himself.

FIRST SENATOR                    Speak, good Cominius.
Leave nothing out for length, and make us think
Rather our state's defective for requital
Than we to stretch it out. [*To the Tribunes.*] Masters o' th'
    people,
We do request your kindest ears, and after,

20. Took off their hats.

Your loving motion toward the common body
To yield what passes here.

SICINIUS                          We are convented [21]
Upon a pleasing treaty, and have hearts
Inclinable to honor and advance
The theme of our assembly.

BRUTUS                              Which the rather
We shall be blest to do, if he remember
A kinder value of the people than
He hath hereto prized them at.

MENENIUS                          That's off, that's off![22]
I would you rather had been silent. Please you
To hear Cominius speak?

BRUTUS                      Most willingly;
But yet my caution was more pertinent
Than the rebuke you give it.

MENENIUS                      He loves your people;
But tie him not to be their bedfellow.
Worthy Cominius, speak.

*Coriolanus rises, and offers to go away.*

                              Nay, keep your place.

FIRST SENATOR   Sit, Coriolanus. Never shame to hear
What you have nobly done.

CORIOLANUS                  Your honors' pardon.
I had rather have my wounds to heal again
Than hear say how I got them.

BRUTUS                          Sir, I hope
My words disbenched you not.

CORIOLANUS                  No, sir. Yet oft,
When blows have made me stay, I fled from words.
You soothed not, therefore hurt not: but your people,
I love them as they weigh—

MENENIUS              Pray now, sit down.

CORIOLANUS   I had rather have one scratch my head i' th' sun
When the alarum were struck than idly sit

21. Convened.
22. Beside the point.

To hear my nothings monstered.[23]

*Exit Coriolanus.*

MENENIUS                                        Masters of the people,
  Your multiplying spawn how can he flatter—
  That's thousand to one good one—when you now see
  He'd rather venture all his limbs for honor
  Than one on's ears to hear it? Proceed, Cominius.
COMINIUS    I shall lack voice. The deeds of Coriolanus
  Should not be uttered feebly. It is held
  That valor is the chiefest virtue, and
  Most dignifies the haver. If it be,
  The man I speak of cannot in the world
  Be singly counterpoised. At sixteen years,
  When Tarquin made a head for Rome,[24] he fought
  Beyond the mark of others. Our then dictator,
  Whom with all praise I point at, saw him fight,
  When with his Amazonian chin he drove
  The bristled lips before him; he bestrid
  An o'erpressed Roman and i' th' consul's view
  Slew three opposers; Tarquin's self he met,
  And struck him on his knee.[25] In that day's feats,
  When he might act the woman in the scene,
  He proved best man i' th' field, and for his meed
  Was brow-bound with the oak. His pupil age
  Man-entered thus, he waxed like a sea,
  And in the brunt of seventeen battles since
  He lurched all swords of the garland. For this last,
  Before and in Corioles, let me say,
  I cannot speak him home.[26] He stopped the fliers,
  And by his rare example made the coward
  Turn terror into sport. As weeds before
  A vessel under sail, so men obeyed
  And fell below his stem; his sword, death's stamp,

23. I would rather lie idle when the call to battle is sounded than have my small
doings overpraised.
24. Raised an army against Rome.
25. To his knees.
26. Say enough.

Where it did mark, it took. From face to foot
He was a thing of blood, whose every motion
Was timed with dying cries. Alone he entered
The mortal gate of th' city, which he painted
With shunless destiny; aidless came off,
And with a sudden reinforcement struck
Corioles like a planet. Now all's his,
When by and by the din of war gan pierce
His ready sense; then straight his doubled spirit
Requickened what in flesh was fatigate,
And to the battle came he; where he did
Run reeking o'er the lives of men, as if
'Twere a perpetual spoil, and till we called
Both field and city ours, he never stood
To ease his breast with panting.

MENENIUS                                Worthy man!

FIRST SENATOR   He cannot but with measure fit the honors
Which we devise him.

COMINIUS                    Our spoils he kicked at,
And looked upon things precious as they were
The common muck of the world. He covets less
Than misery itself would give; rewards
His deeds with doing them; and is content
To spend the time to end it.

MENENIUS                          He's right noble.
Let him be called for.

FIRST SENATOR          Call Coriolanus.

OFFICER   He doth appear.

*Enter Coriolanus.*

MENENIUS   The Senate, Coriolanus, are well pleased
To make thee consul.

CORIOLANUS                I do owe them still
My life and services.

MENENIUS                It then remains
That you do speak to the people.

CORIOLANUS                          I do beseech you,
Let me o'erleap that custom; for I cannot
Put on the gown, stand naked, and entreat them
For my wounds' sake to give their suffrage. Please you

That I may pass this doing.

SICINIUS                              Sir, the people
Must have their voices; neither will they bate
One jot of ceremony.

MENENIUS                      Put them not to't.
Pray you, go fit you to the custom and
Take to you, as your predecessors have,
Your honor with your form.

CORIOLANUS                              It is a part
That I shall blush in acting, and might well
Be taken from the people.

BRUTUS                              [to Sicinius] Mark you that?

CORIOLANUS     To brag unto them, 'Thus I did, and thus!'
Show them th' unaching scars which I should hide,
As if I had received them for the hire
Of their breath only!

MENENIUS                      Do not stand upon't.
We recommend to you, tribunes of the people,
Our purpose to them; and to our noble consul
Wish we all joy and honor.

SENATORS     To Coriolanus come all joy and honor!

*Flourish. Cornets. Then exeunt.*
*Manent Sicinius and Brutus.*

BRUTUS     You see how he intends to use the people.

SICINIUS     May they perceive's intent! He will require them
As if he did contemn what he requested
Should be in them to give.

BRUTUS                              Come, we'll inform them
Of our proceedings here. On th' market-place
I know they do attend us.

[*Exeunt.*]


## Scene 3


*Enter seven or eight Citizens.*

FIRST CITIZEN     Once if he do require our voices, we ought not
    to deny him.

SECOND CITIZEN    We may, sir, if we will.

THIRD CITIZEN    We have power in ourselves to do it, but it is a power that we have no power to do; for if he show us his wounds and tell us his deeds, we are to put our tongues into those wounds and speak for them. So, if he tell us his noble deeds, we must also tell him our noble acceptance of them. Ingratitude is monstrous; and for the multitude to be ingrateful were to make a monster of the multitude; of the which we being members, should bring ourselves to be monstrous members.

FIRST CITIZEN    And to make us no better thought of, a little help will serve; for once we stood up about the corn, he himself stuck not to call us the many-headed multitude.

THIRD CITIZEN    We have been called so of many; not that our heads are some brown, some black, some abram,[27] some bald, but that our wits are so diversely colored; and truly I think if all our wits were to issue out of one skull, they would fly east, west, north, south, and their consent of one direct way should be at once to all the points o' th' compass.

SECOND CITIZEN    Think you so? Which way do you judge my wit would fly?

THIRD CITIZEN    Nay, your wit will not so soon out as another man's will; 'tis strongly wedged up in a block-head; but if it were at liberty, 'twould, sure, southward.

SECOND CITIZEN    Why that way?

THIRD CITIZEN    To lose itself in a fog; where being three parts melted away with rotten dews, the fourth would return for conscience sake, to help to get thee a wife.

SECOND CITIZEN    You are never without your tricks. You may, you may!

THIRD CITIZEN    Are you all resolved to give your voices? But that's no matter, the greater part carries it. I say, if he would incline to the people, there was never a worthier man.

*Enter Coriolanus in a gown of humility, with Menenius.*

Here he comes, and in the gown of humility. Mark his behavior. We are not to stay all together, but to come by

27. Auburn.

him where he stands, by ones, by twos, and by threes. He's to make his requests by particulars;[28] wherein every one of us has a single honor, in giving him our own voices with our own tongues. Therefore follow me, and I'll direct you how you shall go by him.

ALL  Content, content.

[*Exeunt Citizens.*]

MENENIUS  O sir, you are not right. Have you not known The worthiest men have done't?

CORIOLANUS                                   What must I say? 'I pray, sir'—Plague upon't! I cannot bring My tongue to such a pace. 'Look, sir, my wounds! I got them in my country's service, when Some certain of your brethren roared and ran From th' noise of our own drums.'

MENENIUS                                   O me, the gods! You must not speak of that. You must desire them To think upon you.

CORIOLANUS             Think upon me? Hang 'em! I would they would forget me, like the virtues Which our divines lose by 'em.[29]

MENENIUS                                   You'll mar all. I'll leave you. Pray you, speak to 'em, I pray you, In wholesome manner.

*Exit.*

CORIOLANUS                       Bid them wash their faces And keep their teeth clean.

*Enter three[30] of the Citizens.*

                                   So, here comes a brace. You know the cause, sir, of my standing here.

THIRD CITIZEN  We do, sir. Tell us what hath brought you to't.

CORIOLANUS  Mine own desert.

SECOND CITIZEN  Your own desert?

28. To individuals.
29. Fail to teach them.
30. Although the First Folio says "three," it is clear from Coriolanus's "brace" and his "two worthy voices" that only two citizens approach.

CORIOLANUS  Ay, not mine own desire.

THIRD CITIZEN  How not your own desire?

CORIOLANUS  No, sir, 'twas never my desire yet to trouble the poor with begging.

THIRD CITIZEN  You must think, if we give you anything, we hope to gain by you.

CORIOLANUS  Well then, I pray, your price o' th' consulship?

FIRST CITIZEN  The price is to ask it kindly.

CORIOLANUS  Kindly, sir, I pray, let me ha't. I have wounds to show you, which shall be yours in private. Your good voice, sir. What say you?

SECOND CITIZEN  You shall ha't, worthy sir.

CORIOLANUS  A match, sir. There's in all two worthy voices begged. I have your alms. Adieu.

THIRD CITIZEN  But this is something odd.

SECOND CITIZEN  An 'twere to give again—but 'tis no matter.

*Exeunt.*
*Enter two other Citizens.*

CORIOLANUS  Pray you now, if it may stand with the tune of your voices that I may be consul, I have here the customary gown.

FOURTH CITIZEN  You have deserved nobly of your country, and you have not deserved nobly.

CORIOLANUS  Your enigma?

FOURTH CITIZEN  You have been a scourge to her enemies; you have been a rod to her friends. You have not indeed loved the common people.

CORIOLANUS  You should account me the more virtuous that I have not been common in my love. I will, sir, flatter my sworn brother, the people, to earn a dearer estimation of them. 'Tis a condition they account gentle; and since the wisdom of their choice is rather to have my hat than my heart, I will practice the insinuating nod and be off to them most counterfeitly: that is, sir, I will counterfeit the bewitchment of some popular man and give it bountiful to the desirers. Therefore, beseech you, I may be consul.

FIFTH CITIZEN  We hope to find you our friend, and therefore give you our voices heartily.

FOURTH CITIZEN   You have received many wounds for your
  country.
CORIOLANUS   I will not seal your knowledge with showing
  them. I will make much of your voices, and so trouble you
  no farther.
BOTH   The gods give you joy, sir, heartily!

  [*Exeunt.*]

CORIOLANUS   Most sweet voices!
  Better it is to die, better to starve,
  Than crave the hire which first we do deserve.
  Why in this wolvish toge should I stand here,
  To beg of Hob and Dick that does appear
  Their needless vouches? Custom calls me to't.
  What custom wills, in all things should we do't,
  The dust on antique time would lie unswept
  And mountainous error be too highly heaped
  For truth t' o'erpeer. Rather than fool it so,
  Let the high office and the honor go
  To one that would do thus. I am half through;
  The one part suffered, the other will I do.

  *Enter three Citizens more.*

  Here comes moe voices.
  Your voices! For your voices I have fought;
  Watched for your voices; for your voices bear
  Of wounds two dozen odd; battles thrice six
  I have seen and heard of; for your voices have
  Done many things, some less, some more. Your voices!
  Indeed, I would be consul.
FIRST CITIZEN   He has done nobly, and cannot go without any
  honest man's voice.
SECOND CITIZEN   Therefore let him be consul. The gods give
  him joy, and make him good friend to the people!
ALL   Amen, amen. God save thee, noble consul!

  [*Exeunt.*]

CORIOLANUS   Worthy voices!

  *Enter Menenius, with Brutus and Sicinius.*

MENENIUS   You have stood your limitation, and the tribunes
  Endue you with the people's voice. Remains
  That, in th' official marks invested, you
  Anon do meet the Senate.
CORIOLANUS                          Is this done?
SICINIUS   The custom of request you have discharged.
  The people do admit you, and are summoned
  To meet anon upon your approbation.
CORIOLANUS   Where? at the Senate House?
SICINIUS                                There, Coriolanus.
CORIOLANUS   May I change these garments?
SICINIUS                                You may, sir.
CORIOLANUS   That I'll straight do; and, knowing myself again,
  Repair to th' Senate House.
MENENIUS   I'll keep you company. Will you along?
BRUTUS   We stay here for the people.
SICINIUS                                Fare you well.

  *Exeunt Coriolanus and Menenius.*

  He has it now; and by his looks, methinks,
  'Tis warm at's heart.
BRUTUS   With a proud heart he wore his humble weeds.
  Will you dismiss the people?

  *Enter the Plebeians.*

SICINIUS   How now, my masters! Have you chose this man?
FIRST CITIZEN   He has our voices, sir.
BRUTUS   We pray the gods he may deserve your loves.
SECOND CITIZEN   Amen, sir. To my poor unworthy notice,
  He mocked us when he begged our voices.
THIRD CITIZEN                          Certainly
  He flouted us downright.
FIRST CITIZEN   No, 'tis his kind of speech; he did not mock us.
SECOND CITIZEN   Not one amongst us, save yourself, but says
  He used us scornfully. He should have showed us
  His marks of merit, wounds received for's country.
SICINIUS   Why, so he did, I am sure.
ALL                                No, no! No man saw 'em.
THIRD CITIZEN   He said he had wounds, which he could show
    in private;

And with his hat, thus waving it in scorn,
'I would be consul,' says he. 'Aged custom,
But by your voices, will not so permit me.
Your voices therefore.' When we granted that,
Here was 'I thank you for your voices, thank you!
Your most sweet voices! Now you've left your voices,
I have no further with you.' Was not this mockery?

SICINIUS   Why either were you ignorant to see it,
Or, seeing it, of such childish friendliness
To yield your voices?

BRUTUS                Could you not have told him
As you were lessoned? When he had no power,
But was a petty servant to the state,
He was your enemy, ever spake against
Your liberties and the charters that you bear
I' th' body of the weal; and now, arriving
A place of potency and sway o' th' state,
If he should still malignantly remain
Fast foe to th' plebeii, your voices might
Be curses to yourselves. You should have said
That as his worthy deeds did claim no less
Than what he stood for, so his gracious nature
Would think upon you for your voices and
Translate his malice towards you into love,
Standing your friendly lord.

SICINIUS               Thus to have said,
As you were fore-advised, had touched his spirit
And tried his inclination; from him plucked
Either his gracious promise, which you might,
As cause had called you up, have held him to;
Or else it would have galled his surly nature,
Which easily endures not article
Tying him to aught; so putting him to rage,
You should have ta'en the advantage of his choler
And passed him unelected.

BRUTUS              Did you perceive
He did solicit you in free contempt
When he did need your loves, and do you think
That his contempt shall not be bruising to you
When he hath power to crush? Why, had your bodies

No heart among you? Or had you tongues to cry
Against the rectorship[31] of judgment?

SICINIUS                                   Have you,
Ere now, denied the asker? And now again,
Of him that did not ask but mock, bestow
Your sued-for tongues!

THIRD CITIZEN   He's not confirmed; we may deny him yet.

SECOND CITIZEN   And will deny him.
I'll have five hundred voices of that sound.

FIRST CITIZEN   I twice five hundred, and their friends to piece
'em.

BRUTUS   Get you hence instantly, and tell those friends
They have chose a consul that will from them take
Their liberties; make them of no more voice
Than dogs, that are as often beat for barking
As therefore kept to do so.

SICINIUS                             Let them assemble,
And on a safer judgment all revoke
Your ignorant election. Enforce his pride,
And his old hate unto you. Besides, forget not
With what contempt he wore the humble weed,
How in his suit he scorned you; but your loves,
Thinking upon his services, took from you
The apprehension of his present portance,
Which most gibingly, ungravely, he did fashion
After th' inveterate hate he bears you.

BRUTUS                                      Lay
A fault on us, your tribunes: that we labored,
No impediment between, but that you must
Cast your election on him.

SICINIUS                        Say you chose him
More after our commandment than as guided
By your own true affections, and that your minds,
Preoccupied with what you rather must do
Than what you should, made you against the grain
To voice him consul. Lay the fault on us.

BRUTUS   Ay, spare us not. Say we read lectures to you,

31. Guidance, i.e., did you have tongues that contradicted your own good
judgment?

How youngly he began to serve his country,
How long continued, and what stock he springs of,
The noble house o' th' Marcians, from whence came
That Ancus Marcius, Numa's daughter's son,
Who after great Hostilius here was king;
Of the same house Publius and Quintus were,
That our best water brought by conduits hither;
And nobly named, so twice being censor,
Was his great ancestor.[32]

SICINIUS                    One thus descended,
That hath beside well in his person wrought
To be set high in place, we did commend
To your remembrances; but you have found,
Scaling his present bearing with his past,
That he's your fixed enemy, and revoke
Your sudden approbation.

BRUTUS                    Say, you ne'er had done it—
Harp on that still—but by our putting on;
And presently, when you have drawn your number,
Repair to th' Capitol.

ALL                    We will so: almost all
Repent in their election.

*Exeunt Plebeians.*

BRUTUS                    Let them go on.
This mutiny were better put in hazard
Than stay past doubt, for greater.
If, as his nature is, he fall in rage
With their refusal, both observe and answer
The vantage of his anger.

SICINIUS                    To th' Capitol, come.

32. The correctly named ancestor is presumably Censorinus. Editors have always assumed that something is missing, although given Shakespeare's powers of compression in this play one might argue otherwise; he may have doctored the speech to get in the proper name and to fill out the newly added line. Alexander Pope's suggestion at least has some charm of its own: "And Censorinus, darling of the people/(And nobly nam'd so twice being Censor)/Was his great Ancestor." It is probably better not to look too closely at Coriolanus's family tree as it is presented here, since both the building of the aqueduct and Censorinus's service to Rome came long after Coriolanus is supposed to have lived. Just take the speech as an indication that Coriolanus came from high-class stock. For Numa, in another context, see notes, p. 145 and p. 197.

We will be there before the stream o' th' people;
And this shall seem, as partly 'tis, their own,
Which we have goaded onward.

*Exeunt.*

# ACT THREE

## *Scene 1*

*Cornets. Enter Coriolanus, Menenius, all the Gentry, Cominius, Titus
Lartius, and other Senators.*

CORIOLANUS   Tullus Aufidius then had made new head?

LARTIUS   He had, my lord, and that it was which caused
Our swifter composition.[1]

CORIOLANUS   So then the Volsces stand but as at first,
Ready, when time shall prompt them, to make road
Upon's again.

COMINIUS          They are worn, lord consul, so,
That we shall hardly in our ages see
Their banners wave again.

CORIOLANUS                    Saw you Aufidius?

LARTIUS   On safeguard he came to me; and did curse
Against the Volsces, for they had so vilely
Yielded the town. He is retired to Antium.

CORIOLANUS   Spoke he of me?

LARTIUS                    He did, my lord.

CORIOLANUS                              How? what?

LARTIUS   How often he had met you, sword to sword;
That of all things upon the earth he hated
Your person most; that he would pawn his fortunes
To hopeless restitution, so he might
Be called your vanquisher.

CORIOLANUS                    At Antium lives he?

LARTIUS   At Antium.

CORIOLANUS   I wish I had a cause to seek him there,
To oppose his hatred fully. Welcome home.

1. Coming to terms.

*Enter Sicinius and Brutus.*

Behold, these are the tribunes of the people,
The tongues o' th' common mouth. I do despise them;
For they do prank them in authority
Against all noble sufferance.

SICINIUS                              Pass no further.

CORIOLANUS   Ha! What is that?

BRUTUS   It will be dangerous to go on. No further.

CORIOLANUS   What makes this change?

MENENIUS   The matter?

COMINIUS   Hath he not passed the noble and the common?

BRUTUS   Cominius, no.

CORIOLANUS                    Have I had children's voices?

FIRST SENATOR   Tribunes, give way. He shall to th' market-
    place.

BRUTUS   The people are incensed against him.

SICINIUS                                        Stop,
    Or all will fall in broil.

CORIOLANUS                    Are these your herd?
    Must these have voices, that can yield them now
    And straight disclaim their tongues? What are your offices?
    You being their mouths, why rule you not their teeth?
    Have you not set them on?

MENENIUS                    Be calm, be calm.

CORIOLANUS   It is a purposed thing, and grows by plot,
    To curb the will of the nobility.
    Suffer't, and live with such as cannot rule
    Nor ever will be ruled.

BRUTUS                    Call't not a plot:
    The people cry you mocked them; and of late,
    When corn was given them gratis, you repined;
    Scandaled the suppliants for the people, called them
    Time-pleasers, flatterers, foes to nobleness.

CORIOLANUS   Why, this was known before.

BRUTUS                                        Not to them all.

CORIOLANUS   Have you informed them sithence?

BRUTUS                                        How! I inform them!

CORIOLANUS   You are like to do such business.

BRUTUS                                        Not unlike,

Each way, to better yours.

CORIOLANUS   Why then should I be consul? By yond clouds,
Let me deserve so ill as you, and make me
Your fellow tribune.

SICINIUS                You show too much of that
For which the people stir. If you will pass
To where you are bound, you must inquire your way,
Which you are out of, with a gentler spirit,
Or never be so noble as a consul,
Nor yoke with him for tribune.

MENENIUS                Let's be calm.

COMINIUS   The people are abused, set on. This paltering
Becomes not Rome, nor has Coriolanus
Deserved this so dishonored rub, laid falsely
I' th' plain way of his merit.

CORIOLANUS                Tell me of corn!
This was my speech, and I will speak't again—

MENENIUS   Not now, not now.

FIRST SENATOR                Not in this heat, sir, now.

CORIOLANUS   Now, as I live, I will. My nobler friends,
I crave their pardons.
For the mutable, rank-scented meiny, let them
Regard me as I do not flatter, and
Therein behold themselves. I say again,
In soothing them we nourish 'gainst our Senate
The cockle² of rebellion, insolence, sedition,
Which we ourselves have ploughed for, sowed, and scattered
By mingling them with us, the honored number,
Who lack not virtue, no, nor power, but that
Which they have given to beggars.

MENENIUS                Well, no more.

FIRST SENATOR   No more words, we beseech you.

CORIOLANUS                How? no more?
As for my country I have shed my blood,
Not fearing outward force, so shall my lungs
Coin words till their decay against those measles
Which we disdain should tetter us, yet sought
The very way to catch them.

BRUTUS                You speak o' th' people

2. Weed.

As if you were a god to punish, not
A man of their infirmity.

SICINIUS                                   'Twere well
We let the people know't.

MENENIUS                                   What, what? His choler?

CORIOLANUS   Choler!
Were I as patient as the midnight sleep,
By Jove, 'twould be my mind!

SICINIUS                                   It is a mind
That shall remain a poison where it is,
Not poison any further.

CORIOLANUS                           Shall remain!
Hear you this Triton[3] of the minnows? Mark you
His absolute 'shall'?

COMINIUS                           'Twas from the canon.[4]

CORIOLANUS                                   'Shall'?
O good but most unwise patricians! Why,
You grave but reckless senators, have you thus
Given Hydra here to choose an officer,
That with his peremptory 'shall,' being but
The horn and noise o' th' monster's, wants not spirit
To say he'll turn your current in a ditch,
And make your channel his? If he have power,
Then vail your ignorance;[5] if none, awake
Your dangerous lenity. If you are learned,
Be not as common fools; if you are not,
Let them have cushions by you.[6] You are plebeians
If they be senators; and they are no less
When, both your voices blended, the great'st taste
Most palates theirs.[7] They choose their magistrate;
And such a one as he, who puts his 'shall,'
His popular 'shall,' against a graver bench
Than ever frowned in Greece. By Jove himself,

3. Neptune's trumpeter. So far as Coriolanus is concerned, Sicinius does his blowing for the little fish, not for the chief seagod. See "horn and noise" below.

4. Outside the law. The tribunes were supposed to voice the opinion of the people, not impose decisions of their own.

5. You who foolishly gave it to him, bow down (vail).

6. Seats in the Senate. See stage directions at beginning of Act Two, Scene Two.

7. Their voice predominates. The metaphor is that of a strong (Coriolanus might say *rank*) flavor imparting its taste to a mixture.

It makes the consuls base! and my soul aches
To know, when two authorities are up,
Neither supreme, how soon confusion
May enter 'twixt the gap of both and take
The one by th' other.

COMINIUS                    Well, on to th' market-place.

CORIOLANUS    Whoever gave that counsel, to give forth
The corn o' th' storehouse gratis, as 'twas used
Sometime in Greece—

MENENIUS                    Well, well, no more of that.

CORIOLANUS    Though there the people had more absolute
    power—
I say they nourished disobedience, fed
The ruin of the state.

BRUTUS                    Why, shall the people give
One that speaks thus their voice?

CORIOLANUS                         I'll give my reasons,
More worthier than their voices. They know the corn
Was not our recompense, resting well assured
They ne'er did service for't. Being pressed to th' war,
Even when the navel of the state was touched,
They would not thread the gates. This kind of service
Did not deserve corn gratis. Being i' th' war,
Their mutinies and revolts, wherein they showed
Most valor, spoke not for them. Th' accusation
Which they have often made against the Senate,
All cause unborn, could never be the native
Of our so frank donation. Well, what then?
How shall this bosom multiplied digest
The Senate's courtesy? Let deeds express
What's like to be their words: 'We did request it;
We are the greater poll, and in true fear
They gave us our demands.' Thus we debase
The nature of our seats, and make the rabble
Call our cares fears; which will in time
Break ope the locks o' th' Senate, and bring in
The crows to peck the eagles.

MENENIUS                    Come, enough.

BRUTUS    Enough, with over-measure.

CORIOLANUS                         No, take more!

What may be sworn by, both divine and human,
Seal what I end withal! This double worship,
Where one part does disdain with cause, the other
Insult without all reason; where gentry, title, wisdom,
Cannot conclude but by the yea and no
Of general ignorance—it must omit
Real necessities, and give way the while
To unstable slightness. Purpose so barred, it follows,
Nothing is done to purpose. Therefore, beseech you,—
You that will be less fearful than discreet;
That love the fundamental part of state
More than you doubt the change on't; that prefer
A noble life before a long, and wish
To jump[8] a body with a dangerous physic
That's sure of death without it—at once pluck out
The multitudinous tongue; let them not lick
The sweet which is their poison. Your dishonor
Mangles true judgment, and bereaves the state
Of that integrity which should become't,
Not having the power to do the good it would
For th' ill which doth control't.

BRUTUS                                   'Has said enough.

SICINIUS   'Has spoken like a traitor, and shall answer
As traitors do.

CORIOLANUS      Thou wretch, despite o'erwhelm thee!
What should the people do with these bald tribunes?
On whom depending, their obedience fails
To th' greater bench. In a rebellion,
When what's not meet, but what must be, was law,
Then were they chosen. In a better hour,
Let what is meet be said it must be meet,
And throw their power i' th' dust.

BRUTUS   Manifest treason!

SICINIUS                            This a consul? No.

BRUTUS   The ædiles, ho!

*Enter an Ædile.*

                    Let him be apprehended.

8. Risk.

SICINIUS    Go, call the people; [*Exit Ædile.*] in whose name myself
 Attach thee as a traitorous innovator,
 A foe to th' public weal. Obey, I charge thee,
 And follow to thine answer.
CORIOLANUS       Hence, old goat!
ALL [*Patricians*]    We'll surety him.
COMINIUS       Ag'd sir, hands off.
CORIOLANUS    Hence, rotten thing! or I shall shake thy bones
 Out of thy garments.
SICINIUS      Help, ye citizens!

*Enter a rabble of Plebeians, with the Ædiles.*

MENENIUS    On both sides more respect.
SICINIUS    Here's he that would take from you all your power.
BRUTUS    Seize him, ædiles!
ALL [*Plebeians*]    Down with him! down with him!
SECOND SENATOR    Weapons, weapons, weapons!

*They all bustle about Coriolanus.*

ALL    Tribunes!—Patricians!—Citizens!—What, ho!
 Sicinius!—Brutus!—Coriolanus!—Citizens!
 Peace, peace, peace!—Stay, hold, peace!
MENENIUS    What is about to be? I am out of breath;
 Confusion's near; I cannot speak. You, tribunes
 To th' people!—Coriolanus, patience!—
 Speak, good Sicinius.
SICINIUS      Hear me, people. Peace!
ALL [*Plebeians*]    Let's hear our tribune. Peace! Speak, speak, speak!
SICINIUS    You are at point to lose your liberties.
 Marcius would have all from you, Marcius,
 Whom late you have named for consul.
MENENIUS       Fie, fie, fie!
 This is the way to kindle, not to quench.
FIRST SENATOR    To unbuild the city and to lay all flat.
SICINIUS    What is the city but the people?
ALL [*Plebeians*]      True,
 The people are the city.
BRUTUS    By the consent of all we were established

    The people's magistrates.

ALL [*Plebeians*]               You so remain.

MENENIUS   And so are like to do.

COMINIUS   That is the way to lay the city flat,
    To bring the roof to the foundation,
    And bury all, which yet distinctly ranges,
    In heaps and piles of ruin.

SICINIUS               This deserves death.

BRUTUS   Or let us stand to our authority,
    Or let us lose it. We do here pronounce,
    Upon the part o' th' people, in whose power
    We were elected theirs, Marcius is worthy
    Of present death.

SICINIUS         Therefore lay hold of him;
    Bear him to th' Rock Tarpeian, and from thence
    Into destruction cast him.

BRUTUS               Ædiles, seize him!

ALL [*Plebeians*]   Yield, Marcius, yield!

MENENIUS              Hear me one word.
    Beseech you, tribunes, hear me but a word.

AEDILES   Peace, peace!

MENENIUS [*to Brutus*]   Be that you seem, truly your country's
    friend,
    And temperately proceed to what you would
    Thus violently redress.

BRUTUS           Sir, those cold ways,
    That seem like prudent helps, are very poisonous
    Where the disease is violent. Lay hands upon him,
    And bear him to the Rock.

*Coriolanus draws his sword.*

CORIOLANUS           No, I'll die here.
    There's some among you have beheld me fighting:
    Come, try upon yourselves what you have seen me.

MENENIUS   Down with that sword! Tribunes, withdraw awhile.

BRUTUS   Lay hands upon him.

MENENIUS           Help Marcius, help!
    You that be noble, help him, young and old!

ALL [*Plebeians*]   Down with him! down with him!

*Exeunt. In this mutiny the Tribunes, the Ædiles, and the People are beat in.*[9]

MENENIUS   Go, get you to your house! be gone, away!
All will be naught else.

SECOND SENATOR            Get you gone.

CORIOLANUS                           Stand fast!
We have as many friends as enemies.

MENENIUS   Shall it be put to that?

FIRST SENATOR                 The gods forbid!
I prithee, noble friend, home to thy house;
Leave us to cure this cause.

MENENIUS                 For 'tis a sore upon us
You cannot tent yourself. Be gone, beseech you.

COMINIUS   Come, sir, along with us.

CORIOLANUS   I would they were barbarians, as they are,
Though in Rome littered; not Romans, as they are not,
Though calved i' th' porch o' th' Capitol—

MENENIUS                           Be gone;
Put not your worthy rage into your tongue.
One time will owe another.

CORIOLANUS                 On fair ground
I could beat forty of them.

MENENIUS                 I could myself
Take up a brace o' th' best of them; yea, the two tribunes.

COMINIUS   But now 'tis odds beyond arithmetic,
And manhood is called foolery when it stands
Against a falling fabric. Will you hence
Before the tag return? whose rage doth rend
Like interrupted waters, and o'erbear
What they are used to bear.

MENENIUS                 Pray you, be gone.
I'll try whether my old wit be in request
With those that have but little. This must be patched
With cloth of any color.

COMINIUS                 Nay, come away.

*Exeunt Coriolanus and Cominius.*

PATRICIAN   This man has marred his fortune.

9. Driven off stage.

MENENIUS   His nature is too noble for the world.
He would not flatter Neptune for his trident,[10]
Or Jove for's power to thunder. His heart 's his mouth.
What his breast forges, that his tongue must vent;
And, being angry, does forget that ever
He heard the name of death. (*A noise within.*)
Here's goodly work!
PATRICIAN                    I would they were abed!
MENENIUS   I would they were in Tiber! What the vengeance!
Could he not speak 'em fair?

*Enter Brutus and Sicinius, with the Rabble again.*

SICINIUS                         Where is this viper
That would depopulate the city and
Be every man himself?
MENENIUS                    You worthy tribunes—
SICINIUS   He shall be thrown down the Tarpeian Rock
With rigorous hands. He hath resisted law;
And therefore law shall scorn him further trial
Than the severity of the public power,
Which he so sets at nought.
FIRST CITIZEN                      He shall well know
The noble tribunes are the people's mouths,
And we their hands.
ALL [*Citizens*]        He shall, sure on't.
MENENIUS                              Sir, sir,—
SICINIUS   Peace!
MENENIUS   Do not cry havoc, where you should but hunt
With modest warrant.
SICINIUS                       Sir, how comes't that you
Have holp to make this rescue?
MENENIUS                              Hear me speak:
As I do know the consul's worthiness,
So can I name his faults—
SICINIUS                      Consul! what consul?
MENENIUS   The consul Coriolanus.
BRUTUS                              He consul!
ALL [*Citizens*]   No, no, no, no, no!

10. The three-pronged spear was the symbol of Neptune's power.

MENENIUS    If, by the tribunes' leave, and yours, good people,
  I may be heard, I'd crave a word or two;
  The which shall turn you to no further harm
  Than so much loss of time.
SICINIUS                    Speak briefly then;
  For we are peremptory to dispatch
  This viperous traitor. To eject him hence
  Were but our danger, and to keep him here
  Our certain death. Therefore it is decreed
  He dies to-night.
MENENIUS              Now the good gods forbid
  That our renowned Rome, whose gratitude
  Towards her deserved children is enrolled
  In Jove's own book, like an unnatural dam
  Should now eat up her own!
SICINIUS    He's a disease that must be cut away.
MENENIUS    O, he's a limb that has but a disease:
  Mortal, to cut it off; to cure it, easy.
  What has he done to Rome that's worthy death?
  Killing our enemies, the blood he hath lost—
  Which, I dare vouch, is more than that he hath,
  By many an ounce—he dropped it for his country;
  And what is left, to lose it by his country
  Were to us all that do't and suffer it
  A brand to th' end o' th' world.
SICINIUS                    This is clean kam.[11]
BRUTUS    Merely awry. When he did love his country,
  It honored him.
SICINIUS            The service of the foot,
  Being once gangrened, is not then respected
  For what before it was.
BRUTUS                We'll hear no more.
  Pursue him to his house and pluck him thence,
  Lest his infection, being of catching nature,
  Spread further.
MENENIUS          One word more, one word.
  This tiger-footed rage, when it shall find
  The harm of unscanned swiftness, will too late

11. All wrong.

Tie leaden pounds to's heels. Proceed by process,
Lest parties, as he is beloved, break out
And sack great Rome with Romans.

BRUTUS                                    If it were so—

SICINIUS   What do ye talk?
Have we not had a taste of his obedience?
Our ædiles smote? ourselves resisted? Come.

MENENIUS   Consider this: he has been bred i' th' wars
Since 'a could draw a sword, and is ill schooled
In bolted language; meal and bran together
He throws without distinction. Give me leave,
I'll go to him and undertake to bring him
Where he shall answer by a lawful form,
In peace, to his utmost peril.

FIRST SENATOR                Noble tribunes,
It is the humane way. The other course
Will prove too bloody, and the end of it
Unknown to the beginning.

SICINIUS                Noble Menenius,
Be you then as the people's officer.
Masters, lay down your weapons.

BRUTUS                                Go not home.

SICINIUS   Meet on the market-place. We'll attend you there;
Where, if you bring not Marcius, we'll proceed
In our first way.

MENENIUS            I'll bring him to you.
[To the Senators] Let me desire your company. He must
    come,
Or what is worst will follow.

FIRST SENATOR                Pray you, let's to him.

*Exeunt omnes.*


*Scene 2*


*Enter Coriolanus, with Nobles.*

CORIOLANUS   Let them pull all about mine ears, present me
Death on the wheel or at wild horses' heels,

Or pile ten hills on the Tarpeian Rock,
That the precipitation might down stretch
Below the beam of sight, yet will I still
Be thus to them.

NOBLE You do the nobler.

CORIOLANUS I muse my mother
Does not approve me further, who was wont
To call them woollen vassals, things created
To buy and sell with groats, to show bare heads
In congregations, to yawn, be still and wonder,
When one but of my ordinance stood up
To speak of peace or war.

*Enter Volumnia.*

I talk of you:
Why did you wish me milder? Would you have me
False to my nature? Rather say I play
The man I am.

VOLUMNIA O, sir, sir, sir,
I would have had you put your power well on,
Before you had worn it out.

CORIOLANUS Let go.

VOLUMNIA You might have been enough the man you are
With striving less to be so. Lesser had been
The taxings of your dispositions, if
You had not showed them how ye were disposed
Ere they lacked power to cross you.

CORIOLANUS Let them hang!

VOLUMNIA Ay, and burn too!

*Enter Menenius, with the Senators.*

MENENIUS Come, come, you have been too rough, something
too rough.
You must return and mend it.

FIRST SENATOR There's no remedy,
Unless, by not so doing, our good city
Cleave in the midst, and perish.

VOLUMNIA Pray, be counselled.
I have a heart as little apt as yours,
But yet a brain that leads my use of anger

To better vantage.

MENENIUS            Well said, noble woman!
Before he should thus stoop to th' herd, but that
The violent fit o' th' time craves it as physic
For the whole state, I would put mine armor on,
Which I can scarcely bear.

CORIOLANUS            What must I do?

MENENIUS   Return to th' tribunes.

CORIOLANUS            Well, what then? what then?

MENENIUS   Repent what you have spoke.

CORIOLANUS   For them? I cannot do it to the gods.
Must I then do't to them?

VOLUMNIA            You are too absolute;
Though therein you can never be too noble,
But when extremities speak. I've heard you say,
Honor and policy, like unsevered friends,
I' th' war do grow together. Grant that, and tell me,
In peace what each of them by th' other lose,
That they combine not there.

CORIOLANUS            Tush, tush!

MENENIUS            A good demand.

VOLUMNIA   If it be honor in your wars to seem
The same you are not,—which, for your best ends,
You adopt your policy—how is it less or worse,
That it shall hold companionship in peace
With honor, as in war; since that to both
It stands in like request?

CORIOLANUS            Why force you this?

VOLUMNIA   Because that now it lies you on to speak
To th' people, not by your own instruction,
Nor by th' matter which your heart prompts you,
But with such words that are but roted in
Your tongue, though but bastards and syllables
Of no allowance to your bosom's truth.
Now, this no more dishonors you at all
Than to take in a town with gentle words,
Which else would put you to your fortune and
The hazard of much blood.
I would dissemble with my nature where
My fortunes and my friends at stake required

I should do so in honor. I am in this
Your wife, your son, these senators, the nobles;
And you will rather show our general louts
How you can frown than spend a fawn upon 'em
For the inheritance of their loves and safeguard
Of what that want might ruin.

MENENIUS                              Noble lady!—
Come, go with us. Speak fair. You may salve so,
Not what is dangerous present, but the loss
Of what is past.

VOLUMNIA          I prithee now, my son,
Go to them, with this bonnet in thy hand;
And thus far having stretched it,—here be with them—
Thy knee bussing the stones,—for in such business
Action is eloquence, and the eyes of th' ignorant
More learned than the ears—waving thy head,
Which, often thus correcting thy stout heart,
Now humble as the ripest mulberry
That will not hold the handling; or say to them
Thou art their soldier, and being bred in broils
Hast not the soft way which, thou dost confess,
Were fit for thee to use as they to claim,
In asking their good loves; but thou wilt frame
Thyself, forsooth, hereafter theirs, so far
As thou hast power and person.

MENENIUS                              This but done,
Even as she speaks, why, their hearts were yours;
For they have pardons, being asked, as free
As words to little purpose.

VOLUMNIA                    Prithee now,
Go, and be ruled; although I know thou hadst rather
Follow thine enemy in a fiery gulf
Than flatter him in a bower.

*Enter Cominius.*

                              Here is Cominius.

COMINIUS    I have been i' th' market-place; and, sir, 'tis fit
You make strong party, or defend yourself
By calmness or by absence. All's in anger.

MENENIUS  Only fair speech.

COMINIUS                              I think 'twill serve, if he
Can thereto frame his spirit.

VOLUMNIA                          He must, and will.
Prithee now, say you will, and go about it.

CORIOLANUS  Must I go show them my unbarbed sconce?[12]
Must I
With my base tongue give to my noble heart
A lie that it must bear? Well, I will do't.
Yet, were there but this single plot[13] to lose,
This mould of Marcius, they to dust should grind it
And throw't against the wind. To th' market-place!
You've put me now to such a part which never
I shall discharge to th' life.

COMINIUS                          Come, come, we'll prompt you.

VOLUMNIA  I prithee now, sweet son, as thou hast said
My praises made thee first a soldier, so,
To have my praise for this, perform a part
Thou hast not done before.

CORIOLANUS                      Well, I must do't.
Away, my disposition, and possess me
Some harlot's spirit! My throat of war be turned,
Which quired with my drum, into a pipe
Small as an eunuch, or the virgin voice
That babies lulls asleep! The smiles of knaves
Tent in my cheeks, and schoolboys' tears take up
The glasses of my sight! A beggar's tongue
Make motion through my lips, and my armed knees,
Who bowed but in my stirrup, bend like his
That hath received an alms! I will not do't,
Lest I surcease to honor mine own truth
And by my body's action teach my mind
A most inherent baseness.

VOLUMNIA                      At thy choice, then.
To beg of thee, it is my more dishonor
Than thou of them. Come all to ruin! Let
Thy mother rather feel thy pride than fear

12. Uncovered head.
13. Piece of earth, i.e., his own body.

Thy dangerous stoutness; for I mock at death
With as big heart as thou. Do as thou list.
Thy valiantness was mine, thou suck'st it from me;
But owe thy pride thyself.

CORIOLANUS                    Pray, be content.
Mother, I am going to the market-place.
Chide me no more. I'll mountebank their loves,
Cog their hearts from them, and come home beloved
Of all the trades in Rome. Look, I am going.
Commend me to my wife. I'll return consul,
Or never trust to what my tongue can do
I' th' way of flattery further.

VOLUMNIA                    Do your will.

*Exit Volumnia.*

COMINIUS   Away! The tribunes do attend you. Arm yourself
To answer mildly; for they are prepared
With accusations, as I hear, more strong
Than are upon you yet.

CORIOLANUS   The word is 'mildly.' Pray you, let us go.
Let them accuse me by invention, I
Will answer in mine honor.

MENENIUS                    Ay, but mildly.

CORIOLANUS   Well, mildly be't then. Mildly!

*Exeunt.*

*Scene 3*

*Enter Sicinius and Brutus.*

BRUTUS   In this point charge him home, that he affects
Tyrannical power. If he evade us there,
Enforce him with his envy to the people,
And that the spoil got on the Antiates
Was ne'er distributed.

*Enter an Ædile.*

What, will he come?

ÆDILE    He's coming.

BRUTUS                How accompanied?

ÆDILE    With old Menenius, and those senators
That always favored him.

SICINIUS                Have you a catalogue
Of all the voices that we have procured
Set down by th' poll?

ÆDILE                I have; 'tis ready.

SICINIUS    Have you collected them by tribes?

ÆDILE                                I have.

SICINIUS    Assemble presently the people hither;
And when they hear me say, 'It shall be so
I' th' right and strength o' th' commons,' be it either
For death, for fine, or banishment, then let them,
If I say fine, cry 'Fine!'—if death, cry 'Death!',
Insisting on the old prerogative
And power i' th' truth o' th' cause.

ÆDILE                                I shall inform them.

BRUTUS    And when such time they have begun to cry,
Let them not cease, but with a din confused
Enforce the present execution
Of what we chance to sentence.

ÆDILE                Very well.

SICINIUS    Make them be strong, and ready for this hint
When we shall hap to give't them.

BRUTUS                Go about it.

[*Exit Ædile.*]

Put him to choler straight. He hath been used
Ever to conquer, and to have his worth
Of contradiction. Being once chafed, he cannot
Be reined again to temperance; then he speaks
What's in his heart, and that is there which looks
With us to break his neck.

*Enter Coriolanus, Menenius, and Cominius, with others.*

SICINIUS                Well, here he comes.

MENENIUS    Calmly, I do beseech you.

CORIOLANUS    Ay, as an ostler, that for th' poorest piece

Will bear the knave by th' volume. The honored gods
Keep Rome in safety, and the chairs of justice
Supplied with worthy men! plant love among's!
Throng our large temples with the shows of peace,
And not our streets with war!

FIRST SENATOR                              Amen, amen.
MENENIUS   A noble wish.

*Enter the Ædile, with the Plebeians.*

SICINIUS   Draw near, ye people.
ÆDILE   List to your tribunes. Audience! Peace, I say!
CORIOLANUS   First hear me speak.
BOTH TRIBUNES                         Well, say. Peace, ho!
CORIOLANUS   Shall I be charged no further than this present?
   Must all determine here?
SICINIUS                         I do demand,
   If you submit you to the people's voices,
   Allow their officers, and are content
   To suffer lawful censure for such faults
   As shall be proved upon you?
CORIOLANUS                         I am content.
MENENIUS   Lo, citizens, he says he is content.
   The warlike service he has done, consider; think
   Upon the wounds his body bears, which show
   Like graves i' th' holy churchyard.
CORIOLANUS                         Scratches with briars,
   Scars to move laughter only.
MENENIUS                         Consider further,
   That when he speaks not like a citizen,
   You find him like a soldier. Do not take
   His rougher accents for malicious sounds,
   But, as I say, such as become a soldier,
   Rather than envy you.
COMINIUS                         Well, well, no more.
CORIOLANUS   What is the matter
   That being passed for consul with full voice,
   I am so dishonored that the very hour
   You take it off again?
SICINIUS                         Answer to us.
CORIOLANUS   Say, then. 'Tis true, I ought so.

SICINIUS   We charge you that you have contrived to take
   From Rome all seasoned office, and to wind
   Yourself into a power tyrannical,
   For which you are a traitor to the people.

CORIOLANUS   How? traitor?

MENENIUS                     Nay, temperately! your promise.

CORIOLANUS   The fires i' th' lowest hell fold in the people!
   Call me their traitor, thou injurious tribune!
   Within thine eyes sat twenty thousand deaths,
   In thy hands clutched as many millions, in
   Thy lying tongue both numbers, I would say
   'Thou liest' unto thee with a voice as free
   As I do pray the gods.

SICINIUS                     Mark you this, people?

ALL   To th' Rock, to th' Rock with him!

SICINIUS                              Peace!
   We need not put new matter to his charge.
   What you have seen him do and heard him speak,
   Beating your officers, cursing yourselves,
   Opposing laws with strokes, and here defying
   Those whose great power must try him—even this,
   So criminal and in such capital kind,
   Deserves th' extremest death.

BRUTUS                     But since he hath
   Served well for Rome—

CORIOLANUS                What do you prate of service?

BRUTUS   I talk of that, that know it.

CORIOLANUS   You?

MENENIUS   Is this the promise that you made your mother?

COMINIUS   Know, I pray you—

CORIOLANUS                I'll know no further.
   Let them pronounce the steep Tarpeian death,
   Vagabond exile, flaying, pent to linger
   But with a grain a day—I would not buy
   Their mercy at the price of one fair word;
   Nor check my courage for what they can give,
   To have't with saying 'Good morrow.'

SICINIUS                     For that he has,
   As much as in him lies, from time to time
   Envied against the people, seeking means

To pluck away their power; as now at last
Given hostile strokes, and that not in the presence
Of dreaded justice, but on the ministers
That doth distribute it: i' th' name o' th' people
And in the power of us the tribunes, we,
Even from this instant, banish him our city,
In peril of precipitation
From off the Rock Tarpeian, never more
To enter our Rome gates. I' th' people's name,
I say it shall be so.

ALL   It shall be so! it shall be so! Let him away!
He's banished, and it shall be so!

COMINIUS   Hear me, my masters, and my common friends—

SICINIUS   He's sentenced. No more hearing.

COMINIUS                                         Let me speak.
I have been consul, and can show for Rome
Her enemies' marks upon me. I do love
My country's good with a respect more tender,
More holy and profound, than mine own life,
My dear wife's estimate, her womb's increase,
And treasure of my loins. Then if I would
Speak that—

SICINIUS         We know your drift. Speak what?

BRUTUS   There's no more to be said, but he is banished
As enemy to the people and his country.
It shall be so.

ALL   It shall be so! it shall be so!

CORIOLANUS   You common cry of curs, whose breath I hate
As reek o' th' rotten fens, whose loves I prize
As the dead carcasses of unburied men
That do corrupt my air, I banish you!
And here remain with your uncertainty.
Let every feeble rumor shake your hearts!
Your enemies, with nodding of their plumes,
Fan you into despair! Have the power still
To banish your defenders, till at length
Your ignorance—which finds not till it feels,
Making but reservation of yourselves,
Still your own foes—deliver you as most
Abated captives to some nation

That won you without blows! Despising,
For you, the city, thus I turn my back.
There is a world elsewhere.

*Exeunt Coriolanus, Cominius, with [Menenius and the other Senators].*

ÆDILE   The people's enemy is gone, is gone!
ALL   Our enemy is banished! he is gone!

*They all shout, and throw up their caps.*

                              Hoo! hoo!
SICINIUS   Go, see him out at gates, and follow him
As he hath followed you, with all despite;
Give him deserved vexation. Let a guard
Attend us through the city.
ALL   Come, come, let's see him out at gates! Come.
The gods preserve our noble tribunes! Come.

*Exeunt.*


# ACT FOUR

## Scene 1

*Enter Coriolanus, Volumnia, Virgilia, Menenius, Cominius, with the young Nobility of Rome.*

CORIOLANUS   Come, leave your tears. A brief farewell. The
    beast
With many heads butts me away. Nay, mother,
Where is your ancient courage? You were used
To say extremities was the trier of spirits;
That common chances common men could bear;
That when the sea was calm all boats alike
Showed mastership in floating; fortune's blows
When most struck home, being gentle wounded craves[1]
A noble cunning. You were used to load me
With precepts that would make invincible

---

1. The patrician, wounded by fortune, needs . . .

The heart that conned them.

VIRGILIA   O heavens! O heavens!

CORIOLANUS                    Nay, I prithee, woman—

VOLUMNIA   Now the red pestilence strike all trades in Rome,
And occupations perish!

CORIOLANUS               What, what, what!
I shall be loved when I am lacked. Nay, mother,
Resume that spirit when you were wont to say,
If you had been the wife of Hercules,
Six of his labors you'd have done, and saved
Your husband so much sweat. Cominius,
Droop not; adieu. Farewell, my wife, my mother.
I'll do well yet. Thou old and true Menenius,
Thy tears are salter than a younger man's,
And venomous to thine eyes. My sometime general,
I have seen thee stern, and thou hast oft beheld
Heart-hardening spectacles. Tell these sad women
'Tis fond to wail inevitable strokes,
As 'tis to laugh at 'em. My mother, you wot well
My hazards still have been your solace; and
Believe't not lightly—though I go alone,
Like to a lonely dragon, that his fen
Makes feared and talked of more than seen—your son
Will or exceed the common or be caught
With cautelous[2] baits and practice.

VOLUMNIA                    My first son,
Whither wilt thou go? Take good Cominius
With thee awhile. Determine on some course,
More than a wild exposure to each chance
That starts i' th' way before thee.

CORIOLANUS                    O the gods!

COMINIUS   I'll follow thee a month, devise with thee
Where thou shalt rest, that thou mayst hear of us
And we of thee. So, if the time thrust forth
A cause for thy repeal, we shall not send
O'er the vast world to seek a single man,
And lose advantage, which doth ever cool
I' th' absence of the needer.

CORIOLANUS               Fare ye well.

2. Crafty.

Thou hast years upon thee, and thou art too full
Of the wars' surfeits to go rove with one
That's yet unbruised. Bring me but out at gate.
Come, my sweet wife, my dearest mother, and
My friends of noble touch. When I am forth,
Bid me farewell, and smile. I pray you, come.
While I remain above the ground, you shall
Hear from me still, and never of me aught
But what is like me formerly.

MENENIUS                              That's worthily
As any ear can hear. Come, let's not weep.
If I could shake off but one seven-years
From these old arms and legs, by the good gods,
I'd with thee every foot.

CORIOLANUS                    Give me thy hand.
Come.

*Exeunt.*


*Scene 2*


*Enter the two Tribunes, Sicinius and Brutus, with the Ædile.*

SICINIUS   Bid them all home. He's gone, and we'll no further.
The nobility are vexed, whom we see have sided
In his behalf.

BRUTUS         Now we have shown our power,
Let us seem humbler after it is done
Than when it was a-doing.

SICINIUS                      Bid them home.
Say their great enemy is gone, and they
Stand in their ancient strength.

BRUTUS                            Dismiss them home.

[*Exit Ædile.*]

Here comes his mother.

SICINIUS                 Let's not meet her.

BRUTUS                                     Why?

SICINIUS   They say she's mad.

*Enter Volumnia, Virgilia, and Menenius.*

BRUTUS   They have ta'en note of us. Keep on your way.
VOLUMNIA   O, y' are well met. The hoarded plague o' th' gods
  Requite your love!
MENENIUS                 Peace, peace. Be not so loud.
VOLUMNIA   If that I could for weeping, you should hear—
  Nay, and you shall hear some. [*To Brutus*] Will you be gone?
VIRGILIA [*to Sicinius*]   You shall stay too. I would I had the
  power
To say so to my husband.
SICINIUS                 Are you mankind? [3]
VOLUMNIA   Ay, fool, is that a shame? Note but this fool.
  Was not a man my father? Hadst thou foxship
  To banish him that struck more blows for Rome
  Than thou hast spoken words?
SICINIUS                 O blessed heavens!
VOLUMNIA   More noble blows than ever thou wise words,
  And for Rome's good. I'll tell thee what—Yet go.
  Nay, but thou shalt stay too. I would my son
  Were in Arabia, and thy tribe before him,
  His good sword in his hand.
SICINIUS                 What then?
VIRGILIA                           What then?
  He'ld make an end of thy posterity.
VOLUMNIA   Bastards and all.
  Good man, the wounds that he does bear for Rome!
MENENIUS   Come, come, peace.
SICINIUS   I would he had continued to his country
  As he began, and not unknit himself
  The noble knot he made.
BRUTUS                 I would he had.
VOLUMNIA   'I would he had'? 'Twas you incensed the rabble.
  Cats, that can judge as fitly of his worth
  As I can of those mysteries which heaven
  Will not have earth to know!
BRUTUS                 Pray, let us go.
VOLUMNIA   Now, pray, sir, get you gone.

___

3. Are you mad? The assumption is that if she were "mankind" she would be more rational. She takes him literally and, then, gives him "foxship" for "cunning."

You have done a brave deed. Ere you go, hear this:
As far as doth the Capitol exceed
The meanest house in Rome, so far my son,—
This lady's husband here, this, do you see?—
Whom you have banished, does exceed you all.

BRUTUS    Well, well, we'll leave you.

SICINIUS                                Why stay we to be baited
With one that wants her wits?

*Exeunt Tribunes.*

VOLUMNIA                          Take my prayers with you.
I would the gods had nothing else to do
But to confirm my curses. Could I meet 'em
But once a day, it would unclog my heart
Of what lies heavy to't.

MENENIUS              You have told them home;
And, by my troth, you have cause. You'll sup with me?

VOLUMNIA    Anger's my meat. I sup upon myself,
And so shall starve with feeding. Come, let's go.
Leave this faint puling, and lament as I do,
In anger, Juno-like. Come, come, come.

MENENIUS                                Fie, fie, fie!

*Exeunt.*

## Scene 3

*Enter a Roman and a Volsce.*

ROMAN    I know you well, sir, and you know me. Your name, I
think, is Adrian.

VOLSCE    It is so, sir. Truly, I have forgot you.

ROMAN    I am a Roman; and my services are, as you are,
against 'em. Know you me yet?

VOLSCE    Nicanor, no?

ROMAN    The same, sir.

VOLSCE    You had more beard when I last saw you; but your
favor is well appeared by your tongue. What's the news
in Rome? I have a note from the Volscian state to find

you out there. You have well saved me a day's journey.

ROMAN   There hath been in Rome strange insurrections: the people against the senators, patricians, and nobles.

VOLSCE   Hath been? is it ended then? Our state thinks not so. They are in a most warlike preparation, and hope to come upon them in the heat of their division.

ROMAN   The main blaze of it is past, but a small thing would make it flame again; for the nobles receive so to heart the banishment of that worthy Coriolanus that they are in a ripe aptness to take all power from the people and to pluck from them their tribunes for ever. This lies glowing, I can tell you, and is almost mature for the violent breaking out.

VOLSCE   Coriolanus banished?

ROMAN   Banished, sir.

VOLSCE   You will be welcome with this intelligence, Nicanor.

ROMAN   The day serves well for them now. I have heard it said, the fittest time to corrupt a man's wife is when she's fallen out with her husband. Your noble Tullus Aufidius will appear well in these wars, his great opposer, Coriolanus, being now in no request of his country.

VOLSCE   He cannot choose. I am most fortunate, thus accidentally to encounter you. You have ended my business, and I will merrily accompany you home.

ROMAN   I shall, between this and supper, tell you most strange things from Rome, all tending to the good of their adversaries. Have you an army ready, say you?

VOLSCE   A most royal one: the centurions and their charges, distinctly billeted, already in th' entertainment,[4] and to be on foot at an hour's warning.

ROMAN   I am joyful to hear of their readiness, and am the man, I think, that shall set them in present action. So, sir, heartily well met, and most glad of your company.

VOLSCE   You take my part from me, sir. I have the most cause to be glad of yours.

ROMAN   Well, let us go together.

*Exeunt.*

4. The army is already organized into centuries ("distinctly billeted") and has the supplies it needs.

## Scene 4

CORIOLANUS   A goodly city is this Antium. City,
'Tis I that made thy widows. Many an heir
Of these fair edifices 'fore my wars
Have I heard groan and drop. Then know me not,
Lest that thy wives with spits and boys with stones
In puny battle slay me.

*Enter a Citizen.*

                              Save you, sir.
CITIZEN   And you.
CORIOLANUS               Direct me, if it be your will,
  Where great Aufidius lies. Is he in Antium?
CITIZEN   He is, and feasts the nobles of the state
  At his house this night.
CORIOLANUS                         Which is his house, beseech you?
CITIZEN   This, here before you.
CORIOLANUS                         Thank you, sir. Farewell.

*Exit Citizen.*

O world, thy slippery turns! Friends now fast sworn,
Whose double bosoms seem to wear one heart,
Whose hours, whose bed, whose meal and exercise
Are still together; who twin, as 'twere, in love
Unseparable, shall within this hour,
On a dissension of a doit, break out
To bitterest enmity. So, fellest foes,
Whose passions and whose plots have broke their sleep
To take the one the other, by some chance,
Some trick not worth an egg, shall grow dear friends
And interjoin their issues. So with me.
My birthplace hate I, and my love's upon
This enemy town. I'll enter. If he slay me,
He does fair justice; if he give me way,
I'll do his country service.

*Exit.*

## Scene 5

*Music plays. Enter a Servingman.*

FIRST SERVINGMAN   Wine, wine, wine! What service is here? I think our fellows are asleep.

*[Exit.]*
*Enter another Servingman.*

SECOND SERVINGMAN   Where's Cotus? My master calls for him. Cotus!

*Exit.*
*Enter Coriolanus.*

CORIOLANUS   A goodly house. The feast smells well, but I Appear not like a guest.

*Enter the first Servingman.*

FIRST SERVINGMAN   What would you have, friend? Whence are you? Here's no place for you. Pray, go to the door.

*Exit.*

CORIOLANUS   I have deserved no better entertainment, In being Coriolanus.

*Enter second Servant.*

SECOND SERVINGMAN   Whence are you, sir? Has the porter his eyes in his head, that he gives entrance to such companions? Pray, get you out.

CORIOLANUS   Away!

SECOND SERVINGMAN   Away? get you away!

CORIOLANUS   Now th 'art troublesome.

SECOND SERVINGMAN   Are you so brave? I'll have you talked with anon.

*Enter third Servingman; the first meets him.*

THIRD SERVINGMAN   What fellow's this?

FIRST SERVINGMAN   A strange one as ever I looked on. I cannot get him out o' th' house. Prithee, call my master to him.

THIRD SERVINGMAN   What have you to do here, fellow? Pray you, avoid the house.

CORIOLANUS   Let me but stand; I will not hurt your hearth.

THIRD SERVINGMAN   What are you?

CORIOLANUS   A gentleman.

THIRD SERVINGMAN   A marvellous poor one.

CORIOLANUS   True, so I am.

THIRD SERVINGMAN   Pray you, poor gentleman, take up some other station. Here's no place for you. Pray you, avoid. Come.

CORIOLANUS   Follow your function, go, and batten on cold bits.

*Pushes him away from him.*

THIRD SERVINGMAN   What, you will not? Prithee, tell my master what a strange guest he has here.

SECOND SERVINGMAN   And I shall.

*Exit second Servingman.*

THIRD SERVINGMAN   Where dwell'st thou?

CORIOLANUS   Under the canopy.

THIRD SERVINGMAN   Under the canopy?

CORIOLANUS   Ay.

THIRD SERVINGMAN   Where's that?

CORIOLANUS   I' th' city of kites and crows.

THIRD SERVINGMAN   I' th' city of kites and crows? What an ass it is! Then thou dwell'st with daws too?

CORIOLANUS   No, I serve not thy master.

THIRD SERVINGMAN   How, sir? Do you meddle with my master?

CORIOLANUS   Ay, 'tis an honester service than to meddle with thy mistress.

Thou prat'st, and prat'st. Serve with thy trencher. Hence!

*Beats him away.*
*Enter Aufidius with the [second] Servingman.*

AUFIDIUS   Where is this fellow?

SECOND SERVINGMAN   Here, sir. I'd have beaten him like a dog, but for disturbing the lords within.

AUFIDIUS  Whence com'st thou? What wouldst thou? Thy
   name?
  Why speak'st not? Speak, man. What's thy name?
CORIOLANUS                                  If, Tullus,
  Not yet thou know'st me, and, seeing me, dost not
  Think me for the man I am, necessity
  Commands me name myself.
AUFIDIUS                 What is thy name?
CORIOLANUS  A name unmusical to the Volscians' ears,
  And harsh in sound to thine.
AUFIDIUS                 Say, what's thy name?
  Thou hast a grim appearance, and thy face
  Bears a command in't; though thy tackle's torn,
  Thou show'st a noble vessel. What's thy name?
CORIOLANUS  Prepare thy brow to frown. Know'st thou me
  yet?
AUFIDIUS  I know thee not. Thy name?
CORIOLANUS  My name is Caius Marcius, who hath done
  To thee particularly and to all the Volsces
  Great hurt and mischief; thereto witness may
  My surname, Coriolanus. The painful service,
  The extreme dangers, and the drops of blood
  Shed for my thankless country are requited
  But with that surname—a good memory,
  And witness of the malice and displeasure
  Which thou shouldst bear me. Only that name remains.
  The cruelty and envy of the people,
  Permitted by our dastard nobles, who
  Have all forsook me, hath devoured the rest;
  And suffered me by th' voice of slaves to be
  Whooped out of Rome. Now this extremity
  Hath brought me to thy hearth, not out of hope—
  Mistake me not—to save my life; for if
  I had feared death, of all the men i' th' world
  I would have 'voided thee; but in mere spite,
  To be full quit of those my banishers,
  Stand I before thee here. Then if thou hast
  A heart of wreak in thee, that wilt revenge
  Thine own particular wrongs, and stop those maims
  Of shame seen through thy country, speed thee straight,

And make my misery serve thy turn. So use it
That my revengeful services may prove
As benefits to thee; for I will fight
Against my cankered country with the spleen
Of all the under fiends. But if so be
Thou dar'st not this, and that to prove more fortunes
Th' art tired, then, in a word, I also am
Longer to live most weary; and present
My throat to thee and to thy ancient malice;
Which not to cut would show thee but a fool,
Since I have ever followed thee with hate,
Drawn tuns of blood out of thy country's breast,
And cannot live but to thy shame, unless
It be to do thee service.

AUFIDIUS                        O Marcius, Marcius!
Each word thou hast spoke hath weeded from my heart
A root of ancient envy. If Jupiter
Should from yond cloud speak divine things,
And say ' 'Tis true,' I'd not believe them more
Than thee, all-noble Marcius. Let me twine
Mine arms about thy body, whereagainst
My grained ash an hundred times hath broke,
And scarred the moon with splinters. Here I clip
The anvil of my sword, and do contest
As hotly and as nobly with thy love
As ever in ambitious strength I did
Contend against thy valor. Know thou first,
I loved the maid I married; never man
Sighed truer breath. But that I see thee here,
Thou noble thing, more dances my rapt heart
Than when I first my wedded mistress saw
Bestride my threshold. Why, thou Mars, I tell thee,
We have a power on foot; and I had purpose
Once more to hew thy target from thy brawn,
Or lose mine arm for't. Thou hast beat me out
Twelve several times, and I have nightly since
Dreamt of encounters 'twixt thyself and me.
We have been down together in my sleep,
Unbuckling helms, fisting each other's throat,
And waked half dead with nothing. Worthy Marcius,

Had we no other quarrel else to Rome, but that
Thou art thence banished, we would muster all
From twelve to seventy, and, pouring war
Into the bowels of ungrateful Rome,
Like a bold flood o'erbeat. O, come, go in,
And take our friendly senators by the hands,
Who now are here, taking their leaves of me,
Who am prepared against your territories,
Though not for Rome itself.

CORIOLANUS                        You bless me, gods!

AUFIDIUS    Therefore, most absolute sir, if thou wilt have
The leading of thine own revenges, take
Th' one half of my commission; and set down—
As best thou art experienced, since thou know'st
Thy country's strength and weakness—thine own ways,
Whether to knock against the gates of Rome,
Or rudely visit them in parts remote,
To fright them ere destroy. But come in.
Let me commend thee first to those that shall
Say yea to thy desires. A thousand welcomes!
And more a friend than e'er an enemy;
Yet, Marcius, that was much. Your hand. Most welcome!

*Exeunt.*
*Enter two of the Servingmen.*

FIRST SERVINGMAN    Here's a strange alteration!

SECOND SERVINGMAN    By my hand, I had thought to have
strucken him with a cudgel; and yet my mind gave me his
clothes made a false report of him.

FIRST SERVINGMAN    What an arm he has! He turned me about
with his finger and his thumb as one would set up a top.

SECOND SERVINGMAN    Nay, I knew by his face that there was
something in him. He had, sir, a kind of face, methought
—I cannot tell how to term it.

FIRST SERVINGMAN    He had so, looking as it were—Would I
were hanged, but I thought there was more in him than I
could think.

SECOND SERVINGMAN    So did I, I'll be sworn. He is simply the
rarest man i' th' world.

FIRST SERVINGMAN   I think he is. But a greater soldier than he you wot on.

SECOND SERVINGMAN   Who, my master?

FIRST SERVINGMAN   Nay, it's no matter for that.

SECOND SERVINGMAN   Worth six on him.

FIRST SERVINGMAN   Nay, not so neither. But I take him to be the greater soldier.

SECOND SERVINGMAN   Faith, look you, one cannot tell how to say that. For the defense of a town, our general is excellent.

FIRST SERVINGMAN   Ay, and for an assault too.

*Enter the third Servingman.*

THIRD SERVINGMAN   O slaves, I can tell you news. News, you rascals!

BOTH [*First and Second*]   What, what, what? Let's partake.

THIRD SERVINGMAN   I would not be a Roman, of all nations. I had as lief be a condemned man.

BOTH   Wherefore? Wherefore?

THIRD SERVINGMAN   Why, here's he that was wont to thwack our general, Caius Marcius.

FIRST SERVINGMAN   Why do you say, 'thwack our general'?

THIRD SERVINGMAN   I do not say, 'thwack our general,' but he was always good enough for him.

SECOND SERVINGMAN   Come, we are fellows and friends. He was ever too hard for him; I have heard him say so himself.

FIRST SERVINGMAN   He was too hard for him directly, to say the troth on't. Before Corioles he scotched him and notched him like a carbonado.

SECOND SERVINGMAN   An he had been cannibally given, he might have boiled and eaten him too.

FIRST SERVINGMAN   But more of thy news?

THIRD SERVINGMAN   Why, he is so made on here within, as if he were son and heir to Mars; set at upper end o' th' table; no question asked him by any of the senators, but they stand bald[5] before him. Our general himself makes a mistress of him; sanctifies himself with's hand, and turns up the white o' th' eye to his discourse. But the bottom of

5. Bareheaded.

the news is, our general is cut i' th' middle and but one half of what he was yesterday; for the other has half, by the entreaty and grant of the whole table. He'll go, he says, and sowl[6] the porter of Rome gates by th' ears. He will mow all down before him, and leave his passage polled.[7]

SECOND SERVINGMAN    And he's as like to do't as any man I can imagine.

THIRD SERVINGMAN    Do't? he will do't! for, look you, sir, he has as many friends as enemies; which friends, sir, as it were, durst not, look you, sir, show themselves, as we term it, his friends whilst he's in directitude.

FIRST SERVINGMAN    Directitude? what's that?

THIRD SERVINGMAN    But when they shall see, sir, his crest up again, and the man in blood, they will out of their burrows like conies after rain, and revel all with him.

FIRST SERVINGMAN    But when goes this forward?

THIRD SERVINGMAN    To-morrow, to-day, presently. You shall have the drum struck up this afternoon. 'Tis, as it were, a parcel of their feast, and to be executed ere they wipe their lips.

SECOND SERVINGMAN    Why, then we shall have a stirring world again. This peace is nothing but to rust iron, increase tailors, and breed ballad-makers.

FIRST SERVINGMAN    Let me have war, say I. It exceeds peace as far as day does night. It's sprightly, waking, audible, and full of vent. Peace is a very apoplexy, lethargy; mulled, deaf, sleepy, insensible; a getter of more bastard children than war's a destroyer of men.

SECOND SERVINGMAN    'Tis so; and as war, in some sort, may be said to be a ravisher, so it cannot be denied but peace is a great maker of cuckolds.

FIRST SERVINGMAN    Ay, and it makes men hate one another.

THIRD SERVINGMAN    Reason: because they then less need one another. The wars for my money. I hope to see Romans as cheap as Volscians. They are rising, they are rising.

BOTH [*First and Second*]    In, in, in, in!

*Exeunt.*

6. Pull by the ears.
7. Despoiled, from *poll* in the sense of *cut, shear*.

*Scene 6*

*Enter the two Tribunes, Sicinius and Brutus.*

SICINIUS  We hear not of him, neither need we fear him;
  His remedies are tame: the present peace
  And quietness of the people, which before
  Were in wild hurry. Here do we make his friends
  Blush that the world goes well, who rather had,
  Though they themselves did suffer by't, behold
  Dissentious numbers pestering streets than see
  Our tradesmen singing in their shops and going
  About their functions friendly.

BRUTUS  We stood to't in good time.

*Enter Menenius.*

                          Is this Menenius?

SICINIUS  'Tis he, 'tis he! O, he is grown most kind of late.
  —Hail, sir!

MENENIUS      Hail to you both!

SICINIUS                    Your Coriolanus
  Is not much missed, but with his friends.
  The commonwealth doth stand, and so would do,
  Were he more angry at it.

MENENIUS  All's well; and might have been much better, if
  He could have temporized.

SICINIUS                    Where is he, hear you?

MENENIUS  Nay, I hear nothing. His mother and his wife
  Hear nothing from him.

*Enter three or four Citizens.*

ALL  The gods preserve you both!

SICINIUS                    Good-e'en, our neighbors.

BRUTUS  Good-e'en to you all, good-e'en to you all.

FIRST CITIZEN  Ourselves, our wives, and children, on our
    knees,
  Are bound to pray for you both.

SICINIUS                    Live, and thrive!

BRUTUS  Farewell, kind neighbors. We wished Coriolanus
  Had loved you as we did.

CITIZENS                         Now the gods keep you!
BOTH TRIBUNES    Farewell, farewell.

*Exeunt Citizens.*

SICINIUS   This is a happier and more comely time
Than when these fellows ran about the streets,
Crying confusion.
BRUTUS                 Caius Marcius was
A worthy officer i' th' war, but insolent,
O'ercome with pride, ambitious past all thinking,
Self-loving—
SICINIUS            And affecting one sole throne
Without assistance.
MENENIUS                I think not so.
SICINIUS   We should by this, to all our lamentation,
If he had gone forth consul, found it so.
BRUTUS   The gods have well prevented it, and Rome
Sits safe and still without him.

*Enter an Ædile.*

ÆDILE                            Worthy tribunes,
There is a slave whom we have put in prison
Reports the Volsces with two several powers
Are entered in the Roman territories,
And with the deepest malice of the war
Destroy what lies before 'em.
MENENIUS                        'Tis Aufidius,
Who, hearing of our Marcius' banishment,
Thrusts forth his horns again into the world;
Which were inshelled when Marcius stood for Rome,
And durst not once peep out.
SICINIUS                        Come, what talk you
Of Marcius?
BRUTUS   Go see this rumorer whipped. It cannot be
The Volsces dare break with us.
MENENIUS                        Cannot be!
We have record that very well it can,
And three examples of the like hath been
Within my age. But reason with the fellow,
Before you punish him, where he heard this,

Lest you shall chance to whip your information
And beat the messenger who bids beware
Of what is to be dreaded.
SICINIUS                                Tell not me.
I know this cannot be.
BRUTUS                            Not possible.

*Enter a Messenger.*

MESSENGER   The nobles in great earnestness are going
All to the Senate House. Some news is coming
That turns their countenances.
SICINIUS                                'Tis this slave—
Go whip him 'fore the people's eyes—his raising,
Nothing but his report.
MESSENGER                        Yes, worthy sir.
The slave's report is seconded; and more,
More fearful, is delivered.
SICINIUS                                What more fearful?
MENENIUS   It is spoke freely out of many mouths—
How probable I do not know—that Marcius,
Joined with Aufidius, leads a power 'gainst Rome,
And vows revenge as spacious as between
The young'st and oldest thing.
SICINIUS                                This is most likely!
BRUTUS   Raised only, that the weaker sort may wish
Good Marcius home again.
SICINIUS                                The very trick on't.
MENENIUS   This is unlikely.
He and Aufidius can no more atone
Than violent'st contrariety.

*Enter [another] Messenger.*

MESSENGER   You are sent for to the Senate.
A fearful army, led by Caius Marcius
Associated with Aufidius, rages
Upon our territories; and have already
O'erborne their way, consumed with fire, and took
What lay before them.

*Enter Cominius.*

COMINIUS                          O, you have made good work!

MENENIUS    What news? What news?

COMINIUS    You have holp to ravish your own daughters and
   To melt the city leads upon your pates,
   To see your wives dishonored to your noses,—

MENENIUS    What's the news? What's the news?

COMINIUS    Your temples burned in their cement, and
   Your franchises, whereon you stood, confined
   Into an auger's bore.

MENENIUS                     Pray now, your news?—
   You have made fair work, I fear me.—Pray, your news?—
   If Marcius should be joined with Volscians—

COMINIUS                                  If?
   He is their god. He leads them like a thing
   Made by some other deity than nature,
   That shapes man better; and they follow him
   Against us brats with no less confidence
   Than boys pursuing summer butterflies
   Or butchers killing flies.

MENENIUS                          You have made good work,
   You and your apron-men! you that stood so much
   Upon the voice of occupation and
   The breath of garlic-eaters!

COMINIUS                          He will shake
   Your Rome about your ears.

MENENIUS                          As Hercules
   Did shake down mellow fruit.[8] You have made fair work!

BRUTUS    But is this true, sir?

COMINIUS                          Ay, and you'll look pale
   Before you find it other. All the regions
   Do smilingly revolt; and who resists
   Are mocked for valiant ignorance,
   And perish constant fools. Who is't can blame him?
   Your enemies and his find something in him.

MENENIUS    We are all undone, unless
   The noble man have mercy.

COMINIUS                          Who shall ask it?

8. The golden apples of the Hesperides. Actually Hercules did not shake them
down; he held the weight of the heavens on his shoulders, releasing Atlas to get the
apples for him. With a foreign army at the gates, Menenius has reason enough for
mixing up his mythical metaphors.

The tribunes cannot do't for shame; the people
Deserve such pity of him as the wolf
Does of the shepherds. For his best friends, if they
Should say, 'Be good to Rome,' they charged him even
As those should do that had deserved his hate,
And therein showed like enemies.

MENENIUS                                              'Tis true.
If he were putting to my house the brand
That should consume it, I have not the face
To say, 'Beseech you, cease.' You have made fair hands,
You and your crafts! You have crafted fair!

COMINIUS                                      You have brought
A trembling upon Rome, such as was never
S' incapable of help.

TRIBUNES            Say not we brought it.

MENENIUS    How? Was 't we? We loved him; but, like beasts
And cowardly nobles, gave way unto your clusters,
Who did hoot him out o' th' city.

COMINIUS                          But I fear
They'll roar him in again. Tullus Aufidius,
The second name of men, obeys his points
As if he were his officer. Desperation
Is all the policy, strength, and defense
That Rome can make against them.

*Enter a troop of Citizens.*

MENENIUS                              Here come the clusters.
And is Aufidius with him?—You are they
That made the air unwholesome, when you cast
Your stinking greasy caps in hooting at
Coriolanus' exile. Now he's coming;
And not a hair upon a soldier's head
Which will not prove a whip. As many coxcombs
As you threw caps up will he tumble down,
And pay you for your voices. 'Tis no matter.
If he could burn us all into one coal,
We have deserved it.

OMNES    Faith, we hear fearful news.

FIRST CITIZEN                        For mine own part,
When I said banish him, I said 'twas pity.

SECOND CITIZEN   And so did I.

THIRD CITIZEN   And so did I; and, to say the truth, so did very
many of us. That we did, we did for the best; and though
we willingly consented to his banishment, yet it was
against our will.

COMINIUS   Y' are goodly things, you voices!

MENENIUS                                        You have made
Good work, you and your cry! Shall's to the Capitol?

COMINIUS   O, ay, what else?

*Exeunt both.*

SICINIUS   Go, masters, get you home; be not dismayed.
These are a side that would be glad to have
This true, which they so seem to fear. Go home,
And show no sign of fear.

FIRST CITIZEN   The gods be good to us! Come, masters, let's
home. I ever said we were i' th' wrong when we banished
him.

SECOND CITIZEN   So did we all. But come, let's home.

*Exeunt Citizens.*

BRUTUS   I do not like this news.

SICINIUS   Nor I.

BRUTUS   Let's to the Capitol. Would half my wealth
Would buy this for a lie!

SICINIUS                              Pray, let us go.

*Exeunt Tribunes.*


*Scene 7*


*Enter Aufidius, with his Lieutenant.*

AUFIDIUS   Do they still fly to th' Roman?

LIEUTENANT   I do not know what witchcraft's in him, but
Your soldiers use him as the grace 'fore meat,
Their talk at table, and their thanks at end;
And you are darkened in this action, sir,
Even by your own.

AUFIDIUS                I cannot help it now,
   Unless by using means I lame the foot
   Of our design. He bears himself more proudlier,
   Even to my person, than I thought he would
   When first I did embrace him. Yet his nature
   In that's no changeling, and I must excuse
   What cannot be amended.
LIEUTENANT                   Yet I wish, sir,—
   I mean for your particular—you had not
   Joined in commission with him; but either
   Had borne the action of yourself, or else
   To him had left it solely.
AUFIDIUS   I understand thee well; and be thou sure,
   When he shall come to his account, he knows not
   What I can urge against him. Although it seems,
   And so he thinks, and is no less apparent
   To th' vulgar eye, that he bears all things fairly,
   And shows good husbandry for the Volscian state,
   Fights dragon-like, and does achieve as soon
   As draw his sword; yet he hath left undone
   That which shall break his neck or hazard mine,
   Whene'er we come to our account.
LIEUTENANT   Sir, I beseech you, think you he'll carry Rome?
AUFIDIUS   All places yield to him ere he sits down,[9]
   And the nobility of Rome are his;
   The senators and patricians love him too.
   The tribunes are no soldiers, and their people
   Will be as rash in the repeal as hasty
   To expel him thence. I think he'll be to Rome
   As is the osprey to the fish, who takes it
   By sovereignty of nature. First he was
   A noble servant to them, but he could not
   Carry his honors even. Whether 'twas pride,
   Which out of daily fortune ever taints
   The happy man; whether defect of judgment,
   To fail in the disposing of those chances
   Which he was lord of; or whether nature,
   Not to be other than one thing, not moving

9. Lays a siege.

From th' casque to th' cushion, but commanding peace
Even with the same austerity and garb
As he controlled the war; but one of these,
As he hath spices of them all,—not all,
For I dare so far free him—made him feared,
So hated, and so banished. But he has a merit,
To choke it in the utterance. So our virtues
Lie in th' interpretation of the time;
And power, unto itself most commendable,
Hath not a tomb so evident as a chair
T' extol what it hath done.
One fire drives out one fire; one nail, one nail;
Rights by rights founder, strengths by strengths do fail.
Come, let's away. When, Caius, Rome is thine,
Thou art poor'st of all; then shortly art thou mine.

*Exeunt.*

# ACT FIVE

## Scene 1

*Enter Menenius, Cominius; Sicinius, Brutus, the two Tribunes; with others.*

MENENIUS   No, I'll not go. You hear what he hath said
   Which was sometime his general, who loved him
   In a most dear particular. He called me father.
   But what o' that? Go, you that banished him;
   A mile before his tent fall down, and knee
   The way into his mercy. Nay, if he coyed
   To hear Cominius speak, I'll keep at home.
COMINIUS   He would not seem to know me.
MENENIUS                                    Do you hear?
COMINIUS   Yet one time he did call me by my name.
   I urged our old acquaintance, and the drops
   That we have bled together. Coriolanus
   He would not answer to; forbade all names.
   He was a kind of nothing, titleless,

Till he had forged himself a name o' th' fire
Of burning Rome.

MENENIUS                     Why, so.—You have made good work!
A pair of tribunes that have racked for Rome,
To make coals cheap! A noble memory!

COMINIUS   I minded him how royal 'twas to pardon
When it was less expected. He replied,
It was a bare petition of a state
To one whom they had punished.

MENENIUS                                 Very well.
Could he say less?

COMINIUS   I offered to awaken his regard
For's private friends. His answer to me was,
He could not stay to pick them in a pile
Of noisome musty chaff. He said 'twas folly,
For one poor grain or two, to leave unburnt
And still to nose th' offense.

MENENIUS                           For one poor grain or two?
I am one of those! His mother, wife, his child,
And this brave fellow too, we are the grains;
You are the musty chaff, and you are smelt
Above the moon. We must be burnt for you.

SICINIUS   Nay, pray, be patient. If you refuse your aid
In this so-never-needed help, yet do not
Upbraid's with our distress. But, sure, if you
Would be your country's pleader, your good tongue,
More than the instant army we can make,
Might stop our countryman.

MENENIUS                           No, I'll not meddle.

SICINIUS   Pray you, go to him.

MENENIUS                           What should I do?

BRUTUS   Only make trial what your love can do
For Rome toward Marcius.

MENENIUS                           Well, and say that Marcius
Return me, as Cominius is returned,
Unheard—what then?
But as a discontented friend, grief-shot
With his unkindness? Say't be so?

SICINIUS                           Yet your good will
Must have that thanks from Rome, after the measure

As you intended well.

MENENIUS                    I'll undertake't:
I think he'll hear me. Yet, to bite his lip
And hum at good Cominius much unhearts me.
He was not taken well; he had not dined.
The veins unfilled, our blood is cold, and then
We pout upon the morning, are unapt
To give or to forgive; but when we have stuffed
These pipes and these conveyances of our blood
With wine and feeding, we have suppler souls
Than in our priest-like fasts. Therefore I'll watch him
Till he be dieted to my request,
And then I'll set upon him.

BRUTUS   You know the very road into his kindness,
And cannot lose your way.

MENENIUS                    Good faith, I'll prove him,
Speed how it will. I shall ere long have knowledge
Of my success.

COMINIUS          He'll never hear him.

SICINIUS                              Not?

COMINIUS    I tell you, he does sit in gold,[1] his eye
Red as 'twould burn Rome, and his injury
The jailer to his pity. I kneeled before him.
'Twas very faintly he said, 'Rise'; dismissed me
Thus, with his speechless hand. What he would do
He sent in writing after me; what he would not
Bound with an oath to yield to his conditions;
So that all hope is vain
Unless his noble mother and his wife,
Who, as I hear, mean to solicit him
For mercy to his country. Therefore let's hence,
And with our fair entreaties haste them on.

*Exeunt.*

1. Enthroned.

## Scene 2

*Enter Menenius to the Watch on guard.*

FIRST WATCH   Stay. Whence are you?

SECOND WATCH                Stand, and go back.

MENENIUS   You guard like men; 'tis well. But, by your leave,
   I am an officer of state, and come
   To speak with Coriolanus.

FIRST WATCH          From whence?

MENENIUS                From Rome.

FIRST WATCH   You may not pass; you must return. Our general
     Will no more hear from thence.

SECOND WATCH   You'll see your Rome embraced with fire
   before
   You'll speak with Coriolanus.

MENENIUS               Good my friends,
   If you have heard your general talk of Rome
   And of his friends there, it is lots to blanks[2]
   My name hath touched your ears. It is Menenius.

FIRST WATCH   Be't so; go back. The virtue of your name
   Is not here passable.

MENENIUS            I tell thee, fellow,
   Thy general is my lover. I have been
   The book of his good acts, whence men have read
   His fame unparalleled, haply amplified;
   For I have ever verified my friends,
   Of whom he's chief, with all the size that verity
   Would without lapsing suffer. Nay, sometimes,
   Like to a bowl upon a subtle ground,
   I have tumbled past the throw; and in his praise
   Have almost stamped the leasing. Therefore, fellow,
   I must have leave to pass.

FIRST WATCH   Faith, sir, if you had told as many lies in his
    behalf as you have uttered words in your own, you should
    not pass here; no, though it were as virtuous to lie as to
    live chastely. Therefore go back.

---

2. *Good odds.* The lots are winning draws in a lottery compared to the losers, the blanks.

MENENIUS  Prithee, fellow, remember my name is Menenius, always factionary on the party of your general.

SECOND WATCH  Howsoever you have been his liar, as you say you have, I am one that, telling true under him, must say you cannot pass. Therefore go back.

MENENIUS  Has he dined, canst thou tell? For I would not speak with him till after dinner.

FIRST WATCH  You are a Roman, are you?

MENENIUS  I am, as thy general is.

FIRST WATCH  Then you should hate Rome, as he does. Can you, when you have pushed out your gates the very defender of them, and in a violent popular ignorance given your enemy your shield, think to front his revenges with the easy groans of old women, the virginal palms of your daughters, or with the palsied intercession of such a decayed dotant as you seem to be? Can you think to blow out the intended fire your city is ready to flame in, with such weak breath as this? No, you are deceived; therefore back to Rome, and prepare for your execution. You are condemned; our general has sworn you out of reprieve and pardon.

MENENIUS  Sirrah, if thy captain knew I were here, he would use me with estimation.

FIRST WATCH  Come, my captain knows you not.

MENENIUS  I mean thy general.

FIRST WATCH  My general cares not for you. Back, I say, go! lest I let forth your half-pint of blood,—back!—that's the utmost of your having. Back!

MENENIUS  Nay, but, fellow, fellow—

*Enter Coriolanus with Aufidius.*

CORIOLANUS  What's the matter?

MENENIUS  Now, you companion, I'll say an errand for you. You shall know now that I am in estimation; you shall perceive that a Jack guardant cannot office me from my son Coriolanus. Guess but by my entertainment with him. If thou stand'st not i' th' state of hanging, or of some death more long in spectatorship and crueler in suffering, behold now presently, and swound for what's to come upon thee. [*To Coriolanus.*] The glorious gods sit in hourly synod about thy particular prosperity, and love thee no worse than thy old father Menenius does! O my son, my son! Thou art preparing fire for us. Look thee, here's water to quench it. I was hardly moved to come to thee; but being assured none but myself could move thee, I have been blown out of our gates with sighs; and conjure thee to pardon Rome and thy petitionary countrymen. The good gods assuage thy wrath, and turn the dregs of it upon this varlet here—this, who, like a block, hath denied my access to thee.

CORIOLANUS  Away!

MENENIUS  How? away?

CORIOLANUS  Wife, mother, child, I know not. My affairs
Are servanted to others. Though I owe
My revenge properly, my remission lies
In Volscian breasts. That we have been familiar,
Ingrate forgetfulness shall poison, rather
Than pity note how much. Therefore be gone.
Mine ears against your suits are stronger than
Your gates against my force. Yet, for I loved thee,
Take this along. I writ it for thy sake, [*Gives a letter.*]
And would have sent it. Another word, Menenius,
I will not hear thee speak. This man, Aufidius,
Was my beloved in Rome; yet thou behold'st!

AUFIDIUS  You keep a constant temper.

*Exeunt. Manent the Guard and Menenius.*

FIRST WATCH  Now, sir, is your name Menenius?

SECOND WATCH  'Tis a spell, you see, of much power. You know the way home again.

FIRST WATCH  Do you hear how we are shent for keeping your greatness back?

SECOND WATCH  What cause do you think I have to swound?

MENENIUS  I neither care for th' world nor your general. For such things as you, I can scarce think there's any, y' are so slight. He that hath a will to die by himself fears it not from another. Let your general do his worst. For you, be that you are, long; and your misery increase with your age! I say to you, as I was said to, 'Away!'

*Exit.*

FIRST WATCH   A noble fellow, I warrant him.

SECOND WATCH   The worthy fellow is our general. He's the
rock, the oak not to be wind-shaken.

*Exit Watch.*

*Scene 3*

*Enter Coriolanus and Aufidius [with others].*

CORIOLANUS   We will before the walls of Rome to-morrow
Set down our host. My partner in this action,
You must report to th' Volscian lords how plainly
I have borne this business.

AUFIDIUS                              Only their ends
You have respected; stopped your ears against
The general suit of Rome; never admitted
A private whisper, no, not with such friends
That thought them sure of you.

CORIOLANUS                              This last old man,
Whom with a cracked heart I have sent to Rome,
Loved me above the measure of a father;
Nay, godded me indeed. Their latest refuge
Was to send him; for whose old love I have—
Though I showed sourly to him—once more offered
The first conditions, which they did refuse
And cannot now accept. To grace him only,
That thought he could do more, a very little
I have yielded to. Fresh embassies and suits,
Nor from the state nor private friends, hereafter
Will I lend ear to. (*Shout within.*) Ha! What shout is this?
Shall I be tempted to infringe my vow
In the same time 'tis made? I will not.

*Enter Virgilia, Volumnia, Valeria, young Marcius, with Attendants.*

My wife comes foremost; then the honored mould
Wherein this trunk was framed, and in her hand
The grandchild to her blood. But out, affection!

All bond and privilege of nature, break!
Let it be virtuous to be obstinate.
What is that curt'sy worth? or those doves' eyes,
Which can make gods forsworn? I melt, and am not
Of stronger earth than others. My mother bows,
As if Olympus to a molehill should
In supplication nod; and my young boy
Hath an aspect of intercession which
Great nature cries, 'Deny not!' Let the Volsces
Plough Rome and harrow Italy! I'll never
Be such a gosling to obey instinct, but stand
As if a man were author of himself
And knew no other kin.

VIRGILIA                My lord and husband!

CORIOLANUS    These eyes are not the same I wore in Rome.

VIRGILIA   The sorrow that delivers us thus changed
  Makes you think so.

CORIOLANUS         Like a dull actor now,
  I have forgot my part, and I am out,
  Even to a full disgrace. Best of my flesh,
  Forgive my tyranny; but do not say
  For that, 'Forgive our Romans.' O, a kiss
  Long as my exile, sweet as my revenge!
  Now, by the jealous queen of heaven, that kiss
  I carried from thee dear; and my true lip
  Hath virgined it e'er since. You gods! I prate,
  And the most noble mother of the world
  Leave unsaluted. Sink, my knee, i' th' earth;

*Kneels.*

Of thy deep duty more impression show
Than that of common sons.

VOLUMNIA          O, stand up blest!
  Whilst with no softer cushion than the flint
  I kneel before thee, and unproperly
  Show duty as mistaken all this while
  Between the child and parent.

CORIOLANUS         What is this?
  Your knees to me? to your corrected son?

Then let the pebbles on the hungry beach[3]
Fillip the stars! Then let the mutinous winds
Strike the proud cedars 'gainst the fiery sun,
Murdering impossibility, to make
What cannot be, slight work

VOLUMNIA                    Thou art my warrior;
I holp to frame thee. Do you know this lady?

CORIOLANUS   The noble sister of Publicola,
The moon of Rome, chaste as the icicle
That's curded by the frost from purest snow
And hangs on Dian's temple—dear Valeria! [4]

VOLUMNIA   This is a poor epitome of yours,
Which by th' interpretation of full time
May show like all yourself.

CORIOLANUS                  The god of soldiers,
With the consent of supreme Jove, inform
Thy thoughts with nobleness, that thou mayst prove
To shame unvulnerable, and stick i' the wars
Like a great sea-mark, standing every flaw
And saving those that eye thee!

VOLUMNIA                          Your knee, sirrah.

CORIOLANUS   That's my brave boy!

VOLUMNIA   Even he, your wife, this lady, and myself,
Are suitors to you.

CORIOLANUS        I beseech you, peace!
Or, if you'd ask, remember this before:
The thing I have forsworn to grant may never
Be held by you denials. Do not bid me
Dismiss my soldiers, or capitulate
Again with Rome's mechanics. Tell me not
Wherein I seem unnatural. Desire not
To allay my rages and revenges with
Your colder reasons.

VOLUMNIA                O, no more, no more!

3. None of Shakespeare's editors knows why the beach is hungry or what its presumed hunger has to do with Coriolanus's metaphor. It has been suggested that the word was a misprint for *angry*, an explanation that makes a little more sense.

4. Valeria is apparently a good girl (both the moon and Diana, the virgin goddess, intensify the reference to her chastity) of good family (sister to the celebrated consul, Publius Valerius), but these compliments have little to do with the gossipy woman of Act One, Scene Three.

You have said you will not grant us anything;
For we have nothing else to ask but that
Which you deny already; yet we will ask,
That, if you fail in our request, the blame
May hang upon your hardness. Therefore hear us.

CORIOLANUS    Aufidius, and you Volsces, mark; for we'll
Hear naught from Rome in private.—Your request?

VOLUMNIA    Should we be silent and not speak, our raiment
And state of bodies would bewray what life
We have led since thy exile. Think with thyself
How more unfortunate than all living women
Are we come hither; since that thy sight, which should
Make our eyes flow with joy, hearts dance with comforts,
Constrains them weep and shake with fear and sorrow,
Making the mother, wife, and child to see
The son, the husband, and the father tearing
His country's bowels out. And to poor we
Thine enmity's most capital. Thou barr'st us
Our prayers to the gods, which is a comfort
That all but we enjoy. For how can we,
Alas, how can we for our country pray,
Whereto we are bound, together with thy victory,
Whereto we are bound? Alack, or we must lose
The country, our dear nurse, or else thy person,
Our comfort in the country. We must find
An evident calamity, though we had
Our wish which side should win. For either thou
Must as a foreign recreant be led
With manacles through our streets, or else
Triumphantly tread on thy country's ruin,
And bear the palm for having bravely shed
Thy wife and children's blood. For myself, son,
I purpose not to wait on fortune till
These wars determine. If I cannot persuade thee
Rather to show a noble grace to both parts
Than seek the end of one, thou shalt no sooner
March to assault thy country than to tread—
Trust to't, thou shalt not—on thy mother's womb
That brought thee to this world.

VIRGILIA                                    Ay, and mine,

That brought you forth this boy, to keep your name
Living to time.

BOY     A' shall not tread on me!
I'll run away till I am bigger, but then I'll fight.

CORIOLANUS Not of a woman's tenderness to be
Requires nor child nor woman's face to see.
I have sat too long.

[*Rises.*]

VOLUMNIA    Nay, go not from us thus.
If it were so that our request did tend
To save the Romans, thereby to destroy
The Volsces whom you serve, you might condemn us
As poisonous of your honor. No, our suit
Is, that you reconcile them while the Volsces
May say, 'This mercy we have showed,' the Romans,
'This we received,' and each in either side
Give the all-hail to thee and cry, 'Be blest
For making up this peace!' Thou know'st, great son,
The end of war's uncertain, but this certain,
That, if thou conquer Rome, the benefit
Which thou shalt thereby reap is such a name
Whose repetition will be dogged with curses,
Whose chronicle thus writ: 'The man was noble,
But with his last attempt he wiped it out,
Destroyed his country; and his name remains
To th' ensuing age abhorred.' Speak to me, son.
Thou hast affected the fine strains of honor,
To imitate the graces of the gods;
To tear with thunder the wide cheeks o' th' air,
And yet to change thy sulphur with a bolt
That should but rive an oak. Why dost not speak?
Think'st thou it honorable for a noble man
Still to remember wrongs? Daughter, speak you.
He cares not for your weeping. Speak thou, boy.
Perhaps thy childishness will move him more
Than can our reasons. There's no man in the world
More bound to's mother; yet here he lets me prate
Like one i' th' stocks. Thou hast never in thy life
Showed thy dear mother any courtesy,

When she, poor hen, fond of no second brood,
Has clucked thee to the wars, and safely home
Loaden with honor. Say my request's unjust,
And spurn me back; but if it be not so,
Thou art not honest, and the gods will plague thee
That thou restrain'st from me the duty which
To a mother's part belongs. He turns away.
Down, ladies! Let us shame him with our knees.
To his surname Coriolanus 'longs more pride
Than pity to our prayers. Down! An end!
This is the last. So, we will home to Rome,
And die among our neighbors. Nay, behold's!
This boy, that cannot tell what he would have
But kneels and holds up hands for fellowship,
Does reason our petition with more strength
Than thou hast to deny't. Come, let us go.
This fellow had a Volscian to his mother;
His wife is in Corioles, and this child
Like him by chance. Yet give us our dispatch.
I'm hushed until our city be afire,
And then I'll speak a little.

*[Coriolanus] holds her by the hand, silent.*

CORIOLANUS                    O mother, mother!
  What have you done? Behold, the heavens do ope,
The gods look down, and this unnatural scene
They laugh at. O my mother, mother! O!
You have won a happy victory to Rome;
But for your son—believe it, O believe it!—
Most dangerously you have with him prevailed,
If not most mortal to him. But let it come.
Aufidius, though I cannot make true wars,
I'll frame convenient peace. Now, good Aufidius,
Were you in my stead, would you have heard
A mother less? or granted less, Aufidius?
AUFIDIUS   I was moved withal.
CORIOLANUS                    I dare be sworn you were!
  And, sir, it is no little thing to make
Mine eyes to sweat compassion. But, good sir,
What peace you'll make, advise me. For my part,

I'll not to Rome, I'll back with you; and pray you,
Stand to me in this cause. O mother! wife!

AUFIDIUS [*aside*]  I'm glad thou hast set thy mercy and thy
honor
At difference in thee. Out of that I'll work
Myself a former fortune.

CORIOLANUS                [*to Volumnia*] Ay, by and by.
But we will drink together; and you shall bear
A better witness back than words, which we,
On like conditions, will have counter-sealed.
Come, enter with us. Ladies, you deserve
To have a temple built you.[5] All the swords
In Italy, and her confederate arms,
Could not have made this peace.

*Exeunt.*

## Scene 4

*Enter Menenius and Sicinius.*

MENENIUS   See you yond coign o' th' Capitol, yond corner-
stone?

SICINIUS   Why, what of that?

MENENIUS   If it be possible for you to displace it with your
little finger, there is some hope the ladies of Rome,
especially his mother, may prevail with him. But I say
there is no hope in't; our throats are sentenced and stay
upon execution.

SICINIUS   Is't possible that so short a time can alter the
condition of a man?

MENENIUS   There is difference between a grub and a butterfly; yet your butterfly was a grub. This Marcius is
grown from man to dragon. He has wings; he's more than
a creeping thing.

SICINIUS   He loved his mother dearly.

MENENIUS   So did he me; and he no more remembers his

---

5. According to Plutarch, "the Senate ordained that the magistrates, to gratify and
honour these ladies, should grant them all that they would require. And they only
requested that they would build a temple of Fortune for the women . . ."

mother now than an eight-year-old horse. The tartness of
his face sours ripe grapes. When he walks, he moves like
an engine, and the ground shrinks before his treading. He
is able to pierce a corslet with his eye; talks like a knell,
and his hum is a battery. He sits in his state, as a thing
made for Alexander. What he bids be done is finished
with his bidding. He wants nothing of a god but eternity,
and a heaven to throne in.

SICINIUS  Yes, mercy, if you report him truly.

MENENIUS  I paint him in the character. Mark what mercy his
mother shall bring from him. There is no more mercy in
him than there is milk in a male tiger. That shall our
poor city find; and all this is long of [6] you.

SICINIUS  The gods be good unto us!

MENENIUS  No, in such a case the gods will not be good unto
us. When we banished him, we respected not them; and,
he returning to break our necks, they respect not us.

*Enter a Messenger.*

MESSENGER  Sir, if you'd save your life, fly to your house.
The plebeians have got your fellow-tribune,
And hale him up and down; all swearing, if
The Roman ladies bring not comfort home,
They'll give him death by inches.

*Enter another Messenger.*

SICINIUS                              What's the news?

MESSENGER  Good news, good news! The ladies have pre-
vailed,
The Volscians are dislodged, and Marcius gone.
A merrier day did never yet greet Rome,
No, not th' expulsion of the Tarquins.

SICINIUS                              Friend,
Art thou certain this is true? is't most certain?

MESSENGER  As certain as I know the sun is fire.
Where have you lurked that you make doubt of it?
Ne'er through an arch so hurried the blown tide
As the recomforted through th' gates. Why, hark you!

6. Because of.

*Trumpets, hautboys; drums beat; all together.*

The trumpets, sackbuts, psalteries, and fifes,
Tabors and cymbals and the shouting Romans
Make the sun dance. Hark you!

*A shout within.*

MENENIUS                                    This is good news.
I will go meet the ladies. This Volumnia
Is worth of consuls, senators, patricians,
A city full; of tribunes, such as you,
A sea and land full. You have prayed well to-day.
This morning for ten thousand of your throats
I'd not have given a doit. Hark, how they joy!

*Sound still, with the shouts.*

SICINIUS   First, the gods bless you for your tidings; next,
Accept my thankfulness.
MESSENGER                         Sir, we have all
Great cause to give great thanks.
SICINIUS                                  They're near the city?
MESSENGER   Almost at point to enter.
SICINIUS                                We will meet them,
And help the joy.

*Exeunt.*


## Scene 5

*Enter two Senators with Ladies [Volumnia, Virgilia, Valeria] passing over the stage, with other Lords.*
SENATOR   Behold our patroness, the life of Rome!
Call all your tribes together, praise the gods,
And make triumphant fires; strew flowers before them.
Unshout the noise that banished Marcius;
Repeal him with the welcome of his mother.
Cry, 'Welcome, ladies, welcome!'
ALL                                    Welcome, ladies,
Welcome!

*A flourish with drums and trumpets. [Exeunt.]*

*Scene 6*

*Enter Tullus Aufidius, with Attendants.*

AUFIDIUS    Go tell the lords o' th' city I am here.
Deliver them this paper. Having read it,
Bid them repair to the market-place, where I,
Even in theirs and in the commons' ears,
Will vouch the truth of it. Him I accuse
The city ports by this hath entered and
Intends t' appear before the people, hoping
To purge himself with words. Dispatch.

*[Exeunt Attendants.]*
*Enter three or four Conspirators of Aufidius' faction.*

                                              Most welcome!
FIRST CONSPIRATOR    How is it with our general?
AUFIDIUS                                          Even so
As with a man by his own alms empoisoned
And with his charity slain.
SECOND CONSPIRATOR          Most noble sir,
If you do hold the same intent wherein
You wished us parties, we'll deliver you
Of your great danger.
AUFIDIUS                    Sir, I cannot tell.
We must proceed as we do find the people.
THIRD CONSPIRATOR    The people will remain uncertain whilst
'Twixt you there's difference; but the fall of either
Makes the survivor heir of all.
AUFIDIUS                              I know it;
And my pretext to strike at him admits
A good construction. I raised him, and I pawned
Mine honor for his truth; who being so heightened,
He watered his new plants with dews of flattery,
Seducing so my friends; and to this end
He bowed his nature, never known before
But to be rough, unswayable, and free.
THIRD CONSPIRATOR    Sir, his stoutness
When he did stand for consul, which he lost

By lack of stooping—

AUFIDIUS                    That I would have spoke of.
Being banished for't, he came unto my hearth;
Presented to my knife his throat. I took him;
Made him joint-servant with me; gave him way
In all his own desires; nay, let him choose
Out of my files, his projects to accomplish,
My best and freshest men; served his designments
In mine own person; holp to reap the fame
Which he did end all his; and took some pride
To do myself this wrong; till at the last
I seemed his follower, not partner, and
He waged me with his coutenance as if
I had been mercenary.

FIRST CONSPIRATOR          So he did, my lord.
The army marvelled at it; and in the last,
When he had carried Rome and that we looked
For no less spoil than glory—

AUFIDIUS                         There was it!
For which my sinews shall be stretched upon him.
At a few drops of women's rheum, which are
As cheap as lies, he sold the blood and labor
Of our great action; therefore shall he die,
And I'll renew me in his fall. But, hark!

*Drums and trumpets sound, with great shouts of the People.*

FIRST CONSPIRATOR   Your native town you entered like a post,
And had no welcomes home; but he returns,
Splitting the air with noise.

SECOND CONSPIRATOR          And patient fools,
Whose children he hath slain, their base throats tear
With giving him glory.

THIRD CONSPIRATOR          Therefore, at your vantage,
Ere he express himself or move the people
With what he would say, let him feel your sword,
Which we will second. When he lies along,
After your way his tale pronounced shall bury
His reasons with his body.

AUFIDIUS                         Say no more.
Here come the lords.

*Enter the Lords of the city.*

ALL LORDS  You are most welcome home.

AUFIDIUS                                  I have not deserved it.
But, worthy lords, have you with heed perused
What I have written to you?

ALL                                  We have.

FIRST LORD                                  And grieve to hear't.
What faults he made before the last, I think
Might have found easy fines; but there to end
Where he was to begin, and give away
The benefit of our levies, answering us
With our own charge, making a treaty where
There was a yielding—this admits no excuse.

AUFIDIUS  He approaches. You shall hear him.

*Enter Coriolanus, marching with Drum and Colors, the Commoners being with him.*

CORIOLANUS  Hail, lords! I am returned your soldier;
No more infected with my country's love
Than when I parted hence, but still subsisting
Under your great command. You are to know
That prosperously I have attempted, and
With bloody passage led your wars even to
The gates of Rome. Our spoils we have brought home
Do more than counterpoise a full third part
The charges of the action. We have made peace
With no less honor to the Antiates
Than shame to th' Romans; and we here deliver,
Subscribed by th' consuls and patricians,
Together with the seal o' th' Senate, what
We have compounded on.

AUFIDIUS                                  Read it not, noble lords;
But tell the traitor in the highest degree
He hath abused your powers.

CORIOLANUS  Traitor? how now?

AUFIDIUS                                  Ay, traitor, Marcius!

CORIOLANUS                                  Marcius?

AUFIDIUS  Ay, Marcius, Caius Marcius! Dost thou think
I'll grace thee with that robbery, thy stol'n name
Coriolanus in Corioles?

You lords and heads o' th' state, perfidiously
He has betrayed your business and given up,
For certain drops of salt, your city Rome—
I say 'your city'—to his wife and mother;
Breaking his oath and resolution like
A twist of rotten silk; never admitting
Counsel o' th' war; but at his nurse's tears
He whined and roared away your victory,
That pages blushed at him and men of heart
Looked wondering each at other.

CORIOLANUS                               Hear'st thou, Mars?

AUFIDIUS   Name not the god, thou boy of tears!

CORIOLANUS                                   Ha!

AUFIDIUS                                    No more.

CORIOLANUS   Measureless liar, thou hast made my heart
Too great for what contains it. Boy? O slave!
Pardon me, lords, 'tis the first time that ever
I was forced to scold. Your judgments, my grave lords,
Must give this cur the lie; and his own notion—
Who wears my stripes impressed upon him, that
Must bear my beating to his grave—shall join
To thrust the lie unto him.

FIRST LORD   Peace, both, and hear me speak.

CORIOLANUS   Cut me to pieces, Volsces. Men and lads,
Stain all your edges on me. Boy? False hound!
If you have writ your annals true, 'tis there
That, like an eagle in a dovecoat, I
Fluttered your Volscians in Corioles.
Alone I did it. Boy?

AUFIDIUS               Why, noble lords,
Will you be put in mind of his blind fortune,
Which was your shame, by this unholy braggart,
'Fore your own eyes and ears?

ALL CONSPIRATORS                  Let him die for't.

ALL PEOPLE   Tear him to pieces!—Do it presently!—He killed
my son!—My daughter!—He killed my cousin Marcus!
—He killed my father!

SECOND LORD   Peace, ho! No outrage. Peace!
The man is noble and his fame folds in

This orb o' th' earth. His last offenses to us
Shall have judicious hearing. Stand, Aufidius,
And trouble not the peace.
CORIOLANUS                     O that I had him,
With six Aufidiuses, or more, his tribe,
To use my lawful sword!
AUFIDIUS                         Insolent villain!
ALL CONSPIRATORS   Kill, kill, kill, kill, kill him!

*Draw the Conspirators, and kill Marcius, who falls. Aufidius stands
on him.*

LORDS                                    Hold, hold, hold, hold!
AUFIDIUS   My noble masters, hear me speak.
FIRST LORD                            O Tullus—
SECOND LORD   Thou hast done a deed whereat valor will
weep.
THIRD LORD   Tread not upon him. Masters all, be quiet!
Put up your swords.
AUFIDIUS   My lords, when you shall know—as in this rage
Provoked by him you cannot—the great danger
Which this man's life did owe you, you'll rejoice
That he is thus cut off. Please it your honors
To call me to your Senate, I'll deliver
Myself your loyal servant, or endure
Your heaviest censure.
FIRST LORD                    Bear from hence his body,
And mourn you for him. Let him be regarded
As the most noble corse that ever herald
Did follow to his urn.
SECOND LORD               His own impatience
Takes from Aufidius a great part of blame.
Let's make the best of it.
AUFIDIUS                       My rage is gone,
And I am struck with sorrow. Take him up.
Help, three o' th' chiefest soldiers; I'll be one.
Beat thou the drum, that it speak mournfully,
Trail your steel pikes. Though in this city he
Hath widowed and unchilded many a one,
Which to this hour bewail the injury,

Yet he shall have a noble memory.
Assist.

*Exeunt, bearing the body of Coriolanus.*
*A dead march sounded.*

Jack
9213844